# FINDING

# THE HISTORICAL CHURCH

# FINDING THE HISTORICAL CHURCH

## A Resource for the New Evangelization

John M. Redford

Gracewing

First published in 2014 by
Gracewing
2 Southern Avenue
Leominster
Herefordshire HR6 0QF
United Kingdom
www.gracewing.co.uk

No part of this publication may be reproduced, stored in a retrieval system, or transmitted in any form or by any means, electronic, mechanical, photocopying, recording or otherwise, without the written permission of the publisher.

The rights of John M. Redford to be identified as the author of this work have been asserted in accordance with the Copyright, Designs and Patents Act 1988.

© 2014 Literary estate of John M. Redford

ISBN 978 085244 836 6

Typeset by Gracewing

Cover design by Bernardita Peña Hurtado

# CONTENTS

Contents..................................................................v

Foreword................................................................ix

An Invitation to the Reader..................................xi

Abbreviations.....................................................xv

1: The Historical Church and the True Church.........1
   1.1 Salvation of Non-Catholics.........................1
   1.2 Fullness of Visible Unity............................4
   1.3 Some Differences Remaining....................4
   1.4 Authority..................................................6
   1.5 Founded by Christ....................................7
   1.6 *Dominus Jesus*.......................................8
   1.7 Relativism...............................................12
   1.8 The Myth of God Incarnate....................14
   1.9 Demonstration........................................17
   1.10 Historical Evidence...............................19
   1.11 My Story................................................23
   1.12 God and Reason...................................26

2: Newman discovers the Historical Church..........33
   2.1 The Reformation Principle.......................33
   2.2 Development..........................................35
   2.3 Not Mediaeval Accretions.......................37
   2.4 Back to the Fathers.................................41
   2.5 Infallible Authority...................................43
   2.6 Infallibility, Newman and Vatican I...........48

## 3: Modernism and the Quest of the Historical Church.........55
- 3.1 Radical Post-Reformation Criticism................55
- 3.2 Historical Jesus to Historical Church...........57
- 3.3 Change..........................................61
- 3.4 Harnack and Loisy...............................63
- 3.5 Pius X and *Pascendi*...........................65
- 3.6 Thomism.........................................68

## 4: Which Church?....................................71
- 4.1 The Free Churches...............................71
- 4.2 Traditional Churches............................74
- 4.3 Exercising Authority............................76
- 4.4 Necessary.......................................79
- 4.5 Catholic Claims.................................80
- 4.6 Catholic Claims and Critical Scholarship........85

## 5: Building Foundations.............................89
- 5.1 Jesus Existed...................................89
- 5.2 The Critical Minimum............................91
- 5.3 The Three Enigmas...............................94
- 5.4 Unanswered Questions............................96
- 5.5 Jesus Claimed to be the Divine Son of God......99
- 5.6 Blasphemy......................................102
- 5.7 Resurrection..................................104
- 5.8 Basis of Faith.................................105
- 5.9 Building up a Case............................107

## 6: Did Jesus intend to found a Church?.............111
- 6.1 Three Stages..................................111
- 6.2 Jesus was Messiah.............................114
- 6.3 Carry on His Work.............................115

## Contents

    6.4 Authentic References ................................................ 116

    6.5 Unity of Faith and Life ............................................. 119

7: The Apostolic Succession I: the authority of the Apostles themselves ........................................................................ 125

    7.1 Irenaeus .................................................................... 125

    7.2 The Commission of the Risen Christ ...................... 130

    7.3 All Nations ............................................................... 133

    7.4 Exclusivity? .............................................................. 134

    7.5 The Classical Protestant Objection ......................... 136

    7.6 The First Exercise of Apostolic Authority ............... 137

    7.7 The Historical Existence of the Twelve .................. 140

    7.8 Conferred Authority Necessary ............................... 144

    7.9 Paul .......................................................................... 145

    7.10 The Apostles Infallible? ......................................... 148

    7.11 The Apostles: Executive Authority? ..................... 149

    7.12 'Apostle' in the New Testament ........................... 152

    7.13 The Apostles and the Gnostics ............................. 155

    7.14 From 'Sent' to 'Apostles' ...................................... 162

    7.15 Supernatural Selection .......................................... 166

8: The Apostolic Succession II: the monarchical episcopacy ... 175

    8.1 Progress towards the Monarchical Episcopate ....... 175

    8.2 The Challenge of Hans Küng .................................. 177

    8.3 Küng's Ecclesiology ................................................. 180

    8.4 Stage One: Direct Rule from the Apostles ............. 183

    8.5 The First Successors of the Apostles ...................... 187

    8.6 The Authenticity of the Pastorals and I & II Peter .... 189

    8.7 The Pastoral Letters of Paul .................................... 192

    8.8 I & II Peter ............................................................... 194

- 8.9 Stage Three: The Threefold Ministry Of Bishop, Priest, and Deacon..................196
- 8.10 Ignatius' Writings..................198
- 8.11 What Was The Origin Of The Threefold Ministry In Ignatius?..................203

## 9: The primacy of Peter I: the New Testament evidence.....209
- 9.1 The Texts..................209
- 9.2 Introduction..................210
- 9.3 Peter in the New Testament..................213
- 9.4 The Primacy Texts in the Synoptic Gospels..................215
- 9.5 Matthew's added Response..................217
- 9.6 The Messiah and the Rock..................219
- 9.7 The Confession of the Historical Peter..................220
- 9.8 Simon 'The Rock'..................222
- 9.9 Matthew 16 and Isaiah 22..................224
- 9.10 Did the Historical Jesus give Peter Jurisdiction over His Church?..................226
- 9.11 Did Paul accept the Primacy of Peter?..................230
- 9.12 The Role of James..................232
- 9.13 Peter in the later New Testament Literature..........233
- 9.14 Conclusion..................234

## 10: The primacy of Peter II: in the early centuries...........239
- 10.1 Essential Bibliography..................239
- 10.2 Stages of the Development of the Idea of the Primacy..................240
- 10.3 The Historical Jesus and the Apostolic Age.............244
- 10.4 The Second Century..................248
- 10.5 The Third Century..................251
- 10.6 The First Half of the Fourth Century..................253

Contents

    10.7 The Second Half of the Fourth Century..................258
    10.8 The Fifth Century..................................................262
    10.9 Conclusion..........................................................265

11: The Infallibility of the Church.............................................271
    11.1 Vatican I And Vatican II on Infallibility..................271
    11.2 Essential Reading................................................272
    11.3 Introduction.......................................................273
    11.4 Definition of Terms..............................................274
    11.5 Infallible or 'Indefectible' Statements of Faith?......279
    11.6 The Visible Church...............................................283
    11.7 The Primacy and Infallibility.................................285
    11.8 The False Decretals.............................................288
    11.9 The First Vatican Council.....................................291
    11.10 Infallible Fallacies?............................................295
    11.11 *Humanae Vitae*................................................297
    11.12 Chirico and Infallibility......................................303
    11.13 Agreements with Chirico....................................305
    11.14 A Philosophy and a Theology of Infallibility........309
    11.15 Development Again............................................312
    11.16 The Limitation of this Charism............................316

Epilogue..............................................................................323

Bibliography.......................................................................329
    Church Documents......................................................329
    Dictionaries..................................................................329
    Books..........................................................................329

Scriptural Index..................................................................335

Index of Names..................................................................341

# Foreword

Teaching and explaining the Faith was one of Canon John Redford's greatest gifts and he used it to the full. He wanted so much to play his part in fulfilling one of Blessed John Henry Newman's dreams of an educated and articulate laity who would in turn evangelize and witness to the Catholic faith wherever they might find themselves. His voluminous writings, in his books, articles for the Catholic Press and the letters he wrote to those enquiring about the Catholic Faith brought enlightenment and comfort for many people over the years. For John, faith in God and in his Church, was not a passive inheritance but was something to energise, inspire and guide our lives here on earth. It was something to be prayed about, celebrated, cherished and shared with others and he never lost that enthusiasm even in the last few weeks and months of his life, when he decided he should do some more doctoral studies. This book, published posthumously, honours his memory and completes his many years of breaking open the word of God, rooted in his love for the Lord he served so faithfully as a priest of the Archdiocese of Southwark.

✠ Most Reverend Peter Smith
Archbishop of Southwark
Memoria of St Norbert, 6 June 2014

# AN INVITATION TO THE READER

This book is an adaptation of a course book for a distance-learning Master's Degree in Apologetics at the Maryvale Institute. Apologetics is a very ancient discipline in the Church, beginning at the very commencement of the Christian faith. The First Letter of Peter addresses the second or third generation of Christians. The author tells them:

> Have no fear of them, nor be troubled, but in your hearts reverence Christ as Lord. Always be prepared to make a defence (Greek *apologian*) to anyone who calls you to account for the hope that is in you, yet do it with gentleness and reverence. (1 P 3:14b-15)

An *apologia* has a legal connotation, referring to the speech of a defence counsel. Thus John Henry Cardinal Newman replied to a detractor, the novelist author of the *Water Babies* Charles Kingsley, who attacked his integrity, with one of the most famous Victorian works of letters *Apologia Pro Vita Sua* ('In Defence of His Life').

This book is a defence of a truth, for which I hope I would give my life, that the Catholic Church is the true Church founded by Jesus Christ the Son of God himself. I want you as the reader to be challenged by this truth, and maybe you will become a Catholic if you accept its reasons; or if you are already a Catholic, your faith would be strengthened in the context of the New Evangelization.

Much of this book is a straightforward reproduction of that Master's course book *The Quest of the Historical Church*. As I read that book again, I became convinced that any literate intelligent person, with or without prior theological knowledge, could follow its reasoning. A Master's student, of course, will have more involvement, writing essays which will be marked according to academic standards. But a reader without wishing to follow a degree course will I am sure understand my arguments, not because a degree is involved, but because he or she wishes to discover the truth by which we are saved as a human race.

A Master's degree student will already have completed four Modules, the fourth being based partly on my book *Bad, Mad or God? Proving the Divinity of Christ from Saint John's Gospel*. You as a reader not studying that Master's course will need to have introductory material explaining my arguments in *Bad, Mad or God?* I have also written completely from scratch the first Chapter on: *The Historical Church and the True Church*.

Historical arguments are complex, and therefore I could not make this book too easy a read. But I do hope and pray that you will enjoy this quest for the truth, the most important quest which any of us will have on this earth.

# ABBREVIATIONS

| | |
|---|---|
| BMG | Redford, J. *Bad, Mad or God? Proving the Divinity of Christ from St. John's Gospel* (London: Saint Paul's, 2004). |
| Brown II | Brown, R. E. *The Gospel According to John XII-XXI A New Introduction, Translation and Notes* (London: Chapman, 1971). |
| CCC | *Catechism of the Catholic Church* (London: Geoffrey Chapman, 1994). |
| DCD | Newman, J. H. *An Essay on the Development of Christian Doctrine* (Notre Dame Series in the Great Books). Foreword by Ian Ker. |
| DJ | Congregation for the Doctrine of the Faith, *Dominus Iesus, Declaration on the Unicity and Salvific Universality of Jesus Christ and the Church* (London: Catholic Truth Society, 2003). |
| DV | *Dogmatic Constitution of the Second Vatican Council on Divine Revelation Dei Verbum* ('The Word of God'). The version used in this book is in Tanner, N. P. II, 971–981 (ed.) *Decrees of the Ecumenical Councils.* II Vols. (London & Washington: DC, Sheed & Ward and Georgetown University Press, 1990). |
| ECD | Kelly, J. N. D. *Early Christian Doctrines* (London: Adam and Charles Black, 1968). |
| ET | Benoit, P. *Exégèse et Théologie* (Paris: Les Éditions du Cerf, 1961). |

| | |
|---|---|
| FG | Funk, R. and Hoover, R. W. and the 'Jesus Seminar', *The Five Gospels The Search for the Authentic Words of Jesus.* (New York: Scribner, 1993). |
| GA | Newman, J. H. *An Essay in Aid of a Grammar of Assent.* New edition, edited and introduced by Harold, C. F. (New York: Longmans, Green and Company, 1947). |
| HJCG | Theissen, G., and Merz, A. *The Historical Jesus: A Comprehensive Guide* (London: SCM, 1998). |
| HST | Bultmann, R. *The History of the Synoptic Tradition.* Translated Marsh, J. Revised Edition 1968. |
| IFG | Dodd, C. H. *The Interpretation of the Fourth Gospel* (Cambridge University Press, 1953). |
| INF | Küng, H. *Infallible? An enquiry.* Translated from the German by Mosbacher, E. (London: Collins, 1971). |
| INT | Brown, R. E. *An Introduction to the New Testament* (London, Doubleday, 1997). |
| JN | Pope Benedict XVI. *Jesus of Nazareth. Volume 1, From the Baptism in the Jordan to the Transfiguration* (London: Bloomsbury, 2007). |
| JVG | Wright, N. T. *Jesus and the Victory of God. Volume 2 of Christian Origins and the Question of God* (London: SPCK, 1996). |
| LG | *The Dogmatic Constitution On the Church Lumen Gentium,* Tanner, N. P., (ed.) *Decrees of the Ecumenical Councils.* II Vols. (London & Washington: DC, |

|        | Sheed & Ward and Georgetown University Press, 1990). |
|--------|--|
| LJCE   | Hodgson, P. C. (ed.), Strauss, D. F. *The Life of Jesus Critically Examined* (London: SCM, 1973). |
| MJ1    | Meier, J. P. *Rethinking the Historical Jesus. Volume One: The Roots of the Problem and the Person* (New York: Doubleday, 1991). |
| MJ2    | Meier, J. P. *Rethinking the Historical Jesus, Volume Two: Mentor, Message, and Miracles* (New York: Doubleday, 1994). |
| MJ3    | Meier, J. P. *Rethinking the Historical Jesus, Volume Three, Companions and Competitors* (New York: Doubleday, 2001). |
| MLM    | Bockmuehl, M. *This Jesus: Martyr, Lord, Messiah* (Edinburgh: T and T Clark, 1994). |
| ND     | Neuner, J. and Dupuis, J. *The Christian Faith in the Doctrinal Documents of the Catholic Church* (London: Collins, 1983). |
| NJBC   | Brown, R. E., Fitzmyer, J. A., Murphy, R. E. (ed.) *The New Jerome Biblical Commentary* (London: Geoffrey Chapman, 1989). (The system of numbering in this commentary we adopt also in this book: the article number, followed by a colon and the paragraph number of that particular article (all bold), followed finally by the page number in normal type, for instance: (NJBC, **42:75**, 653). |
| NTHIP  | Kúmmel, W.G. *The New Testament: The History of the Investigation of its Problems* |

|  |  |
|---|---|
|  | Transl. Mclean Gilmour S. and Kee, H. C. (London: SCM, 1973). |
| NTI | Wickenhauser, A. *New Testament Introduction* (New York: Herder and Herder, 1958). |
| OC | Moule, C. F. D. *The Origins of Christology* (Cambridge University Press: 1977). |
| ODCC | Cross, F. L. & Livingstone, E. A. (eds.) *The Oxford Dictionary of the Christian Church* (Oxford University Press, 1974). |
| ODP | Kelly, J. N. D. (ed.) *The Oxford Dictionary of Popes* (Oxford University Press, 1986). |
| PNT | Brown, R. E., Donfried, K. P., and Reumann. J. (eds.) *Peter in the New Testament: A Collaborative Assessment by Protestant and Roman Catholic Scholars*. Reprint edition (Wipf and Stock Publishers, 2002). |
| QHJ | Schweitzer, A. *The Quest of the Historical Jesus. A Critical Study of its Progress from Reimarus to Wrede*. Transl. W. Montgomery. (London: A. and C. Black, 3rd Edition, 1954). |
| Tanner | Tanner, N. P. (ed.) *Decrees of the Ecumenical Councils*. II Vols. (London & Washington: DC, Sheed & Ward and Georgetown University Press, 1990). |
| WWJ | Redford, J. *Who Was John? The Fourth Gospel Debate After Pope Benedict XVI's Jesus of Nazareth* (London: Saint Pauls, 2008). |

# 1

# THE HISTORICAL CHURCH AND THE TRUE CHURCH

## 1.1 SALVATION OF NON-CATHOLICS

*Baptised non-Catholic Christians are members of the true Church of Christ.*

The Second Vatican Council, 1962 to 1965, was innovative, if not revolutionary in many ways. Perhaps its most important innovation was the promotion of ecumenism between the Christian churches. While some consider that the impetus towards Christian unity has faded somewhat in the past two decades after disagreements caused by changes such as the ordination of women; continued debate as to the possibility of intercommunion; and disagreements as to sexual ethics; others would be more positive in their assessment. They would point to the fact that hostility between Christian churches, in particular between the Roman Catholic Church and the Church of England, has been replaced by increasing co-operation. If there are differences still remaining, these could be seen as an increasing realism that all cannot be solved by agreed statements, but rather that an honest recognition of our differences could lead to an attitude of prayer to the Lord that he will solve those differences in his own way and in his own time.

The ecumenical movement from the Catholic point of view has been founded on a developed new theology of the Church. The popular film *The Cardinal* pictures a young and intelligent priest, eventually promoted to bishop and cardinal, returning from his studies in Rome to his home city of Boston as a curate. His parish priest details him to teach catechism. He asks the class, "Where do people who are not Catholics go when they die?" The answer came back immediately. "Father, they go to hell." "Why do they go to hell?" Father asks. "Cos they ain't Catholics." the class replies.

The Catholic Church in its official teaching never taught such a thing. In fact, a priest was censured who taught that all non-Catholics will go to hell.[1] The Church always taught that anyone of whatever religion or none could be saved and go to heaven if they followed truly their conscience. But the popular attitude which came across even to Catholics was that anyone who did not join the 'true church' was damned. In any case, it was considered that such a non-Catholic was saved not by membership of their own church, but by the mercy of God who would not condemn to hell anyone but through their own fault.

This is where the Second Vatican Council's Decree on Ecumenism *Unitatis Redintegratio* ('The Restoration of Unity') was so clear and original. It speaks of those who are Christians but not members of the Catholic Church:

> The differences that exist in varying degrees between them and the Catholic Church—whether in doctrine and sometimes in discipline, or concerning the structure of the Church—do indeed create many obstacles, sometimes serious ones, to full ecclesiastical communion. The ecumenical movement is striving to overcome these obstacles. *But even in spite of them it remains true that all who have been justified by faith in Baptism are incorporated into Christ; and therefore have a right to be called Christian, and with good reason are accepted as brothers by the children of the Catholic Church.*[2]

It was a huge revolution for the bishops of the Catholic Church to recognise formally that non-Catholic Christians are members of the Church. The Bull of Pope Boniface VIII, *Unam Sanctum*, promulgated November 18, 1302 would seem at first sight to support those in the catechism class who told the future Cardinal that all those who were not Catholics would go to hell,

> Urged by faith, we are obliged to believe and to maintain that the Church is one, holy, catholic, and also apostolic. We believe in her firmly and we confess with simplicity that outside of her there is neither salvation nor the remission of sins, as the Spouse in the Canticles (Song of Songs 6:8) proclaims: 'One is my dove, my perfect one. She is the only one, the chosen of her who bore her', and she represents one sole mystical body whose Head is Christ and the Head of Christ is God (1 Co 11:3). In her then is one Lord, one faith, one baptism (Ep 4:5). There had been at the time of the deluge only one ark of Noah, prefiguring the one Church, which ark, having been finished to a single cubit, had only one pilot and guide, i.e., Noah, and we read that, outside of this ark, all that subsisted on the earth was destroyed.[3]

This statement of Pope Boniface can be turned on its head by what the Decree on Ecumenism says about non-Catholic Christians. 'Outside the Church there is no salvation' can equally be interpreted as meaning that, if baptised members of other Christian denominations are partially members of the Church, then they can be saved as within the Church, even if their membership lacks complete fulfilment.

The same Vatican Council in its Pastoral Constitution on the Church in the Modern World *Gaudium et Spes* ('Joy and Hope') goes even further, and states that those who are not members of the Church, for example Jews, Moslems, even atheists, can be saved through the Paschal Mystery, but 'in ways known only to God'.[4] However the salvation of non-Catholic Christians is not 'in ways known only to God' but is very specifically through their membership of their own church, in partial though real communion with the Catholic Church.

## 1.2 FULLNESS OF VISIBLE UNITY

*Non-Catholic Christians lack that fullness of visible unity which can only be achieved by full membership of the Catholic Church.*

However, as with much Church doctrine, there is a sting in the tail. Often a doctrine can only be expressed by stating two opposites. It was heresy for Arius to deny that Jesus Christ was true God. But it was also heresy for Apollinarius to deny the humanity of Christ by saying that the human mind of Jesus was replaced by the divine *logos*.[5] Thus, non-Catholic Christians will have been encouraged by being told that the Catholic Church saw them as members of the Church. However they might not have been so pleased to be told that they were not full members of the Church. *Unitatis Redintegratio,* goes on to say:

> Nevertheless, our separated brethren, whether considered as individuals or as communities and Churches, are not blessed with that unity which Jesus Christ wished to bestow on all those to whom he has given new birth into one body, and whom he has quickened to newness of life—that unity which the Holy Scriptures and the ancient Tradition of the Church proclaim. For it is through Christ's Catholic Church alone, which is the universal help towards salvation, that the fullness of the means of salvation can be obtained. It was to the apostolic college alone, of which Peter is the head, that we believe that Our Lord entrusted all the blessings of the New Covenant in order to establish the one Body of Christ into which all those should be fully incorporated who belong in any way to the people of God.[6]

## 1.3 SOME DIFFERENCES REMAINING

*Ecumenical Dialogue has not resolved all serious differences between the Catholic Church and other Christian Communities.*

In the heady days after the Second Vatican Council, the emphasis was clearly on the first paragraph of *Unitatis Redintegratio*, that those who were non-Catholic Christians were at least partially members of the Church. It was the time when many very important agreed statements were written by groups of Catholic theologians working together with theologians of other churches to find out where agreement lay, and where disagreements remained. No doubt many hoped and prayed that those disagreements would be resolved.

Some important differences would not go away, such as the Real Presence of Christ in the Eucharist,[7] and perhaps above all the ordination of women to the priesthood, which in 1992 was passed by the General Synod of the Church of England.[8] Pope John Paul II used his full papal authority to insist that the Church has no power from Christ to ordain women to the priesthood.[9]

Disagreements as to sexual ethics dated from the decision of the Lambeth Conference 1930, which recommended to the Anglican Church worldwide that diverse methods could be used to prevent conception if sound reasons require it.[10] Pope Paul VI on the contrary issued his famous, to some infamous, encyclical *Humanae Vitae* ('Of Human Life') in 1968 in which he strongly condemned the use of condoms and the contraceptive pill which prevented the act of intercourse from bearing its fruit in a new human life.[11]

Finally, although the Anglican/Roman Catholic International Commission agreed on the historical threefold ministry of bishop, priest, and deacon,[12] the Catholic Church refused to reverse the statement of Pope Leo XIII's encyclical *Apostolicæ Curae* ('of Apostolic Care') of 1896 'we pronounce and declare that ordinations carried out according to the Anglican rite have been, and are, absolutely null and utterly void'[13] because the Edwardine Anglican Prayer Book Ordinal had refused to accept that the Eucharist was a sacrifice.[14] This meant that intercommunion between Anglicans and Roman Catholics was still not possible.

## 1.4 AUTHORITY

*The most serious obstacle to visible unity is the question as to by what authority the Catholic Church can dictate to other Christian communities what to believe and what to practice.*

These continued unresolved differences, and others, have thrown the emphasis back on the question of authority. At the end of the day, whatever theological reasons have been given by the Pope and the Vatican for the Catholic position on these disputed issues, the real question is by what authority the Catholic Church claims to dictate to other Christian communions what to believe and what to practice; because on each separate issue, the Catholic Church clearly claims to have such an authority. Whatever agreed statements are issued, it seems the Roman Catholic Church reserves to itself the final decision as to whether such disagreements can be resolved, since disagreements must be resolved on its own terms.

Anglicans and Roman Catholics have discussed the question of Authority in depth. In 1998 ARCIC (Anglican/Roman Catholic International Commission) produced its document *The Gift of Authority*[15] which itself was a further reflection upon the *Final Report* it had produced in 1981. *The Gift of Authority* concluded:

> Even though progress has been made, some serious difficulties have emerged on the way to unity. Issues concerning authority have been raised acutely for each of our communions. For example, debates and decisions about the ordination of women have led to questions about the sources and structures of authority and how they function for Anglicans and Roman Catholics.[16]

The question of authority is therefore the key. If the Anglicans on ARCIC had agreed with the Catholic view of authority in the Church, it is difficult to see how they could have done anything else than seek full communion with the Roman Catholic Church. The Second Vatican Council in its Decree on Ecumenism has made it clear that it is only if one becomes a full member of the Catholic Church that the fullness of visible unity is achieved; and that visible unity can only be achieved if the authority of that Church, represented above all by the Bishop of Rome as the successor of Peter, is accepted on each issue debated.

The issue then reveals itself in all its stark reality. Fullness of visible unity can only be achieved as far as the Catholic Church is concerned if a Christian becomes united with the visible Catholic Church. Only thereby does one receive all the 'blessings of the covenant'. Moreover such visible unity can only be achieved if one seeking such unity is prepared to accept all the authoritative decisions of the Pope as representing the Catholic Church.

## 1.5 FOUNDED BY CHRIST

*The Catholic Church maintains that its authority is based on the fact that it has received the final revelation of Jesus as the Son of God, and that the Bishop of Rome is the successor of Saint Peter with the gift of infallibility together with the worldwide college of bishops with him.*

This seems at first sight to be a bold, even an arrogant, attitude on the part of the Catholic Church. What right has any Christian community to dictate terms over other Christians? That is because the Catholic Church makes two absolute claims for its own authority which are either true or incredibly arrogant. The Church claims that God sent his Son, God become Man, to live a human life and to save us by his life, death, and resurrection. This is the final revelation from God to the human race. As Peter said to the Jewish Council and to all his own Jewish people regarding Jesus, 'There is no one else for there is no other name under heaven given among men by which we must be saved'. (Ac 4:12)

Many Christians, if not the majority, would agree. But the second absolute claim is that Jesus Christ during his life on earth established Peter as the head of his church after him, and that Peter and the other Apostles were to rule his Church through their successors the Pope and the Bishops of the Catholic Church. This primacy over the whole church was given to Peter by Jesus according to Matthew's Gospel. On retreat in Caesarea Philippi, Jesus asked his disciples who people said he was. Then, finally he challenged them: 'Whom do *you* say I am?'

> Simon Peter replied, 'You are the Christ, the Son of the living God.' And Jesus answered him, 'Blessed are you, Simon Barjona! For flesh and blood has not revealed this to you, but my Father who is in heaven. And I tell you, you are Peter, and on this rock I will build my church, and the powers of death shall not prevail against it. I will give you the keys of the kingdom of heaven, and whatever you bind on earth shall be bound in heaven, and whatever you loose on earth shall be loosed in heaven.' (Mt 16:16–19)

The Catholic Church makes the further claim that in consequence, and to make this rule effective, Peter and his successors the Bishops of Rome, together with the college of bishops in union with him were given the gift of infallibility, to be guided into all truth by the Holy Spirit (cf. Jn 16:13) in order to keep that truth inviolate until Christ comes again. The reader is asked to excuse the author for not giving references at this point, since it is the precise purpose of this book to demonstrate these doctrines, and full references will be given later. However the reader must understand that this question of the historical evidence for the infallibility of the Church will be our main point of controversy, together with the executive primacy of the Pope, the successor of Simon the Rock.

## 1.6 *DOMINUS JESUS*

*In AD 2000, the Vatican issued the Declaration* **Dominus Jesus** *('The Lord Jesus') in which the intimate connection between Christ as the final revelation of God and the Catholic Church as the visible body of Christ was affirmed.*

On 6 August 2000, the senior ministry of the Vatican, the Sacred Congregation for the Doctrine of the Faith issued its *Declaration Dominus Jesus on the Unity and Salvific Universality of Jesus Christ and the Church* [DJ]. This document was issued with the full authority of Pope John Paul II. In fact, the Prefect of that Congregation, Joseph Cardinal Ratzinger less than five years later was himself elected Pope. For a good number of years, he had been the senior theological consultor of Pope John Paul II. It is obvious that the Pope shared Ratzinger's vision of the Church, and that his ratification of *Dominus Jesus* was no mere rubber stamp.

This document caused some controversy, to say the least. One reaction on the internet was by J. Shelby Spong who entitled his response *Dominus Iesus: The Voice of Rigor Mortis: The Vatican's exclusionist document exposes a hierarchy that refuses to face reality*.[17] More sober reactions from ecumenists expressed the fear that particularly in its view of the Church this document was going back a step to pre-ecumenical days in claiming once again that the Catholic Church was the 'true church'.

However *Dominus Jesus* was no more than a reiteration of the doctrine of the Church which we have already seen in the Decree on Ecumenism. If the blessings of the new covenant are exclusively gained in full by membership of the visible Catholic Church, then the Second Vatican Council decreed that exclusivity in 1964. This was further clarified in 1973 by the Sacred Congregation for the Doctrine of the Faith's *Mysterium Ecclesiae* ('The Mystery of the Church') *Declaration in Defence of the Catholic Doctrine on the Church against Certain Errors of the Present Day*,[18] which affirmed in 2 the infallibility of the teaching authority of the Catholic Church. This document freely acknowledges with Vatican II that those baptised Christians not in full communion with the Catholic Church are in partial yet real communion with her. This is a great stimulus to seek for that partial unity to become complete. Yet in part 1: *The Oneness of Christ's Church, Mysterium Ecclesiae* insists:

But at the same time Catholics are bound to profess that through the gift of God's mercy they belong to that Church which Christ founded and which is governed by the successors of Peter and the other Apostles, who are the depositories of the original Apostolic tradition, living and intact, which is the permanent heritage of doctrine and holiness of that same Church.

Asserted here is the historical identity between the Church which Jesus came to found, and the visible reality of the Roman Catholic Church. We cannot say that this is anything less than the old claim that the Roman Catholic Church is the 'true Church'.

A word here about the expression 'Roman Catholic Church', which ecumenists within the Catholic Church have willingly accepted in dialogue with other churches, for example, the very title of ARCIC, 'The Anglican/Roman Catholic International Commission'. The term 'Roman Catholic' is ambiguous, since it can mean 'Catholics of the Roman rite', that is the Western or Latin discipline, as distinct from Catholics of the Eastern rite, in full communion with Rome but celebrating and following the discipline of the Eastern rites, in Greek, Slavic or the Maronite Aramaic liturgy.

What the term 'Roman Catholic' cannot mean in terms of what we have discussed above is the claim of some non-Catholic Christians that 'We are English or Swedish Catholics, you are Roman Catholics'. In all church documents, the term 'Catholic Church' is used without the prefix 'Roman' precisely to convey the meaning that the Church of Christ subsists visibly in the Catholic Church, that body which on earth is governed by the Pope and the bishops of the world in union with him, and only in the Catholic Church.

There has been much discussion on the use of the word 'subsists' regarding the way in which the Church is present in the Catholic Church. The Fathers of the Second Vatican Council avoided the expression 'The Church of Christ *exists* in the Catholic Church' to emphasise that the Church also genuinely exists in Christian communities separate from Rome. *Dominus Jesus* agrees that 'subsists' means this but this does not deny for DJ that the full visible unity of the body of Christ exists only in the Catholic Church, and that it does really exist there now, and not only in hope or desire:

> Therefore, there exists a single Church of Christ, which subsists in the Catholic Church, governed by the Successor of Peter and by the Bishops in communion with him ... The Christian faithful are therefore not permitted to imagine that the Church of Christ is nothing more than a collection—divided, yet in some way one—of Churches and ecclesial communities; nor are they free to hold that today the Church of Christ nowhere really exists, and must be considered only as a goal which all Churches and ecclesial communities must strive to reach.[19]

This had already been affirmed in the earlier document *Mysterium Ecclesiae* 1, that the verb 'subsists' was used in order to affirm the salvific potential of churches and groups of separated Christians, but not to deny that only the Catholic Church (or if one wishes to use the expression 'The Roman Catholic Church') rejoices in that fullness of visible unity. What was new in *Dominus Jesus* was the explicit *connection* established between the doctrine of the divinity of Christ as the final revelation of God, and the Catholic Church as having the unique mission from Jesus to proclaim that Good News. *Dominus Jesus* was reiterating that connection two thousand years after Peter had named Christ as the Son of God, and Jesus had replied to Simon, calling him 'Rock', just as Peter had called him 'Messiah'.

This intimate connection between Christ as the final revelation of God and the Catholic Church as uniquely possessing the fullness of visible unity of the body of Christ is made with full emphasis in *Dominus Jesus* because it addresses a particular theological challenge, the challenge of 'relativism'.

## 1.7 RELATIVISM

*The Declaration* **Dominus Jesus** *was a response to a growing atmosphere of religious and moral relativism in the Church and in the world.*

> The Church's constant missionary proclamation is endangered today by relativistic theories which seek to justify religious pluralism, not only *'de facto'* but also *'de iure'* (or in principle). As a consequence, it is held that certain truths have been superseded; for example, the definitive and complete character of the revelation of Jesus Christ, the nature of Christian faith as compared with that of belief in other religions, the inspired nature of the books of Sacred Scripture, the personal unity between the Eternal Word and Jesus of Nazareth, the unity of the economy of the Incarnate Word and the Holy Spirit, the unicity and salvific universality of the mystery of Jesus Christ, the universal salvific mediation of the Church, the inseparability—while recognizing the distinction—of the kingdom of God, the kingdom of Christ, and the Church, and the subsistence of the one Church of Christ in the Catholic Church.[20]

Towards the close of the Second Millennium, many factors had led Europeans, and indeed Christians who lived in places far from Europe, to consider the question of different faiths and their relationship with Christianity and with the Catholic Church. In Britain, immigration was rendering it necessary for even Catholic schools to teach religious education in other faiths. And the general atmosphere in modern society was against the idea that any one religious system could represent the final truth.

The Second Vatican Council had not ignored this issue. In its Declaration *Nostra aetate*, ('In Our Era') it had insisted that 'The Catholic Church rejects nothing of what is true and holy in these religions'.[21] However a general attitude was developing, fed now by some theories of religious education and of religious truth, that each religion only expressed a partial view of the truth, thus denying the final quality of Christian revelation and hence a denial that the Catholic Church can be 'the true Church' in any absolute sense.

We do not need to demonstrate the existence of such relativistic attitudes in reality either from scholarly writing or from statistical surveys. It is a view obviously prevalent in our society. *Dominus Jesus* was addressing a widespread problem; but it had a problem particularly in mind raised by theories of comparative religion. It mentions a particular view which it declares is contrary to Christian faith:

> In contemporary theological reflection there often emerges an approach to Jesus of Nazareth that considers him a particular, finite, historical figure, who reveals the divine not in an exclusive way, but in a way complementary with other revelatory and salvific figures. The Infinite, the Absolute, the Ultimate Mystery of God would thus manifest itself to humanity in many ways and in many historical figures: Jesus of Nazareth would be one of these. More concretely, for some, Jesus would be one of the many faces which the Logos has assumed in the course of time to communicate with humanity in a salvific way... These theses are in profound conflict with the Christian faith. The doctrine of faith must be *firmly believed* which proclaims that Jesus of Nazareth, son of Mary, and he alone, is the Son and the Word of the Father.[22]

Such a view here denominated as an error by the Sacred Congregation is a detachment from concrete history of the Word which John's Gospel has said has become flesh in Jesus of Nazareth (Jn 1:14). In such a view, the Word can now roam freely through all the religions of the world leading human beings to God. But the Word is not now truly incarnate in Jesus, giving us 'life through his name' (Jn 20:31).[23]

*Dominus Jesus* paragraph 4 which we have quoted above names a wide variety of views both in Christology (the doctrine of Christ) and Ecclesiology (the doctrine of the Church) which it insists are against Catholic faith. It is impossible in a small book to encompass all these theories. My aim in this book is to concentrate on one particular scholarly movement in the Anglo-Saxon world, the 'historical Jesus' school, which has had profound repercussions in the thinking of lay Christians as well as among scholars in Britain and in America. In this view, 'the historical Jesus' was not the final revelation of God as in the Catholic faith, but rather a Jewish prophet who suffered the supreme penalty under the Roman Governor Pontius Pilate because of rebellion against the religious establishment. Jesus as the final revelation of God, if he is to be taken into account at all, is in this view only a reflection of 'the Christ of faith', of what Christians traditionally believe, and not of 'the historical Jesus', what the prophet of Nazareth actually taught about himself and his mission.

It goes without saying that a community which preached the message of such a Jesus two thousand years after his crucifixion would not rejoice in any special authority, certainly not infallible authority. We will now consider therefore challenges made in the name of 'the historical Jesus' to see how they undermine Christian and Catholic faith both in Jesus Christ as the final revelation of God and the Church as his authoritative body, before following the main agenda of this book, which is to argue in favour of the truth that 'the historical Jesus' was truly God become man, and that he came to found a Church which we identify today as the Catholic Church.

## 1.8 THE MYTH OF GOD INCARNATE

*'The Jesus Seminar' in the USA and 'The Myth of God Incarnate' in Great Britain challenged Christian faith that Jesus Christ was God Incarnate on the grounds that 'the historical Jesus' never made such a claim.*

In 1977, our British summer was disturbed by the publication of a symposium entitled *The Myth of God Incarnate*, in which a number of leading Christian academics questioned whether we had any more to believe in the doctrine of the Incarnation, that Jesus of Nazareth was truly God become man. John Hick, in the leading article of that symposium, raises the whole question as to whether in this day and age the concept of God becoming incarnate in Jesus is still intelligible, and perhaps whether Christianity itself needs the doctrine of the Incarnation any more.[24] For him, the key question is that of the historical reliability of the Fourth Gospel:

> ... the later stages of that development (i.e. the early Christian development of the doctrine of the Incarnation) were greatly influenced by the evidence of the Fourth Gospel understood in a straightforwardly historical way. How else could one interpret a Jesus who said 'Before Abraham was, I am' and 'I and my Father are one'? As I was still being taught in my confirmation class, such a Jesus must be either 'mad, bad or God'. But if the Fourth Gospel is understood in a less straightforwardly historical way (as on general critical grounds I believe it has to be) then its implications for doctrine may prove to be somewhat different from what they appeared to earlier ages to be.[25]

A similar link between scepticism regarding the Incarnation and scepticism concerning the historicity of the Fourth Gospel was made by a group of American scholars who led what they called the *Jesus Seminar* in the United States, which also attracted some media attention.[26] In 1985, thirty scholars accepted an invitation to lead a Seminar together with 'more than 200 professionally trained specialists'.[27] The Seminar then took a poll of views on which words attributed to Jesus had actually been said by him, and what had been added later by the Church. The participants dropped coloured beads into a box to signify whether they considered this or that saying consisted of Jesus' own words, or were probably more or less his or expressed ideas close to his.

The verdict of the *Jesus Seminar* on the historical Jesus in the Gospel of John was less than favourable. Not only the Jesus saying in John 8:58 'Before Abraham was, I AM' was judged to be inauthentic; virtually all the words attributed to Jesus in the Fourth Gospel were black coded;[28] that is to say, came under the heading, 'Jesus did not say this; it represents the perspective or content of a later or different tradition'.[29]

According to the *Jesus Seminar*, therefore, the Fourth Gospel contains virtually nothing which even approximates to what Jesus said. No, according to the *Jesus Seminar*, St John's Gospel deliberately misleads us about the historical Jesus, that is, what he really said and did during his life on earth. This Gospel, the *Jesus Seminar* claims, is patently untrue. It replaces the historical Jesus with the mythical Jesus of the Christian Creed, which although defined by early church tradition, very much expressed the theology of the Fourth Gospel:

> I believe in God the Father almighty.
> Creator of heaven and earth,
> I believe in Jesus Christ, God's only Son, our Lord,
> who was conceived by the Holy Spirit, born of the Virgin Mary
> suffered under Pontius Pilate, was crucified, died, and was buried; he descended into hell
> On the third day he rose again;
> he ascended into heaven, he is seated at the right hand of the Father, and he will come again to judge the Living and the dead.[30]

How can we continue to believe this mythology about Jesus, say the *Jesus Seminar*, when the historical Jesus never said anything like this, nor can we verify that he did anything remotely as miraculous as stated in the Christian Creed?[31]

## 1.9 DEMONSTRATION

*On the contrary, I shall attempt to demonstrate in this book, that the historical Jesus of Nazareth claimed to be God become man, and that he came to earth to found a Church which became the Catholic Church.*

In 2004, I published a book which was the fruit of a life's study *Bad, Mad or God? Proving the Divinity of Christ from Saint John's Gospel*.[32] In that book, I demonstrated that the old argument advocated by Christian apologetes such as C. S. Lewis was still valid: that Jesus could not have been just a good man, since his claim to be God meant that he was either bad, mad, or was truly God. In that book, I emphasised evidence from the Gospel of John, where explicit claims are made for example in John 8:58, and where Jesus says to his shocked hearers, 'Before Abraham was, I am', and later 'I and the Father are One' (Jn 10:30). I argued that contrary to the Jesus Seminar and the Myth of God Incarnate symposium, the Fourth Gospel is telling us the sober truth that the historical Jesus truly claimed to be God.

Indeed, what John tells us about Jesus is precisely what *Dei Verbum* ('The Word of God') of Vatican II tells us as Catholic faith, namely that the historical Jesus came to reveal himself as the final revelation of God:

> To see Jesus is to see His Father (Jn 14:9). For this reason Jesus perfected revelation by fulfilling it through his whole work of making Himself present and manifesting Himself: through His words and deeds, His signs and wonders, but especially through His death and glorious resurrection from the dead and final sending of the Spirit of truth. Moreover He confirmed with divine testimony what revelation proclaimed, that God is with us to free us from the darkness of sin and death, and to raise us up to life eternal.[33]

Thus I argue in *Bad, Mad or God?* that this statement of Vatican II, which is a summary of what the four Gospels say, and most explicitly in John, is authentic historically, as testified by the four Gospel writers. Many, I am sure, will deny the veracity of the Gospels and thus of my book; but I am still waiting for sceptics to produce arguments against what I wrote in 2004. Rather than tediously rehearsing the demonstrations in that book (although I shall be referring to it from time to time as appropriate), I refer the reader to *Bad, Mad or God?*, and promise to attempt to respond to any criticisms of it; but now claim the right to proceed forward to the next stage in the process, from Christ to the Church.

The revelation of God in Jesus is therefore no myth for the Dogmatic Constitution for Divine Revelation *Dei Verbum*, but a revelation in history. Furthermore, that same Dogmatic Constitution proclaims that this revelation, which it claims to be God's final revelation to the human race,[34] has been handed on effectively from Jesus through the Apostles right down the centuries to us in the third millennium:

> In His gracious goodness, God has seen to it that what He had revealed for the salvation of all nations would abide perpetually in its full integrity and be handed on to all generations. Therefore Christ the Lord in whom the full revelation of the supreme God is brought to completion (see 2 Co 1:20; 3:13; 4:6), commissioned the Apostles to preach to all men that Gospel which is the source of all saving truth and moral teaching.[35]

With *Dominus Jesus*, it is easy to see how the unbreakable link between Christ as the final revelation of God and the Catholic Church as his body can be immediately established. If Jesus was only a failed revolutionary, then it is difficult to see how any church he founded could be effective. But if Christ was true God become man, and he came to earth in order to save the human race, we presume that he came to be effective in what he decided to achieve. That is the reason why he would wish to found a Church, led by the Apostles and their successors, to ensure that his message of salvation would last until the end of time, when he told us that he would return.

How could this be demonstrated? One piece of evidence which is by no means to be immediately dismissed is that the Catholic Church still exists visibly, with a billion members. It has four thousand bishops worldwide, who claim to be successors of the apostles, as the college of Catholic bishops have so claimed for two millennia since the foundation of the Church. The Bishops of Rome, who claim to be the successors of Saint Peter, have also been there for two millennia. I would submit that the continued existence and impressive size of the Catholic Church right to the present day itself is an argument for its claims to be at least seriously examined.

## 1.10 HISTORICAL EVIDENCE

*Our aim is to examine the historical evidence that Jesus while on earth founded a Church, led by Peter and the Apostles, and that he gave them and their successors the Spirit of Truth to interpret infallibly the faith and morals of the Gospel.*

Our task is to demonstrate the 'historical continuity' between what was originally founded by Christ on earth and the Catholic Church as outlined in *Dominus Jesus*:

> The Catholic faithful are required to profess that there is an historical continuity—rooted in the apostolic succession— between the Church founded by Christ and the Catholic Church: 'This is the single Church of Christ... which our Saviour, after his Resurrection, entrusted to Peter's pastoral care (cf. Jn 21:17), commissioning him and the other Apostles to extend and rule her (cf. Mt 28:18ff.), erected for all ages as 'the pillar and mainstay of the truth' (1 Tm 3:15). This Church, constituted and organized as a society in the present world, subsists in (*subsistit in*) the Catholic Church, governed by the Successor of Peter and by the Bishops in communion with him.[36]

As with the historical evidence for the life of Jesus as we researched in *Bad, Mad or God?* we must consider the relationship between historical evidence and the act of faith. The Church teaches that to come to faith in Jesus, historical investigation is not sufficient in itself. The gift of the Holy Spirit needs to be given to the enquiring person in order for faith to exist at all. The First Vatican Council, which met in 1869 to counter growing secularism and materialism in Europe, with many losing their faith, said in the Dogmatic Constitution *Dei Filius* on the Catholic Faith:

> Since human beings are totally dependent on God as their creator and lord, and created reason is completely subject to uncreated truth, we are obliged to yield to God the revealer full submission of intellect and will by faith. This faith, which is the beginning of human salvation, the Catholic Church *professes* to be a supernatural virtue, by means of which, with the grace of God inspiring and assisting us, we believe to be true what He has revealed, not because we perceive its intrinsic truth by the natural light of reason, but because of the authority of God himself, who makes the revelation and can neither deceive nor be deceived. Faith, declares the Apostle, 'is the assurance of things hoped for, the conviction of things not seen' (Heb 11:1).[37]

As Paul said, 'No one can say Jesus is Lord except by the Holy Spirit'. (1 Co 12:3). Yet, as with so many Catholic doctrines, there are again two sides to it. The same *Dei Filius* immediately goes on to say that reason also has a part to play in the road to faith:

> Nevertheless, in order that the submission of our faith should be in accordance with reason, it was God's will that there should be linked to the **internal assistance** of the Holy Spirit **external indications** of his revelation, that is to say divine acts, and first and foremost **miracles** and **prophecies**, which clearly demonstrating as they do the omnipotence and infinite knowl-

edge of God, are the most certain signs of revelation and are suited to the understanding of all.[38]

In *Bad, Mad or God?* we noted the importance of the miracles in the life of Jesus, particularly those miracles which indicated his divinity such as the Walking on the Water, the Multiplication of the Loaves, and above all his bodily resurrection. These we saw as not myths, but as 'most certain signs of revelation' as Vatican I states, not dispensing with the need for faith, but rather being linked with 'the internal assistance of the Holy Spirit' in the investigation of the historical evidences of revelation.

In this volume, we look at the miracle of the Church, and we note that, however imperfect and even sinful are her members, she fulfils the mission given to her by her founder Jesus himself, because in her life she is the beneficiary of the miracle of his grace and his truth, which she has received from the beginning of her foundation from Jesus himself. *Dei Filius,* Chapter 3 continues:

> What is more, the Church herself by reason of her astonishing propagation, her outstanding holiness and her inexhaustible fertility in every kind of goodness, by her catholic unity and her unconquerable stability, is a kind of great and perpetual motive of credibility and an incontrovertible evidence of her own divine mission. So it comes about that, like a standard lifted up for the nations she both invites to herself those who have not yet believed, and likewise assures her sons and daughters that the faith they profess rests on the firmest of foundations. To this witness is added the effective help of power from on high.
>
> For, the kind Lord stirs up those who go astray and helps them by his grace so that they may come to the knowledge of the truth; and also confirms by his grace those whom he has translated into his admirable light, so that they may persevere in this light, not abandoning them unless he is first abandoned.

Many might see the above as a somewhat idealistic picture of the Church. Admittedly, it has the style of a church document of a previous age. But the Church *is* a miracle, because over the centuries it has brought so many millions to the truth handed on by Christ, and communicated the holiness of God by signs which we call 'sacraments' in the unity of the body of Christ. Many of us would say that, but for the wonderful grace of the Holy Spirit, the Church would have perished many centuries ago through the imperfections and sins of those of us who are her members.

A note on the use of the feminine singular personal pronoun 'her' with reference to the Church. In traditional theology, which goes back to the New Testament, the Church is feminine as the 'spouse of Christ':

> Husbands, love your wives, as Christ loved the church and gave himself up for her, that he might sanctify her, having cleansed her by the washing of water with the word, that he might present the church to himself in splendour, without spot or wrinkle or any such thing, that she might be holy and without blemish. (Ep 5:25–27)

The new English translation of the Roman Missal, authorised internationally, has restored this usage, for instance in the prayer for Peace in the Communion Rite of the Mass:

> Lord Jesus Christ, who said to your apostles: Peace I leave you, my peace I give you; look not on our sins, but on the faith of your Church, and graciously grant her peace and unity in accordance with your will. Who live and reign for ever and ever. Amen.[39]

In the traditional theology of the Church, Christ is himself as Man redeemer and King of the human race. The Church is his Spouse, united body and soul with her Lord.

Jesus himself said 'seek and you will find' (Mt 7:7). With all of us, that seeking is a combination of the instinct of faith given by the Holy Spirit together with some honest and

## 1.11 MY STORY

*I narrate the story of my own seeking and finding fullness of Catholic unity.*

At the age of sixteen, I left grammar school with three O. Levels. I said to my headmaster, "There is no point on my staying on to the sixth form, is there, sir?" He replied, "No, Redford, there isn't". My teenage laziness rendered poor my chances of going to University. He ended his comment with "You won't stop writing, will you?" I have followed his advice in that aspect, at least, down the years.

Failing to find employment with the local paper as a trainee journalist, I became a library assistant. Regarding religion, I was lapsing from attending the local Anglican church where I had been baptised as an infant, and where I had been a choirboy during my school years. Wisely, my widowed mother, a very good evangelical Anglican Christian, put no pressure on me, but invited my sister and me to spend a holiday at a Christian Conference Centre called Lee Abbey. It was beautiful country, in North Devon, and I was immediately attracted to the community there, a team of young people being on what would today be called 'a gap year'.

There were excellent daily talks on the Bible each morning. I began to read the letters of Saint Paul in a modern version by J. B. Philips called *Letters to Young Churches*, and to read the brilliant apologetic writings of C. S. Lewis such as *Broadcast Talks* and *The Screwtape Letters*. When I returned home, I became a fully committed member of the church from which I had lapsed, a church which had a vibrant and well attended young people's weekly Sunday meeting after the church service.

It was also the time when the great American evangelist Billy Graham came to Britain, and filled Haringey arena six nights of the week for three months with twelve thousand people. I went to a meeting one evening, but something held me back from going forward with hundreds of others at the invitation of the hymn *Just as I am, without one plea, But that Thy Blood was shed for me, and that Thou bidst me come to Thee, O Lamb of God, I come.* Instead, my conversion experience, as such it was, took place on the top of a London bus, when I became powerfully aware of the presence of the unseen God, to whom I knew from then on I must give my life.

It was while working at the public library that I first considered the role of the Catholic Church. Full of my fervour as an evangelical Christian, I said to a colleague who had recently become a Catholic, "I believe in the Bible as my source of faith". "But," he asked, "who gave you that Bible?" "Of course, the Church", I responded. "That is why I am a Catholic", he said.

After two years working in the library, at eighteen years of age, I was due for National Service. Walking up the steps of the Town Hall after lunch, I then had an experience similar to my awareness of God two years before. I was certain that I would have to be ordained a minister of the Church. My Vicar was very encouraging, and I was accepted at a theological college after completing two years of National Service in the Army.

I was very happy indeed at the College, but intellectually dissatisfied. I could not solve the problem of biblical criticism, which was really the problem of authority. I could not be a fundamentalist, and accept that the world was created by God in six days. But if I did not accept the six days of creation, then how much of the Bible should I accept? I was at an Evangelical college, but the Anglo-Catholics I met only raised the question still further. If I accepted the authority of the Church to determine belief, then why should I not become a Catholic, since that Church exercised such authority, while the Church of England did not?

At the same time as the intellectual questions, I began emotionally to desire to become a Catholic. Such feelings came to a height when I saw a Corpus Christ procession emerging from the church opposite, that of Our Lady of Grace at Charlton, South London, where I was eventually ordained a Catholic priest. The sight of the priest at the back of a long procession carrying the host under a canopy gave me what Anglicans call 'Roman fever'.

I put such feelings aside, because I was soon to be ordained a deacon in the Anglican Church. I went ahead with ordination, but the 'Roman fever' increased, and I only survived three months in the Anglican ministry. After Christmas, I returned to my parish after a break, and I experienced a deep yearning in my heart to become a Catholic. That had been increased by reading the Spanish mystic John of the Cross for my Anglican priestly ordination studies. I opened the volume, and read:

> O living flame of love, that tenderly woundest my soul at its deepest centre, perfect me now if it be Thy will. Break the web of this sweet encounter.

John of the Cross describes his experience of being so close to God that all he needs to fulfil complete union with divine love is death itself, bodily life being the only 'web of this sweet encounter' which needed to be broken for that fullness of union to be finally fulfilled. That I knew was a mystical Catholic union, a union which could only be found in the visible body of Christ. I then opened the Bible at random, and I read:

> There is one body and one Spirit, just as you were called to the one hope that belongs to your call, one Lord, one faith, one baptism, one God and Father of us all, who is above all and through all and in all. (Ep 4:4–6)

## 1.12 GOD AND REASON

*Upon reflection, it became clear that my acceptance of the Catholic faith involved both the work of the Holy Spirit and human reasoning.*

It is manifest to the reader, surely, that my journey towards the fullness of Catholic unity was not a purely intellectual one. I was drawn by the Holy Spirit, just as the First Vatican Council had said. However it was also an intellectual journey. I saw the necessity of the Church as the authority to determine what inspired scripture was and what was not. In fact, Karl Barth, the foremost Protestant theologian of the twentieth century, said that he could not in truth be certain as to which books constituted canonical scripture; because if he did, he was implicitly asserting the infallibility of the Church, which he could not do as a Protestant.

Furthermore, I would not have become a Catholic had I not considered that the arguments for the truth of the historical Catholic Church were true, and could be verified. I believed that the historical Jesus was God, and had revealed himself as God become Man, as C. S. Lewis had argued in his Bad, Mad or God apologetics. I also believed that Jesus while on earth had made Simon Peter the head of his Church after him. You could say that I 'believed' this; but such a faith was what could be called 'an historical faith'. I was rationally convinced of the twin historical truths, that Jesus was God and had founded the Catholic Church. If I had not accepted this, I would not have become a Catholic.

As the First Vatican Council said therefore, there is a twin operation, of faith and of reason, in coming to faith in the revelation of Jesus and the Church. At the time, my rational argumentation was primitive, yet I was completely convinced of the historical truth of the claims of the Catholic Church.

This gives the main agenda for this book. During more than half century that I have been a Catholic, I have taken particular interest in the historical Jesus, and more recently in the historical reasons for the authenticity of Jesus handing on his authority to the Catholic Church. My studies are now coming to fruition. More and more people realise that historical reasons cannot be absolute. Yet I will submit that they are convincing and, together with faith, make sound reasons for a person to submit in faith to the visible unity of the Catholic Church.

We began this Introductory Chapter by stating that members of other Christian denominations are members of the Catholic Church, albeit not fully. My own story, and the story of many others, testifies that many of us cannot be satisfied with such incomplete membership. We seek for that fullness of visible unity which is a seeking for fullness of the truth.

The Second Vatican Council's document *Dignitatis Humanae* ('Of Human Dignity') states that all must have the freedom to search for the truth without coercion. But then it states the other side of the coin, that all have the obligation to seek the truth:

> It is in accordance with their dignity as persons—that is, beings endowed with reason and free will and therefore privileged to bear personal responsibility—that all men should be at once impelled by nature and also bound by a moral obligation to seek the truth, especially religious truth. They are also bound to adhere to the truth, once it is known, and to order their whole lives in accord with the demands of truth.[40]

I know personally that if I had not followed my path towards visible unity in the Catholic Church, I would have been profoundly frustrated all my life. Whether or not, in terms of that catechism class we mentioned at the beginning narrated in the film *The Cardinal*, I would have been condemned to eternal loss if I had not sincerely sought the truth, I just do not know. But I am glad that I did not take the chance.

## Notes

1. http://alcazar.net/Feeney2.html [accessed 18 February 2013] Father Leonard Feeney was suspended from his priestly duties for disobedience in 1949, and further refused to obey his Jesuit superiors. The Holy Office in Rome summoned him to account for his view which seemed to say that all non-Catholics would go to hell; but he refused to go to Rome to answer the charge against him of teaching error. He was therefore formally excommunicated by the Vatican on 13 February 1953.
2. Second Vatican Council, Decree on Ecumenism: *Unitatis Redintegratio* (1964) 3.1 translated by A. Flannery, *Vatican Council II The Conciliar and Post-Conciliar Documents* 1992. Italics mine.
3. http://www.americancatholictruthsociety.com/docs/unamsanctum.htm [accessed 18 February 2013].
4. See Vatican II, *Gaudium et Spes*, 22: "All this holds true not only for Christians, but for all men of good will in whose hearts grace works in an unseen way. For, since Christ died for all men, and since the ultimate vocation of man is in fact one, and divine, we ought to believe that the Holy Spirit in a manner known only to God offers to every man the possibility of being associated with this paschal mystery."
5. http://www.newadvent.org/cathen/01615b.htm [accessed 18 February 2013]
6. Second Vatican Council, Decree on Ecumenism: *Unitatis Redintegratio* (1964), 3.4, translated by A. Flannery, *Vatican Council II The Conciliar and Post-Conciliar Documents* 1992
7. In its critique of the Anglican/Roman Catholic *ARCIC Agreement on Eucharistic Doctrine*, Full Text, Windsor, 1971, No.12. http://www.prounione.urbe.it/dia-int/arcic/doc/e_arcic_eucharist.html [accessed 18 February 2013] the Congregation for the Doctrine of the Faith listed a series of doctrines on which ARCIC claimed to have reached agreement, but without formulating them in a manner that safeguarded Catholic teaching. It noted: 'Certain formulations in the Report are not sufficiently explicit and hence can lend themselves to a twofold interpretation, in which both parties can find unchanged the expression of their own position. This possibility of contrasting and ultimately incompatible readings of formulations which are apparently satisfactory to both sides gives rise to a question about the real consensus of the two Communions, pastors and faithful alike, In effect, if a formulation which has received the agreement of experts can be diversely interpreted, how could it serve as a basis for reconciliation on the level of Church life and practice?' http://www.ad2000.com.au/articles/1992/apr1992p10_750.html [accessed 18 February 2013].
8. http://news.bbc.co.uk/onthisday/hi/dates/stories/november/11/newsid_2518000/2518183.stm [accessed 18 February 2013].

9   http://www.vatican.va/holy_father/john_paul_ii/apost_letters/ documents/hf_jp-ii_apl_22051994_ordinatio-sacerdotalis_en.html [accessed 18 February 2013] *Ordinatio Sacerdotalis*, 4: 'Wherefore, in order that all doubt may be removed regarding a matter of great importance, a matter which pertains to the Church's divine constitution itself, in virtue of my ministry of confirming the brethren (cf. Lk 22:32) I declare that the Church has no authority whatsoever to confer priestly ordination on women and that this judgment is to be definitively held by all the Church's faithful.'

10  Resolutions from 1930 Resolution 15: The Life and Witness of the Christian Community — Marriage and Sex. Where there is clearly felt moral obligation to limit or avoid parenthood, the method must be decided on Christian principles. The primary and obvious method is complete abstinence from intercourse (as far as may be necessary) in a life of discipline and self-control lived in the power of the Holy Spirit. Nevertheless in those cases where there is such a clearly felt moral obligation to limit or avoid parenthood, and where there is a morally sound reason for avoiding complete abstinence, the Conference agrees that other methods may be used, provided that this is done in the light of the same Christian principles. The Conference records its strong condemnation of the use of any methods of conception control from motives of selfishness, luxury, or mere convenience. Voting: For 193; Against 67. http://www.lambethconference.org/resolutions/1930/1930–15.cfm [accessed 18 February 2013].

11  http://www.vatican.va/holy_father/paul_vi/ encyclicals/documents/ hf_p-vi_enc_25071968_humanae-vitae_en.html [accessed 18 February 2013].

12  http://www.prounione.urbe.it/dia-int/arcic/doc/ e_arcic_ministry.html [accessed 18 February 2013] A Statement on the Doctrine of the Ministry, Anglican/Roman Catholic International Commission, Canterbury, 1973, No.16 Both presbyters and deacons are ordained by the bishop. In the ordination of a presbyter the presbyters present join the bishop in the laying on of hands, thus signifying the shared nature of the commission entrusted to them. In the ordination of a new bishop, other bishops lay hands on him, as they request the gift of the Spirit for his ministry and receive him into their ministerial fellowship. Because they are entrusted with the oversight of other churches, this participation in his ordination signifies that this new bishop and his church are within the communion of churches. Moreover, because they are representative of their churches in fidelity to the teaching and mission of the apostles and are members of the episcopal college, their participation also ensures the historical continuity of this church with the apostolic church and of its bishop with the original apostolic ministry. The communion of the churches in mission, faith and holiness, through time and space, is thus symbolised and maintained

in the bishop. Here are comprised the essential features of what is meant in our two traditions, by ordination in the apostolic succession.

13  Leo XIII, *Apostolicae Curae*,36.
14  *Apostolicae Curae*, 25. But the words which until recently were commonly held by Anglicans to constitute the proper form of priestly ordination namely, 'Receive the Holy Ghost,' certainly do not in the least definitely express the sacred Order of Priesthood (*sacerdotium*) or its grace and power, which is chiefly the power 'of consecrating and of offering the true Body and Blood of the Lord' (Council of Trent, Sess. XXIII, de Sacr. Ord. , Canon 1) in that sacrifice which is no 'bare commemoration of the sacrifice offered on the Cross' (Ibid, Sess XXII., de Sacrif. Missae, Canon 3).
15  http://www.ewtn.com/library/Theology/Arcicgf3.htm [accessed 18 February 2013].
16  ARCIC, *The Gift of Authority*, 3.
17  http://www.beliefnet.com/Faiths/Christianity/2000/11/Dominus-Iesus-The-Voice-Of-Rigor-Mortis.aspx [accessed 19 February 2013].
18  http://www.saint-mike.org/library/curia/congregations/faith/mysterium_ecclesiae.html [accessed 19 February 2013].
19  DJ 17.
20  DJ 4.
21  Tanner II, p. *969.
22  DJ 9–10. The Declaration *Dominus Jesus* has almost certainly in mind J. Dupuis, *Christianity and the Religions: from Confrontation to Dialogue*.
23  F. Clark, *Godfaring On Reason, Faith, and Sacred Being* (Washington, D.C.: Catholic University of America Press, 2000). Clark counters views among theologians who deny the essential relationship between faith and the Incarnate Word.
24  There was a rapid and competent reply from the viewpoint of orthodox Christology to the symposium M. Green, (ed.) *The Truth of God Incarnate* (London: Hodder and Stoughton, 1977).
25  J. Hick, *The Myth of God Incarnate* (London, SCM, 1977), p. 4.
26  There is a fierce and sustained attack on the *Jesus Seminar* in T. L. Johnson, *The Real Jesus: The Misguided Quest for the Historical Jesus and the Truth of the Traditional Gospel* (San Francisco: Harper Collins, 1997), pp. 1–27.
27  FG, p. 34.
28  Cf. FG pp. 401–470. Only John 4:43b (pink: 'Jesus probably said something like this') and 12:24–5 (gray: 'Jesus probably did not say this, but the ideas contained in it are close to his own').
29  *Ibid.*, p. 36.
30  *Ibid.*, p. 7.
31  This section about *The Myth of God Incarnate* and The Jesus Seminar is adapted from *Bad, Mad, or God?* [BMG] pp. 22–25.

32. J. Redford, *Bad, Mad or God? Proving the Divinity of Christ from Saint John's Gospel* (London: St. Paul's Publications, 2004).
33. DV 4.
34. The Christian dispensation, therefore, as the new and definitive covenant, will never pass away and we now await no further new public revelation before the glorious manifestation of our Lord Jesus Christ (see 1 Tm 6:14 and Tt 2:13).
35. DV 7.
36. DJ 16.
37. Vatican I, *Dei Filius*, Chapter 3 on Faith.
38. *Ibid*.
39. The CTS New Daily Missal, People's Edition, with the New Translation of the Mass, London: Catholic Truth Society, 2012, p. 1067.
40. Vatican II, *Dignitatis Humanae*, 2.

# 2

# NEWMAN DISCOVERS THE HISTORICAL CHURCH

## 2.1 THE REFORMATION PRINCIPLE

*Luther introduced the principle of sola scriptura ('scripture alone') as the rule of faith rather than church authority. The Church of England after the Reformation accepted this principle, although with some traditional elements remaining from the pre-Reformation church.*

Western Christendom in the sixteenth century was rent asunder by two conflicting views of the Church. The traditional Catholic ecclesiology maintained that the Church was a visible society with Christ's authority at its head. Salvation was achieved for everyone through its sacramental life. However, now a new revolutionary theology of the church was claiming half of the European states after the revolution by the Augustinian friar Martin Luther. For Protestants who followed Luther, and other Reformers such as Calvin and Zwingli, the Church was essentially a community of individual believers who were saved directly by their personal assurance from God that their sins were forgiven, by faith alone (*sola fide*).

This meant that Protestants went about differently in order to discover what the true Christian doctrine was. Catholics could rely on the Creeds and the magisterial teaching of the Church under the authority of the Pope and bishops. But for the new faith, the individual must rely on the Word of God written, scripture alone (*sola scriptura*). It was expected that each Christian would be able to read the newly printed Bible, and no more be enslaved by Popish superstition.

However the Church of England, which broke away from Rome under Henry VIII with the Act of Supremacy, did not follow the principle of *sola scriptura*, but in general accepted the Catholic doctrines of the pre-Reformation Church. Henry declared himself Supreme Head of the Church of England, and accepted all the Catholic doctrines except that of the Primacy of the Bishop of Rome. He even burnt Protestants as heretics who denied Catholic doctrines. What we might call this 'Catholic' element never entirely disappeared from Anglicanism. The Anglican compromise was, from Elizabeth I onwards, that Protestantism simply co-existed with the traditional Catholic elements, just as the mediaeval churches and the Episcopal structures of the Church of England maintained at least that outward continuity with pre-Reformation Catholic England.

Under the next King, Edward VI, more and more Protestant ideas from Germany entered the Church of England. In general it subscribed to the Catholic creeds as defined by the Council of Nicaea onwards. After all, the Athanasian Creed[1] was sung liturgically.[2] Why, then, was there need for a restatement of Christian doctrine in the *Ecclesia Anglicana* after the English monarchy had declared itself Head of the Church of England? It was here that the Church of England post-Henry VIII linked strongly with the Protestant Reformation. Like the German Lutherans and the Scottish, Welsh, and Swiss Calvinists, it taught that certain doctrines found in the mediaeval Catholic Church were the result of corruptions which had crept in since the definitions of the Catholic Creeds from Nicaea 325 to Chalcedon 451. This was the continuous legacy of *sola scriptura* in English Christianity.

This also reinforced the Church of England's theological ambiguity. Both traditional pre-Reformation Catholicism and *sola scriptura* Lutheranism co-existed in the same ecclesiastical body.

Those British Christians who dissented from the Church of England were more radical in their ecclesiology. Presbyterians, forming the official 'Kirk of Scotland', for instance, denied a position for bishops because they argued that the New Testament church had presbyters, and not bishops. Welsh Congregationalists had neither presbyters nor bishops, but independent church communities led by a preacher. Baptists argued that only those who can make a personal act of faith should be baptised, in what they thought was in keeping with the doctrine of the New Testament, where the baptism of infants is not easily demonstrable. But the *sola scriptura* principle meant that scripture reading could always revise positions originally considered to be part of the historical constitution of the church. The entry into Christianity of this critical principle meant that no position could be considered as in itself authoritative; otherwise there would be a return to an authoritative church, which Protestantism precisely was resolved to abandon. This critical theology would affect both Anglican and Dissenting Christians.

By the eighteenth century, with the Enlightenment, the Church of England had become a State religion with worldly clergy needing religious reform. The Evangelicals, led by John Wesley,[3] eventually driven into the Methodist schism, saw the resolution of this problem as the preaching of the Gospel, based upon the Scriptures and conversion. The early nineteenth-century Tractarians reacted similarly to what they saw as Anglican Erastianism,[4] the rule of the State over the Church. However their solution was not the preaching of the Gospel on horseback with a Bible in the saddle bag, but reading heavy tomes of the Greek and Latin Fathers in the Oxford University Library. Into this movement, in the early nineteenth century came an inspiring leader, John Henry Newman.

## 2.2 DEVELOPMENT

*For Newman, a doctrine is not a matter of faith because it is stated in a text of scripture, but because as an idea it develops in tradition to become articulated as a doctrine of faith.*

It is here that we see the vital importance of Newman's *Essay on the Development of Christian Doctrine*,[5] written in the first half of the nineteenth century (first edition 1845). Newman's *Advertisement to the First Edition* contained a *Postscript* informing the reader that 'the Author has joined the Catholic Church'.[6] For Newman, the writing of *The Development* became a written road into the Catholic Church. He argued that the Roman Catholic Church was the only true development of the Church of the Fathers.

The real problem for Newman is that

> ... Creeds and dogmas live in the one idea which they are designed to express, and which alone is substantive; and are necessary, because the human mind cannot reflect upon that idea except piecemeal, cannot use it in its oneness and entireness, or without resolving it into a series of aspects and relations'.[7]

In Christianity, the idea is that of the Incarnation, which develops in various modes: 'Taking the Incarnation as its central doctrine, the Episcopate, as taught by St Ignatius, will be an instance of political development, the *Theotokos* of logical, the determination of the date of our Lord's birth of historical, the Holy Eucharist of moral, and the Athanasian Creed of metaphysical'.[8]

That is why for Newman the doctrine of sola scriptura cannot explain or justify the development of doctrine.

> Nor could it surely be maintained without extravagance that the letter of the New Testament, or of any assignable number of books, comprises a delineation of all possible forms which a divine message will assume when submitted to a multitude of minds'.[9]

> What prominence has the Royal Supremacy in the New Testament, or the lawfulness of bearing arms, or the duty of public worship, or the substitution of the first day of the week for the seventh, or infant baptism, to say nothing of the fundamental principle that the Bible and the Bible only is the religion of

> Protestants? These doctrines, and usages, true or not, which is not the question here, are surely not gained by the direct use and immediate application of Scripture, nor by a mere exercise of argument upon words and sentences placed before the eyes, but by the unconscious growth of ideas suggested by the letter and habitual to the mind.[10]

Newman concludes: 'From the necessity, then, of the case, from the history of all sects and parties in religion, and from the analogy and example of Scripture, we may fairly conclude that Christian doctrine admits of formal, legitimate, and true developments, that is, of developments contemplated by its Divine Author'.[11] This harmonises with God at work in nature. 'And there is a plan of things beforehand laid out, which, from the nature of it, requires various systems of means, as well as length of time, in order to the carrying on its several parts into execution'.[12]

It may be added here that Newman is very much at home with an evolutionary concept of creation, contemporary with Darwin's Origin of Species.

## 2.3 NOT MEDIAEVAL ACCRETIONS

*For Newman, a significant example of the development of doctrine is purgatory, which Protestants would argue is an example of mediaeval accretion, but which Newman argued was a development from the traditional teaching on post-baptismal sin.*

Newman gives as an example of logical development the Catholic doctrine of purgatory. The question which bothered the early church was that of the reconciliation of those who committed serious post-baptismal sin. As Newman recounts, Novatian[13] (200 to 258) held the doctrine judged to be heretical that 'those who had once fallen from the faith could in no case be received again'.[14] Long penances, even till death, were given in some quarters.[15] The question arose as to: 'Were these punishments merely signs of contrition, or in any sense satisfaction for sin?'[16] The Fathers clearly thought the latter, claims Newman.

Newman quotes Bishop Kaye focussing on the teaching of Clement of Alexandria ('died about the year 215.')[17]

> Clement distinguishes between sins committed before and after baptism: the former are remitted at baptism; the latter are purged by discipline ... The necessity of this purifying discipline is such, that if it does not take place in this life, it must after death, and is then to be effected by fire, not by a destructive, but a discriminating fire, pervading the soul which passes through it.[18]

Cyprian also seems to refer not just to penance on this earth, but after death:

> ... one thing to be tormented for sin in long pain, and so to be cleansed and purged a long while by fire (*purgari diu igne*) another to be washed from all sin in martyrdom; one thing, in short, to wait for the Lord's sentence in the Day of Judgement, another at once to be crowned by Him'.[19]

St Perpetua prays for her brother who had died at the age of seven. 'Then I knew' she says, 'that he was translated from his place of punishment'. [20] 'Thus we see how, as time went on, the doctrine of Purgatory was brought home to the minds of the faithful as a portion or form of Penance due for post-baptismal sin'.[21] The Church became more merciful as the faithful became more lax, as the days of imperial persecution became more spasmodic.

This, of course, undermined completely the Lutheran doctrine of *sola fide*. For Luther, because the forgiveness of sins is only a cloak for God forgetting what is a fact, namely the total depravity of human nature after the Fall, then any suggestion that post-baptismal sin with its final punishment after death in purgatory can be remitted by works of the penitent must for him be unscriptural.

Against Luther, 2 Corinthians 3:11–15, referring to a person 'saved by fire' could be interpreted with reference to cleansing by fire of the person after death;[22] but the only explicit and unambiguous biblical reference to belief in Purgatory is 2 Maccabees 12:40–46, 'where the hero Judas Maccabeus, finding amulets of gods on dead soldiers, prayed for them '... he had this expiatory sacrifice offered for the dead, so that they might be released from their sin.' (v. 44).

Needless to say, Luther led the Reformers to exclude the books of Maccabees together with all the books of the Old Testament written originally in Greek, in agreement with the Jewish rabbinical canon.[23] Newman would have argued back that the very decision one made to accept certain books as inspired and others as 'apocryphal' is itself a case of the development of doctrine. Centuries after the apostles, Newman argues in *Development*, that in the early centuries of Christianity 'the Canon of the New Testament was still undetermined'.[24] How, he would argue, can one base one's faith upon scripture alone, when what constitutes scripture is itself uncertain, only finally to be determined by the developing mind of the Church?

However, if one accepts the canonical status of Maccabees, then paradoxically the doctrine of purgatory could be authenticated by the doctrine of *sola scriptura*. After the battle where the Jewish rebels defeated Gorgias, the governor of Idumea's army, the Jews went around to inspect the bodies of the slain:

> Then under the tunic of every one of the dead they found sacred tokens of the idols of Jamnia, which the law forbids the Jews to wear. And it became clear to all that this was why these men had fallen. So they all blessed the ways of the Lord, the righteous Judge, who reveals the things that are hidden; and they turned to prayer, beseeching that the sin which had been committed might be wholly blotted out. And the noble Judas exhorted the people to keep themselves free from sin, for they had seen with their own

> eyes what had happened because of the sin of those who had fallen. He also took up a collection, man by man, to the amount of two thousand drachmas of silver, and sent it to Jerusalem to provide for a sin offering. In doing this he acted very well and honourably, taking account of the resurrection. For if he were not expecting that those who had fallen would rise again, it would have been superfluous and foolish to pray for the dead.But if he was looking to the splendid reward that is laid up for those who fall asleep in godliness, it was a holy and pious thought. Therefore he made atonement for the dead, so that they might be delivered from their sin. (2 M 12:40–45)

This is a perfect statement of the Catholic doctrine of purgatory, a century or so before the coming of Christ. The slain have not committed a mortal sin, but what later moral theology calls a 'venial sin', the wearing of little statues of the gods for luck. For this venial or 'light' sin, the survivors of the battle sent an offering to Jerusalem for the dead to be 'released from their sins'. In this case, the offering of the Mass for those who have died, a hugely popular mediaeval custom, would be justified as the obvious development prefigured in the Old Testament sacrifices offered for the dead.

It was the sale of indulgences which for Luther was the spark for the German Reformation, throwing down the gauntlet to challenge the whole Catholic doctrine of justification and merit. There is no question that, in the late Middle Ages, the sale of indulgences was a great scandal, Dominican preachers throughout Europe collecting for the building of St Peter's in Rome. The Council of Trent rid that particular abuse by the following decree, from Session 21, Canon 9:-

> And the Council Decrees that any indulgences or spiritual favours, of which the faithful should not be deprived by this ruling, should henceforth be published to the people at the appropriate times by the local bishops through the agency of two members

of their Chapter, who will also be empowered to make an honest collection of alms and other offerings for charity, without receiving any payment for the task. And may all thereby understand that these treasures of the church are administered to increase devotion and not private gain.[25]

Thus Newman, no doubt in this supported by his fellow Tractarians, including those like Pusey[26] who never made the spiritual journey to Rome, was challenging fundamental tenets of Protestantism within the Anglican Church. To pray for the dead, with the indulgence of pleading the merits of the saints was close to blasphemy. On the contrary, for Newman in the *Development*, the doctrine of purgatory, linked logically with the doctrine of the need to remedy post-baptismal sin by the merit of good works done as penance, is a prime example of authentic development attested with clear evidence in the early Fathers of the Church.

## 2.4 BACK TO THE FATHERS

*The Oxford Tractarians, of whom Newman was a leading light, were convinced that the purification of the Church could only come with a return to the ancient Fathers of Christendom.*

For Evangelicals, the reform of the Church could only come from the preaching of the Gospel from the scriptures based upon the doctrine of the saving blood of Christ for each individual. For the Tractarians, so named because of a series of *Tracts for the Times* which they published, the salvation of the Church of England would come with a return to that faith preached in particular by the Fathers of the early Councils of the Church, in particular from Nicaea 325 to Chalcedon 451. It was to this faith that the mediaeval Church of England was heir, and the Tractarians were calling Anglicans to return to it.

What mattered to the early nineteenth century Anglo-Catholics was that there was a true historical continuity between the Church of the Ecumenical Councils of the fourth and fifth centuries and the Church of England in their own time.

They did not question whether there was such a genuine continuity between the post-Nicene Church and the original Church of the apostles, still less whether the church of the apostles was genuinely continuous with the teaching of Jesus of Nazareth. They assumed that this was so. The Quest of the Historical Jesus, which we have already mentioned, but which we will consider further in chapter three, had not yet made the journey across the Channel from Germany to England, or, if the Tractarians had heard of it, they did not feel that they had to deal with such impiety as Strauss' *Leben Jesu* as worthy of intellectual consideration.

What mattered to the nineteenth-century Anglo-Catholics was that the *Ecclesia Anglicana* was authentically continuous with the Church of the Fathers, and therefore that they could call themselves Catholics. They did not consider themselves Protestants. Their doctrines did not come from the reading of scripture in isolation from the tradition of the Church, but as an integral part of that tradition. They would have accepted, with Newman, the whole concept of development.

Anglo-Catholics adhered strongly to the infallibility of the apostles, and to the doctrines of the Ecumenical Councils of the fourth and fifth centuries. Anglo-Catholics of the nineteenth century solved the problem of infallibility by positing that the whole body of bishops represents the apostles and its decrees carry their authority, with the Pope considered as one of the bishops, even the most senior as the successor of St Peter. However the Bishop of Rome did not have full executive authority over all the bishops, as given in Catholic ecclesiology. The Pope was simply one member of the College of Bishops which was itself the successor of the apostles, even if he could be given senior status within that College. This became a firm article of the Anglo Catholic creed right into the twentieth century.

This Anglo-Catholic view of the superiority of the General Council even held some sway in the Roman Catholic Church, in a mediaeval canonical theory called Conciliarism: that a general council of the church has greater authority than the Pope and may, if necessary, depose him.[27] These views were finally condemned with the definition of papal primacy and infallibility at the First Vatican Council, which we will look at much more closely later. But three decades before that Council, while still an Anglican, Newman had seen the fallacy of such a view, leading him to seek and find full communion with the Catholic Church.

## 2.5 INFALLIBLE AUTHORITY

*The General Councils of the Church, Newman insisted, only in the end were effective because of the infallible authority of the Bishop of Rome.*

Newman asked, how was the Catholic Church in those early fourth and fifth centuries able to provide such cohesion across the world, and for its name 'Catholic' even to be accepted by those who were outside of its visible ranks, calling those who disagreed, who chose to follow particular doctrines rather than the whole, 'heretics'? It is here that Newman came to his life-changing conclusion; that the doctrine of papal supremacy was the final glue which held together the visible Catholic communion. As the church began, so it continued until Newman's day in the Roman Catholic Church. He realised that he must join that Church, however much pain it would cause to his fellow Anglicans.

What convinced Newman that any form of Conciliarism was untenable was what Pope Leo the Great nicknamed the Council of 449 'The Latrocinium', or 'Robbers' Council'. This Council, summoned by the Emperor, took place in Ephesus, The Pope sent legates to the Council. The Council was dominated by Dioscorus the Patriarch of Alexandria.[28]

Since the death of Cyril of Alexandria, the great promoter of the doctrine of the Hypostatic Union, defined at Ephesus (431) more extreme positions had been taken up in Alexandria by Cyril's less able successors. Cyril had ensured that Catholics held that the union of divine and human in Christ was substantial, a union of hypostasis, not a loose *prosópon*, a 'mask' linking divine and human as the Nestorians had claimed. However the successors of Cyril, in particular the monk Eutyches,[29] more and more referred to the Incarnate Saviour as not only one person (*hypostasis*) but also one nature (*ousios*). The Monophysite formula was 'before the Incarnation, two natures divine and human: after the Incarnation, one nature'.

At the 449 Council of Ephesus, as Newman says, 'Eutyches was supported by the Imperial Court, and by Dioscorus the Patriarch of Alexandria'.[30] On the other hand the Patriarch Flavian of Constantinople was against Eutyches. Pope Leo the Great sent his delegates, and addressed his famous Tome of Leo, 13 June 449[31] to Flavian,[32] in which he condemned Eutyches and Monophysitism as heresy.

The supporters of the Pope were defeated by Dioscorus and his supporters. The Latrocinium ended with Flavian being attacked by an armed mob of the Monophysites, receiving wounds from which he died, 'The proceedings ended by Dioscorus excommunicating the Pope, and the Emperor issuing an edict in approval of the decision of the Council'. Eustathius of Berytus even quoted from Cyril at Ephesus; (even though Cyril had later supported the Antiochene formula which asserted the two natures divine and human after the Incarnation)[33] 'We must not then conceive two natures, but one nature of the Word Incarnate'.[34] What Newman saw as the impossibility of holding to a Conciliarist position was that by all the criteria alleged by Conciliarist theory, the Latrocinium was a legitimate Council whose decrees were legitimately promulgated. That the Emperor summoned the Council would not have been a problem, since Emperors generally summoned all the Councils. Just as the first Council of Ephesus (431) had been. It has always been recognised as a General Council, it claimed to be representative of all the Catholic bishops in the world. Its conclusions were, as Newman stated, validly arrived at. The Council of the Latrocinium 'seems to have been unanimous, with the exception of the Pope's legates, in the restoration of Eutyches; a more complex decision can hardly be imagined.'[35] Regarding its conclusions, General Councils present their conclusions as the view of the Episcopal body, not of the Pope. The Latrocinium did seem to represent the general view of the Bishops, and the disagreement of the papal legates would not necessarily invalidate those conclusions.

> Such was the state of Eastern Christendom in the year 449; a heresy, appealing to the Fathers, to the Creed, and, above all, to Scripture, was by a general Council, professing to be Ecumenical, received as true in the person of its promulgator. If the East could determine a matter of faith independently of the West, certainly the Monophysite heresy was established as Apostolic truth in all its provinces from Macedonia to Egypt.

> There has been a time in the history of Christianity, when it had been Athanasius against the world, and the world against Athanasius. The need and straitness of the Church had been great, and one man was raised up for her deliverance. In this second necessity, who was the destined champion of her who cannot fail? Whence did he come, and what was his name? He came with an augury of victory upon him, which even Athanasius could not show; it was Leo, Bishop of Rome.'[36]

The papal legates at the Council of Chalcedon (451) exercised such infallible authority in the name of the Pope, overturning the decrees of the Latrocinium and defining the doctrine of the two natures divine and human in the incarnate Christ against Monophysitism. Even Protestants, says Newman, recognise this as an exercise of claimed infallible authority on the part of Pope Leo the Great.

The Pope exercised his full papal authority through his legates at the Council of Chalcedon, 451.[37] Unlike Athanasius at the Council of Nicaea 325, the Pope was not just a voice, even the dominating voice. He exercised his authority rather as the successor of Peter, overturning all the decrees of what was considered the legitimate General Council of Ephesus 449, and anathematizing all those in the East as well as in the West who refused to accept Chalcedon. When the papal legates had spoken, defending the two natures of Christ before and after the Incarnation, all the bishops in the Council proclaimed 'Peter has spoken through Leo'.

St Peter Chrysologus urged Eutyches 'to submit to what has been written by the blessed Pope of Rome; for St Peter, who lives and presides in his own See, gives the true faith to those who seek it.'[38] From the beginning, the Pope exercises significant control of the Council of Chalcedon. Leo demanded first, as the head of all the Churches that Dioscorus should not sit, on the grounds that 'he had presumed to hold a Council without the authority of the Apostolic See, which had never been done nor was lawful to do'.[39]

Regarding Theodoret[40] who had been deposed by the Latrocinium as not supporting Monophysitism, he was restored to the Council, having been restored to the Episcopal Office by Pope Leo.[41] Dioscorus was then tried and condemned, sentence pronounced against him by the Pope's legates: 'The most holy Archbishop of Rome, Leo, through us and this present Council with the Apostle St Peter, who is the rock and foundation of the Catholic Church and of the orthodox faith, deprives him of the Episcopal dignity and every sacerdotal ministry.'[42]

The Council, after its termination, addressed a letter to Pope Leo. In it the Fathers acknowledge him as 'constituted voice of the interpreter Peter' (with an allusion to St Peter's

Confession in Mt 16) and speak of him as 'the very one commissioned with the guardianship of the vine by the Saviour'.[43] Newman concludes:

> Such is the external aspect of those proceedings by which the Catholic faith has been established in Christendom against the Monophysites. That the definition passed at Chalcedon is the Apostolic Truth once delivered to the Saints is most firmly to be received, from faith in that overruling Providence which is by special promise extended over the acts of the Church ; moreover, that it is in simple accordance with the faith of St Athanasius, St Gregory Nazianzen, and all the other Fathers, will be evident to the theological student in proportion as he becomes familiar with their works : but the historical account of the Council is this, that a formula which the Creed did not contain, which the Fathers did not unanimously witness, and which some eminent Saints had almost in set terms opposed, which the whole East refused as a symbol, not once, but twice, patriarch by patriarch, metropolitan by metropolitan, first by the mouth of above a hundred, then by the mouth of above six hundred of its Bishops, and refused upon the grounds of its being an addition to the Creed, was forced upon the Council, not indeed as being such an addition, yet, on the other hand, not for subscription merely, but for acceptance as a definition of faith under the sanction of an anathema,—forced on the Council by the resolution of the Pope of the day, acting through his Legates and supported by the civil power.[44]

Protestant apologetic against Catholicism quite rightly sees Chalcedon as the first clear and full expression of papal authority over the universal church in matters of doctrine. For Newman, it meant that he had to pack his bags and move from Littlemore in Oxford to what he later called 'Maryvale' or *Sancta Maria in Valle*, a house in Oscott, South Staffordshire, in what is now north Birmingham. It had been for many years a Catholic seminary for the Midland District and continued in Newman's day as a 'Mass House'. From Maryvale, Newman was ordained a Catholic priest in Rome, and soon moved a few miles south to found the Birmingham Oratory. His quest for the historical Church had at last been successful.

> The present day Roman Catholic Church was that historical Church: ... that amid its disorders and its fears there is but one Voice for whose decisions the people wait with trust, one Name and one See to which they look with hope, and that name Peter, and that See Rome; such a religion is not unlike the Christianity of the fifth and sixth Centuries.[45]

## 2.6 INFALLIBILITY, NEWMAN AND VATICAN I

*Newman freely accepted the doctrine of the infallibility of the Church, and in consequence the doctrine of the infallibility of the Pope as defined by Vatican I. He had argued in DCD that it is antecedently probable that, if God were to give a final revelation to the human race, he would grant his infallible authority to the Church. However he considered that the definition of Vatican I was 'inopportune'.*

We will be discussing later in more detail the whole concept of infallibility. However we must say from the outset that Newman would not have become a Catholic had he not believed that the Catholic Church was given the gift of infallibility to discern and interpret revelation correctly. Newman accepted the principle of the infallibility of the Church as a Tractarian, as his Oxford colleagues did also.

Newman was persuaded that true development of doctrine was not possible without infallibility of the external authority monitoring such development. Granted that developments are necessary in matters of doctrine in the divine order of things, Newman then argues to the need for an external authority to monitor such development. This,

Newman argues, is antecedently probable. He introduces Section II. *An Infallible Developing Authority to be Expected:*[46]

> Reasons shall be given in this Section for concluding that, in proportion to the probability of true developments of doctrine and practice in the Divine Scheme, so is also the probability of the appointment in that scheme of an external authority to decide upon them, thereby separating them from the mass of mere human speculation, extravagance, corruption, and error, in and out of which they grow. This is the doctrine of the infallibility of the Church; for by infallibility I suppose is meant the power of deciding whether this, that, and a third, and any number of theological or ethical statements are true.[47]

What, as we have seen, distinguished Newman from his fellow Anglo-Catholics was that he saw that the primacy of the Pope could over-trump a General Council as had happened at Chalcedon and that as a result the infallible decisions of a Council could be expressed by a Pope or the Pope's legates without question from the other bishops.

In writing *Essay on the Development of Christian Doctrine,* you might say that Newman had written himself into the Catholic Church. He argues, on the principle of development, for the infallibility of the Church and for Papal Supremacy. Many have quite legitimately wondered, therefore, why, when the First Vatican Council was summoned by Pope Pius IX in 1868, Newman was against the definition of papal infallibility. He joined the party of what were somewhat ineptly called the 'Inopportunists'. They held that the doctrine of papal infallibility was 'inopportune' to define at the time of the First Vatican Council. Such a minority included, with Newman, those inclined to Conciliarism in the French ('Gallican') Church, Monsignor Dupanloup, and Dr Döllinger, the Bavarian church historian (1799–1890); although the latter was more extreme, and after the definitions of Vatican I left the Church.[48]

Newman and the Inopportunists would have had two major problems with the late nineteenth century timing of any definition of papal primacy and infallibility. The first was **political**. During the nineteenth century the political power of the papacy was declining together with the collapse of the Austro-Hungarian Empire, what was left of the 'Holy Roman Empire'. The Popes still ruled the 'papal states', from which they drew both financial support for the papacy and political power in Europe. But with growing Italian Nationalism, in 1860 the Papal States were mostly absorbed into the Kingdom of Italy, and finally even the city of Rome was absorbed in 1870.

This of course left the Pope in a precarious position in Rome, a problem which was not resolved finally until 1929, when the Lateran Treaty was signed,[49] giving the Pope Vatican City, a square mile of his own territory over which he was sovereign. Until then, there was always a fear (real or imagined) among the political powers in Europe that the Pope would once more attempt a political coup to restore his political fortunes.

The concern was, therefore, that if papal primacy and infallibility was dogmatised by the First Vatican Council, this would only spark off alarm in Europe that the Pope was once more after his ancient powers.

It is this political fear which explains what a 'liberal' comment is to some from Newman in his *Letter to the Duke of Norfolk*. Newman is quoted as saying in that letter 'I would drink to the Pope. But I would drink to my own conscience first.' However that comment is in the context of the attacks on the Pope from Europe's politicians fearful of papal political ambition. Newman could not accept the infallibility of the Church without using his conscience to make that judgement. It was not therefore a political but a moral choice.

The second major problem for the Inopportunists was their fear that the right wing papal party within the Church (called the 'Ultramontanes', that is, the views of those 'beyond the mountains', south over the Alps) would dominate the Church. The Ultramontanes were strong in the newly emancipated Catholic Church in England, headed by Cardinal Manning, Archbishop of Westminster, 1865–1892,[50] a convert widower clergyman from Anglicanism.

A friend of Gladstone, if Manning had stayed in the Church of England no doubt he would have become Archbishop of Canterbury. Manning was a consummate ecclesiastical politician, and was one of the dominant forces at the First Vatican Council. He saw Newman as insufficiently strong in his Catholic theology; but in the end, the formula of the definition of the Infallibility of the Pope was itself weaker than Manning and the Ultramontanes would have liked. It is said that Wilfred Ward, a rampant Ultramontane, would have liked an infallible decree of the Pope every morning at breakfast with his copy of *The Times*!

Newman, as we have seen, accepted both the infallibility of the Church and the supremacy of the Pope. He would not have become a Catholic unless he had. But his *model* of the *exercise* of papal authority was different to that of the Ultramontanes. In the Anglo-Catholic tradition, the prime organ of the definition of doctrine was the Ecumenical Council, not the Pope. After all, it was not until after four hundred years from the founding of the Christian faith that the Pope made an explicit and effective intervention at the Council of Chalcedon. Newman's Pope was always more laid-back, only entering into situations when there was an emergency.

Newman was what we might call a 'moderate infallibilist'. More specifically, as a nineteenth-century ecclesiastical historian, we might say, he was a fifth century papalist, seeing the Pope's role precisely as did Leo the Great. At that time, the Christian empire was dependant on local Episcopal authority, with much of its universal rule under imperial authority, the great Sees such as Constantinople, Alexandria, and Carthage, and indeed Rome, very much ruling themselves by their bishops. Only at moments such as Ephesus in 431 and Chalcedon in 451 was it necessary for the Pope to intervene, in order to provide that unity of the whole Church in matters of essential doctrine which the Bishop of Rome alone could provide.

It is only in more recent centuries, and particularly since the forming of the Vatican State in the twentieth century, that the global nature of the Church has required structures in the Vatican 'square mile' equivalent to ministries in the modern State, and day to day executive authority from the centre. The exercise of such authority is still controversial within the Catholic Church herself. But Newman must have foreseen such a process at least beginning at the end of the nineteenth century, towards the end of his life. Having accepted papal infallibility defined by Vatican I as a legitimate development of his own theology, indeed his own faith, he would have seen the potential of such development into the structures of the modern papacy as likewise a legitimate development of the doctrine of the primacy and infallibility of the successor of Peter. A major spur for such development was the advent of Modernism.

## Notes

1. For the text of the Athanasian Creed (historically most probably later than Athanasius) http://anglicansonline.org/basics/athanasian.html [accessed 19 February 2013].
2. For a critical introduction to the Athanasian Creed, cf. http://www.ccel.org/ccel/schaff/creeds1.iv.v.html [accessed 19 February 2013].
3. http://www.bbc.co.uk/humber/famous_folk/wesley/biography.shtml [accessed 19 February 2013].
4. http://www.britannica.com/EBchecked/topic/191050/Erastianism. [accessed 19 February 2013].
5. J. H. Newman, *An Essay on the Development of Christian Doctrine* (Notre Dame Series in the Great Books). Foreword by I. Ker .
6. I possess a copy of the 1890 edition of the *Essay on the Development of Christian Doctrine*, the seventh, Longmans, Green and Co. In this edition, the *Advertisement to the First Edition* is on pp. ix-xi.
7. DCD, p. 53.
8. *Ibid.*, p. 54.
9. *Ibid.*, p. 56–7.

10   *Ibid.*, pp. 58–9.
11   *Ibid.*, p. 74.
12   *Ibid.*, p. 75
13   http://mb-soft.com/believe/txc/novation.htm [accessed 19 February 2013]
14   DCD, p. 385
15   *Ibid.*, p. 386.
16   *Ibid.*, pp. 386–7.
17   http://www.newadvent.org/cathen/04045a.htm. [accessed 19 February 2013] The Catholic Encyclopaedia tells us 'Date of birth unknown; died about the year 215. St Clement was an early Greek theologian and head of the catechetical school of Alexandria.'
18   DCD, p. 388.
19   *Ibid.*
20   *Ibid.*, p. 389.
21   *Ibid.*, p. 390.
22   http://www.purgatoryisreal.blogspot.com/
23   For discussion of canonicity, see my Maryvale course book *The Theology of Revelation*. For the list of canonical books of scripture of the Old and New Testament defined by the Council of Trent, cf. CCC 120.
24   DCD, p. 68.
25   Tanner, II, p. 732*.
26   http://www.newadvent.org/cathen/12582a.htm. 1800–1882. [accessed 19 February 2013] After whom was named Pusey House Oxford.
27   http://www.britannica.com/EBchecked/topic/131168/conciliarism [accessed 19 February 2013].
28   http://www.newadvent.org/cathen/05495a.htm [accessed 19 February 2013].
29   http://www.newadvent.org/cathen/05631a.htm [accessed 19 February 2013]. This article makes a subtle distinction between Eutychianism and Monophysitism. But the essential doctrine of both Monophysites and Eutychians was that Jesus was two natures divine and human before the Incarnation, and one nature after it.
30   DCD, p. 299.
31   http://www.newadvent.org/fathers/3604028.htm.
32   DCD, p. 299.
33   Scholastic theology came to make a clear distinction between *natura*, the specific essence of a thing, and *persona*, the individual existent intellectual being. Thus Jesus Christ is two natures, divine and human, and one person, the person of the Word. But for Cyril, there was a tendency to make *phusis* (nature) approximated to, without being actually synonymous with, *hupostasis* (person). In this sense, therefore, Cyril could easily say that before the Incarnation, there were two natures, divine and human, and after it, one, since by that he could mean what we mean by one 'person'. However, Cyril clearly rejected

the view that there was a fusion of natures after the Incarnation. And he accepted the compromise formula for peace with the Antiochenes approved at Ephesus 431, which clearly affirmed the two natures divine and human after the Incarnation. Cyril's more militant right-wing supporters, however, such as Euthyches and Dioscorus, were resentful of Cyril's acceptance of this formula, and after Cyril's death in 444 pursued a more explicitly Monophysite path. Cf. ECD, pp. 321–328.

34  DCD, p. 300.
35  Ibid., p. 305.
36  Ibid., pp. 306–7.
37  http://en.wikipedia.org/wiki/Council_of_Chalcedon [accessed 19 February 2013].
38  DCD, p. 307.
39  Ibid., p. 308.
40  Theodoret of Cyrus, http://en.wikipedia.org/wiki/Theodoret. [accessed 19 February 2013]. His life is full of ambiguities, seeming on the one hand to support the Nestorians, then the Monophysites. The Pope simply restored him to his rightful place as a bishop at the Council of Chalcedon.
41  DCD, p. 308.
42  Ibid., p. 309
43  Ibid., p. 311.
44  Ibid., p. 312.
45  Ibid., p. 322.
46  Ibid., p. 75.
47  Ibid., p. 78–9.
48  http://en.wikipedia.org/wiki/Johann_Joseph_Ignaz_von_D%C3%B6llinger [accessed 20 February 2013].
49  http://en.wikipedia.org/wiki/Vatican_City [accessed 20 February 2013].
50  http://www.newadvent.org/cathen/09604b.htm [accessed 20 February 2013].

# 3

# MODERNISM AND THE QUEST FOR THE HISTORICAL CHURCH

## 3.1 RADICAL POST-REFORMATION CRITICISM

*The historical study of the scriptures inspired by Protestantism led, with the Enlightenment, to a radical criticism of the sources of Christian revelation itself.*

The Anglo-Catholic Tractarians were to a large extent immune from the investigation of the scriptures inspired by the Reformation. The Anglo-Catholics were less interested in what critical and historical investigation revealed, and much more interested in that meaning of scripture handed on by the tradition of the Fathers.

Luther was deeply suspicious of the spiritual sense as practiced by the Fathers of the Church. He favoured the historical method, because for him that alone uncovered what God actually wanted to say to the believing individual. For Luther, the scriptures explained themselves, and needed no Church or Tradition to explain them. 'For Luther, the scriptures have one meaning, a simple unequivocal one.'[1] This, together with the classical revival of the Renaissance, led to a boom in the study of scripture, both the Old and New Testaments.

In Germany, once the authority of the Church was abandoned, the critical method went still further to question the sources of Revelation itself. Luther had already questioned the canon of the New Testament, seeing contradictions between the Epistle of James (2:14) which emphasised the necessity of works as well as faith, and Paul's doctrine of justification by faith (Rm 5:1), which was the lynchpin of Luther's *sola fidei* soteriology. 'If anyone can harmonize these sayings, I'll put my doctor's cap on him and let him call me a fool'.[2]

Early criticisms of the Gospels led Eichhorn in the eighteenth century to propose a primitive Gospel in Aramaic, Jesus' own language, which the Gospels we have embellished.[3] He had hoped by this critical analysis to stave off even more radical criticisms of scripture stemming from the seventeenth century, proposed by the English Deists such as Lord Herbert of Cherbury, which denied the supernatural character of revelation. These were influenced by the growth of scientific knowledge that led to the denial of miracles, reverting to a 'natural religion', although they accepted the existence of a God of reason.[4]

This prepared the way for a radical examination of the Gospels within the German Lutheran Church of the eighteenth and nineteenth century, and in consequence, a correspondingly radical view of the Church emerged. For Herbert Samuel Reimarus, in *The Aims of Jesus and His Disciples*, Jesus was not the eternal Son of God become Man, but a Jewish prophet who led a failed revolution in Jerusalem. His disciples, preferring the new life as preachers to which Jesus had introduced them, rather than their previous fishing career, stole away his body and invented the myth of his resurrection. A Church founded on such fantasies could hardly with any credibility claim that Jesus had founded an infallible church, or that Peter was the leader of anything but a bunch of charlatans.

As I point out in *Bad, Mad or God*,[5] rejection of the Incarnation and of the miraculous in the life of Jesus was a presupposition of Reimarus and those in the nineteenth century, most notably David Friedrich Strauss, who followed what came to be called 'The Quest of the Historical Jesus'. It was never formally proved. The great Albert Schweitzer recorded the history of this Quest up to his own day at the end of the nineteenth century, admitted freely:

> This dogma had to be shattered before men could once more go in quest of the historical Jesus, before

they could even grasp the thought of his existence. That the historic Jesus is something different from the Jesus Christ of the doctrine of the Two Natures seems to us now self-evident. [6]

Of course, there had been intense philosophical discussion of the Incarnation post-Reformation, the doctrine of the two natures being denied for instance by the Socinians.[7] Those such as the nineteenth-century Berlin professor Friedrich Schleiermacher sometimes named 'the father of modern theology', also attempted to work out a Christology, which however the radical critic Strauss himself claimed was 'not meeting the requirements either of the faith of the Church, or of science'.[8] What was lacking, however, was any attempt by scholars of orthodox faith to attempt systematically to reconcile the dogma of the two natures with the historical-critical investigation of the four Gospels, or if they did so attempt, to make any impact on the world of scholarship. For that we had to wait until the twentieth century, and even the twenty-first.

## 3.2 HISTORICAL JESUS TO HISTORICAL CHURCH

*In the nineteenth century, attempts were made to develop the 'historical church' from the 'historical Jesus'.*

The critical scholars investigating 'The Quest of the Historical Jesus' were not long in applying their methods to consideration of the origins of the Christian Church. If Jesus was just a religious fanatic becoming unpopular with the Jewish authorities, any community which bore his name could hardly have a promising beginning.

For Ferdinand Christian Baur,[9] Professor of Church History and Dogmatics at Tübingen University 1826–60,[10] and rooted in Hegelian evolutionary philosophy, there were two factions in the primitive church. The first, the 'Petrine', saw Peter as the leader appointed to be the Rock by Christ. This for Baur was the 'thesis', this party favouring continuance of the Jewish Law in the new Christian community. Then there was the Pauline school, which demanded freedom from the Law. This was the 'antithesis'. According to Baur, what we see in 1 Peter and most of all in the Acts of the Apostles in particular is a compromise. Peter and Paul agree in Acts 15 that there should be no demand for Gentile Christians to be circumcised, but there was the demand that they should obey certain Jewish legal precepts, as for instance to eat *kosher*. 'It has been decided by the Holy Spirit and by ourselves not to impose on you any burden beyond these essentials: you are to abstain from food sacrificed to idols, from blood, from the meat of strangled animals and from illicit marriages. Avoid these, and you will do what is right. Farewell!' This was the Hegelian 'synthesis' resolving the supposed conflict between the Petrine and the Pauline parties. (Ac 15:28–29)

Implicit in this Hegelian analysis was an anti-institutionalist bias. The 'baddies' were the Petrine party, wishing to take the first Christians back to the Jewish Law. The 'goodies' were the Pauline charismatics, breaking out into freedom from the Law (cf. Ga 2:4). Implicit also in this analysis was a negative view of the Jewish Law, particularly in its later history, promoted by critical Old Testament scholars such as Julius Wellhausen, who saw the Jewish Law as a late and very negative development from the spontaneous 'natural religion' practised by the early Israelite community.[11]

What Baur and the nineteenth-century German Lutheran critical movement could not accept was that the apostles, whether Peter or Paul, were handed on genuine authority from the historical Jesus. Indeed, the Tübingen University scholars of the nineteenth century, of whom Baur was a most notable representative, did not have any firm conviction that the historical Jesus actually existed at all. Authority coming from such a mythical figure could hardly be a convincing foundation for a Christian community.

In the second half of the nineteenth century, Liberal Protestantism was born, which proposed its own compromise, modifying the extremes of the Hegelians. Holtzmann persuaded German theology that Mark's Gospel was first, and that it presented a fundamentally reliable picture of the life and teaching of Jesus of Nazareth. For Holtzmann, Jesus of Nazareth did indeed exist, although he shared German scepticism regarding the miracles of Jesus, his resurrection, and his divine nature. Holtzmann believed that Jesus preached an ethical kingdom of God, did not expect a future kingdom, or the Church which actually emerged. It must be rejected as a supernatural additive. But the historical Jesus was indeed a good man, even a prophet, whose mission ultimately failed because it was too idealistic.[12]

Holtzmann's view of Jesus appealed to many sceptical German Lutherans of the nineteenth century, as indeed it has a general appeal to a modern public who cannot accept that Jesus was truly the Son of God become Man, and who truly rose from the dead. However it can agree he was truly a good man who had a good influence on his contemporaries, and indeed on later generations. In this way, Jesus is comparable with Buddha, Mohammed, Ghandi and many other great religious leaders. This view is popular in the world of scholarship, and even as presented in stage productions such as Jesus Christ, Superstar.

Albert Schweitzer, compiling his masterly summary of the Quest of the Historical Jesus up to his own day, was scathing of Holtzmann's liberal Jesus. Schweitzer claimed that it was no better than an image of a bourgeois German of the nineteenth century, not of the historical Jesus at all. But we must wonder whether Schweitzer's Jesus was any more credible. For Schweitzer, Jesus was in reality a Jewish prophet who thought that the end of the world was coming. He went up to Jerusalem to prepare for that coming kingdom, but was mistaken, and was put to death by the Jewish authorities. Holtzmann's popular social reformer is replaced by a religious fanatic. Schweitzer's Jesus thought that his death would be the prelude to the coming of the kingdom. Instead, what happened was only his death. For Schweitzer, Jesus preached during his life only an 'interim ethic', the dogma and canon law of the Catholic Church actually emerging after his death and entirely outside of his intention. 'Jesus preached the kingdom, and the Church came into being' claimed Schweitzer, the Church which therefore came to be having little in common with the message which the historical Jesus preached.

After having published his epoch-making work *The Quest of the Historical Jesus* (the German title being *Von Reimarus zu Wrede*, 'From Reimarus to Wrede') Schweitzer considered that there was in reality nothing more to be said regarding the historical Jesus. Indeed, the final paragraph of his book indicated that, for him, the quest of the historical Jesus was at an end, to be replaced by the Jesus that could be found in human experience:-

> He comes to us as One unknown, without a name, as of old, by the lakeside, He came to those men who knew him not. He speaks to us the same word: 'Follow thou me!' and sets to us the tasks which He has to fulfil for our time. He commands. And to those who obey Him, whether they be wise or simple, He will reveal Himself in the toils, the conflicts and the sufferings which they shall pass through in His fellowship, and, as an ineffable mystery, they shall learn in their experience who He is.[13]

Schweitzer then took himself off as a Lutheran missionary to found a hospital in Africa, where he achieved fame as a surgeon and as a sage. Jesus was now for Schweitzer one 'without a name' who could only be encountered through experience, not through searching for the historical Jesus. But others would have to continue that search, wherever it led.

## 3.3 CHANGE

*Both Protestant and Catholic Modernism arose from the perceived need to adapt the Christian faith to a world of change. We look at Strauss' Life of Jesus as a prime example of such attempted adaptation.*

How far was revelation, the living tradition of the Church, itself changeable, and how could it develop without losing its identity? This was the central question addressed by Modernism, a movement which profoundly affected both the Protestant and Catholic Churches at the end of the nineteenth century and the beginning of the twentieth.

Modernism was rooted in a very complex set of ideas. Perhaps the best single presentation of these ideas, albeit as presented in a hostile way, is in Pope Pius X's Encyclical Letter *Pascendi*, which we will examine a little more closely later. However since we have begun our own quest with consideration of the Quest of the Historical Jesus, a fruitful approach for us might be to look at the ideas of David Friedrich Strauss. His philosophy illuminates Modernism in his approach to the Gospels.

Strauss was a Lutheran pastor, appointed early on as Professor because of his prestigious intellect. In 1838, he published his most famous, and to some notorious work, *Das Leben Jesu Kritisch Bearbeitet*. ('The Life of Jesus Critically Examined.'). He was soon expelled from the Lutheran Seminary for his unorthodoxy, but was appointed Professor in the Swiss Protestant town of Zurich. The people of the city revolted against such a heretic being appointed. Strauss could not take up his post as Professor, but because he had been formally appointed, he was given a pension for life. He continued to produce editions of his *Life of Jesus*, but none made any impact comparable with his early work.

*Das Leben Jesu* in its 1838 edition was translated into English by none other than George Eliot, author of *Middlemarch* and other novels.[14] She was the sceptical daughter of a parson. She eventually became tired out with translating

Strauss' massive work, although completing the task, and wondering whether anyone would read it. Certainly, in choosing to write novels rather than to continue translating scholarly works, she made a good decision in terms of readership.

We have already referred to the philosophy of Hegel, which was all the rage in early nineteenth-century Germany. Strauss was a radical Hegelian, and interpreted Hegel's philosophy of change in a way which he hoped would provide a convincing new presentation of the Christian faith; although on reflection, at the end of his life, he had to admit that he was no longer a Christian, but was, he insisted, 'spiritual'.

Strauss was the first historical-Jesus scholar to call the Gospels 'myth'. The early Rationalists after Reimarus had accepted the Gospels as recounting historical fact, but had interpreted that fact as non-miraculous. Thus the miracle of the five thousand fed miraculously with five loaves and two fishes was interpreted by the Rationalists as being when in reality all shared their lunches which they had brought; and Paulus, perhaps the Prince of Rationalists, Professor at the Catholic University of Heidelberg, interpreted the Transfiguration story as the early morning sunlight shining on Jesus, together with two strangers who appeared from somewhere, but by no means supernaturally, on the mountain top.

Strauss, with the Rationalists, shared the rejection of the possibility of the miraculous, and therefore of the incarnation of Jesus. He went even further: for him the story was itself without any historical foundation, a 'myth' based often on an Old Testament story applied to Jesus by the credulous Gospel writers. Thus there was no feeding of the five thousand even by sharing. The whole story was only an upgrading of the prophet Elishah's feeding the two hundred men at Baal Shalisha with a small quantity of loaves and fishes (2 K 4:42–44).

Underlying Strauss' investigation of the Gospels was a distinctive Hegelian philosophy. Hegel had distinguished between the *Vorstellung* ('Representation') and the *Begriff* ('Concept'). The Concept could remain the same, while its Representation was a changeable phenomenon. Thus for Strauss, the Gospel stories recounting supernatural events such as Jesus walking on the water or rising from the dead were examples of Representation, a myth. But the Concept which underlay those mythical stories was fixed and serviceable for the modern world.

In Strauss' project of finding a modern replacement for the old Presentation of the Christian faith could be seen as in reality the project of the whole of the Modernist movement. The world, it seemed, could no longer accept that Jesus appeared bodily to the amazed disciples; but was there not some valuable truth which could be salvaged as the true *Begriff* of these old Gospel *Vorstellungen*?

Strauss himself had to admit that he had not by the end of his sad life replaced the dogmas of Christian faith with any satisfactory alternative. His own solution was the demythologisation of Christ by making Jesus not God but the symbol of true humanity although it is difficult to see how this new *Vorstellung* differs from a straightforward atheistic presentation of human evolution. This was the whole problem of Modernism. It was easier to tear down than to rebuild.

## 3.4 HARNACK AND LOISY

*The Protestant Harnack and the Catholic Loisy attempted to provide a systematic theology of the Church to present to the twentieth century as a viable alternative to orthodox Christianity.*

The classical Liberal Protestant position was developed by Adolf Harnack, who extended Holtzmann's studies of the historical Jesus, applied those principles much further to the early history of the Church, and worked out a full ecclesiology based upon the Gospel criticism of the previous century. For Harnack, the early Church evolved more and more in a Catholic direction, converting the simple religion of Jesus of Nazareth. He developed Holtzmann's view of Jesus as an ethical reformer, to that institution which soon was dominated by Greek Hellenist philosophy. 'In the winter of 1899–1900 he delivered a celebrated course of lectures stressing the moral side of Christianity, especially the claims of human brotherhood, to the exclusion of all that was doctrinal'.[15]

For Harnack, the historical Jesus 'expected his imminent return, but by regarding as the real content of Jesus' thought faith alone in the inwardness of God's kingdom and by assuming that the disciples at a very early time abandoned Jesus' way of thinking in favour of a mere hope for the future'.[16]

Early Reformers had viewed the Middle Ages as the time when the simple biblical religion of Jesus had been converted by the Catholic Church into the system which Luther had brought down in German Protestant lands. However, Harnack, a consummate church historian, had realised that such a judgement did not at all conform to the facts. He realised that early Catholicism (*Frühkatholizismus*) began in apostolic times, immediately after the death of Jesus. Building on Albert Schweitzer's reconstruction of the historical Jesus together with his own knowledge of the history of the apostolic church, Harnack proposed that the Catholic system in fact began with those first Christians, who had to cope with the harsh reality that Jesus did not return immediately to bring about the kingdom of God. The Catholic system therefore in fact began at this earliest time, early Catholicism compensating for the non-return of Jesus by forming a Hellenistic church, centred on the worship of Jesus as a Greek God. For Harnack, this Hellenistic Church had no serious connection with the life and teaching of the historical Jesus.

The most famous Catholic Modernist, Alfred Loisy, was closer to Schweitzer than to Holtzmann, refusing to agree with Harnack that Jesus preached an ethical message. Rather, as with Schweitzer, 'the primitive Gospel was the proclamation of a sudden and definitive coming of a Kingdom of God that was quite foreign to this world and swooped upon it only to do away with it.'[17] But importantly, Loisy accepted that the message of the historical Jesus was not that of Catholic orthodoxy. Jesus' expectation of a whirlwind kingdom did not actually come to pass, and, like the Protestant Modernists, he thought that the Church was created in an image totally unlike that which the historical Jesus either predicted or expected. Loisy rejected entirely the historicity of the Gospel of John, which proclaimed explicitly the divinity of Christ. Loisy's dictum 'They were expecting the Kingdom of God, and it was the Church that came.' was a statement while sounding innocuous enough, was an explicit contradiction of Catholic ecclesiology because the church which emerged after the death of Jesus was not in any sense a fulfilment of Jesus' own expectations.

It was at first encouraging that like Harnack, Loisy located *Frühkatholizismus* in the apostolic age, immediately after the death of Jesus; but that still was not early enough for Pope Pius X. The obvious problem for the Pope and for orthodox Catholics was that there seemed to be zero compatibility between the Schweitzerian religious fanatic Jesus of Nazareth who mistakenly thought that the kingdom of God was coming in his own lifetime when it did not; and the Christ of the Catholic creeds who was of one substance (*homóousios*) with God his eternal Father and who knew all things (Jn 21:17).

## 3.5 PIUS X AND *PASCENDI*

*Pope Pius X tackled Modernism philosophically in his Encyclical* **Pascendi**, *and practically in removing from office and excommunicating those seen as tainted with Modernism.*

Pope Saint Pius X was born on 2 June 1835, baptised Giuseppe Melchiorre Sarto, the son of a postman. He studied hard, earned a scholarship to seminary, and rose to become bishop of Mantua in 1884, then Patriarch of Venice and Cardinal, June 1893, and after the death of Pope Leo XIII was elected Pope on Sunday, 9 August, 1903.[18]

Pius X is adjudged by history to be harsh and oppressive regarding what he saw as the new heresy of Modernism, initiating a programme of repression of modernist ideas in the training of priests, and the censorship of books. The anger of a man born into a poor family who rose to the highest office in the Church, and saw the need to defend the faith against the ravening wolves of modern thought is clear in his famous encyclical *Pascendi*, ('Pasturing', that is, 'the flock'). The encyclical breathes deep anger. Pius X was no ecumenist! Yet the encyclical is masterly in its analysis of the problems raised by the Modernist crisis; and we would be naïve to think that a century later we have put to bed all the issues raised by *Pascendi*

The real issue is that Modernism is not a heresy like the denial by Arius of the divinity of Christ, but rather a way of thinking which permeates one's whole approach to religious faith. Thus it can co-exist with many orthodox ideas. This is where *Pascendi* is useful today, since Pius X exposes Modernism first as a subjectivist philosophy, then as the reduction of religion to experience, thirdly as a defective view of faith, fourthly as destructive of the relationship between faith and science, fifthly as denying the divine inspiration of the scriptures, sixthly as undermining the divinity of Christ, and finally as relativising magisterium and dogma.

We cannot deal with each of these issues raised in *Pascendi*. The Pope reveals himself as fully aware of Strauss' view, which we considered earlier, regarding the reducing of dogma to a changeable representation of the truth. According to Pius X, the Modernist holds that God is immanent in us and that 'the representations of the object of faith are merely symbolical' (para.19). We have seen that this is central to the critique of orthodoxy in Strauss' Life of Jesus.

The Pope also demonstrates that he is aware of the debates regarding the historical Jesus. Historical science for the Modernist, according to Pius X, 'sees in Christ nothing more than a man whose religious consciousness has been, like that of all men, formed by degrees.' (Para. 20). Orthodoxy would not deny that the mind of Jesus developed, as we are told in Luke's Gospel, that 'Jesus increased in wisdom and in stature, and in favour with God and man.' (Lk 3:52). However this would be for the orthodox Christian the developing consciousness of one who was truly God become Man. However for Holtzmann Jesus was a mere man with a developing messianic consciousness to provide social change in the environment of his day.

So, for the Pope, the Modernist now defines the Church: 'What, then, is the Church? It is the product of the collective conscience that is to say of the society of individual consciences which by virtue of the principle of vital permanence, all depend on one first believer, who for Catholics is Christ. Now every society needs a directing authority to guide its members towards the common end, to conserve prudently the elements of cohesion which in a religious society are doctrine and worship. Hence the triple authority in the Catholic Church, disciplinary, dogmatic, liturgical.' (Para. 23). Catholic Modernists would distinguish themselves from the Protestant Modernist in this insistence upon the Church. However now, in the Modernist version of the Catholic Church, the Pope explains in the same paragraph: 'For in the same way as the Church is a vital emanation of the collectivity of consciences, so too authority emanates vitally from the Church itself. Authority therefore, like the Church, has its origin in the religious conscience, and, that being so, is subject to it. Should it disown this dependence it becomes a tyranny.' As we shall see later, such a view of the Church is by no means redundant among Christian communities in the new millennium.

## 3.6 THOMISM

*The Thomist philosophy revived by Pope Leo XIII, Pope Pius X's predecessor, expresses some principles which are essential foundations in response to Modernism.*

Pope Pius X's predecessor, Pope Leo XIII, had restored the study of Thomism in seminaries and Catholic institutes of higher education. This scholastic revival, based on the philosophy and theology of St Thomas Aquinas, is for Pius X the key intellectual response to cure the malaise of Modernism. As the Successor of Peter, the Pope orders his brother bishops, members of the Apostolic College 'On this philosophical foundation the theological edifice is to be solidly raised.'[19]

This commendation of Aquinas is reiterated almost a century later in the encyclical *Fides et Ratio*, Faith and Reason, 1998 of Pope John Paul II: 'More radically, Thomas recognized that nature, philosophy's proper concern, could contribute to the understanding of divine Revelation. Faith therefore has no fear of reason, but seeks it out and has trust in it.'[20]

Thomism was the theological underpinning of the First Vatican Council, summoned in 1870 to counter the growing threat of agnosticism and secularism in Europe. Vatican I, less than forty years before *Pascendi*, provides for Pius X the counter to the destructive revelation theology of Modernism:

- Vatican I insists that God can be objectively known by reason alone. We are not restricted as the German philosopher, Kant claimed only to what appears to us, the phenomena.[21]
- Faith is not just an expression of religious sentiment, but is 'the full homage of intellect and will to God who reveals himself'.[22]
- Although faith is a gift of God's Holy Spirit, reason works with faith in discerning the truth of divine

revelation through 'divine facts' (*facta divina*). Thus miracles and prophecies are not myths, but rather 'the most certain signs of the divine revelation, adapted to the intelligence of all men'.[23]

- The Church is not merely the collective consciousness of believers, but the infallible transmitter of truths which are not subject to the corruption of the evolutionary process, but 'through her ordinary and universal teaching office, are proposed for belief as having been divinely revealed'.[24]

These principles we will utilise in the next chapter, in order to provide a philosophical and theological underpinning of our case that the historical Jesus truly was God become Man, and that he came to earth to found a Church which we now call the Catholic Church.

## Notes

1   NTHIP, p. 22.
2   Ibid., p. 26.
3   Ibid., pp. 78–79.
4   Ibid., pp. 51–61.
5   BMG, pp. 39–42.
6   QHJ, pp. 3–4.
7   LJCE, p. 764.
8   LJCE, p. 772.
9   NTHIP, p. 127 ff., cf. especially pp. 129–30.
10  Ibid., p. 467.
11  'Wellhausen follows well the impulses of Hegel and Vatke in the presentation of the historical process, but his estimation of this process and its teleology is totally otherwise. Vatke attempted to follow Hegel in building a bridge to the New Testament, in order to find there the last phase of the self-realisation of the absolute Spirit. Where Wellhausen is concerned, there is no such pathway'. Kraus, Hans-Joachim, *Geschichte der historisch-kritischen Erforschung des Alten Testaments*. Neukirchener Verlag, Rev. Ed., p. 268.
12  Holtzmann, *The New Testament: The History of the Investigation of its Problems*, pp. 151–2. So also Dungan, 1999, p. 327: 'Holtzmann's book (*Die Synoptischen Evangelien: Ihr Ursprung und geshichlichen Character*, 1863), with a few exceptions, was greeted as a masterpiece, not only

because it seemed to proceed with such caution and deft mastery of the best of modernist Protestant Gospel scholarship, but also because it appeared to give a solid answer to the doubts raised by Strauss about the historical Jesus'.

13  QHJ, 401.
14  LJCE.
15  ODCC, p. 620.
16  NTHIP, p. 178.
17  L. Bouyer, *The Church of God: Body of Christ and Temple of the Spirit*, translated by Charles Underhill Quinn, (Chicago: Franciscan Herald Press, 1982), p. 4. First Edition *L'Église de Dieu* (Paris: Les Editions du Cerf, 1970).
18  http://www.newadvent.org/cathen/12137a.htm [accessed 20 February 2013]
19  Pope St Pius X, *Pascendi*, 46.
20  Pope John Paul II, *Fides et Ratio*, 43.
21  ND **113**.
22  *Ibid.*, **118**.
23  *Ibid.*, **119**.
24  *Ibid.*, **121**.

# 4

# WHICH CHURCH?

## 4.1 THE FREE CHURCHES

*Christian communities without links to a tradition split up into groups which either claim each one the truth of their reading of scripture, or rely on the direct movement of the Spirit, which also leads to different interpretations and even to further scepticism.*

Roughly speaking, those Protestant Christian communities which have formed since the Reformation without formal links to the historic threefold ministry of the Church (of which historic ministry much more later) can be divided roughly into Evangelical based upon the reading of scripture as the Word of God, and Pentecostal, based upon the experience of the Holy Spirit in the community.

From the early twentieth century onwards, all the churches of Christendom had to take some account of the biblical criticism inspired by the Enlightenment. Some, called often without too much definition Fundamentalist, would see Modernism as the work of the devil. They would reject evolution and maintain that the world was created in six days exactly according to the book of Genesis. They would see their own church community as a true successor of the apostles, teaching the true Gospel originally taught by Jesus himself.

They would be the contemporary upholders of Luther's *sola scriptura*. The Bible, and the Bible alone, will be for them the sole norm of doctrine. They would not need the Magisterium to define doctrine. That is clearly stated in Luther's plain meaning of scripture. Nor would they need sophisticated biblical scholars to dissect the sacred text for them and strip away that plain meaning, or scientists to contradict it. They need neither bishops nor professors to tell them what the Bible means. As Luther says, scripture is its own interpreter (*ipsi suis interpres*).

And yet, if the Bible were that plain in meaning, then why do Fundamentalists disagree so much among themselves? Why are there so many churches all claiming to be based upon scripture alone?

It is in these church communities stemming more directly from the Protestant tradition that the Modernist crisis has in many cases been a destructive force. Without any reliance on church tradition, the British Free Churches have had their congregations decimated in the twentieth century, and surely one factor must have been the critical study of the scriptures. When the Fundamentalist begins to question his or her Fundamentalism, then it is quite possible to undermine one's whole faith, if that faith is based upon scripture alone.

It is surely no accident that the most powerful movement in twentieth century post-Modernist Christianity has been the phenomenal growth worldwide of Pentecostalism. In its origin, this stemmed from the Methodist Holiness Movement in the United States, looking for a 'second blessing' that same Holy Spirit poured out on the apostles on the Day of Pentecost. In 1905, at the Azuza Street Mission in Los Angeles, the congregation began to speak in tongues, and a fire was lit which spread not only over the United States, but into South America and other continents such as Africa, where there are said to be 20,000 separate and distinct Pentecostal Church communities.

Strictly speaking, Pentecostals are not *sola scriptura* Christians. What lights the Pentecostal fire is not the text of scripture, although that is of course vitally important as the Word of God. What moves the Spirit is nothing other than the Spirit itself, causing most of all the phenomenon of speaking in tongues, but giving other gifts such as prophecy and healing. The biblical critic is silenced when the Spirit actually moves. There is nothing more to be said or discussed.

But Pentecostals will often admit that the Spirit sometimes does not seem to be there. At the beginning, all is the power and the glory of the Spirit's presence. However is there the same spontaneity and fervour after weeks of services? What of the second generation of Pentecostals in a given church? Are the children of the first members of the Pentecostal congregation just as filled with the Spirit? An observer might go to a Pentecostal service, and find it little different from a standard Free Church act of worship, plus a short time of speaking in tongues, apparently quite a controlled affair as part of the service. Such a service would not be such as to set alight the community at Azuza Street.

Without perhaps being even aware of it, modern Pentecostals are successors of what was called 'the left wing of the Reformation'. These were groups in Europe who disagreed with Luther and the 'right wing' in that they did not consider the plain meaning of scripture the basis of faith, but rather the 'Holy Spirit within' (the *Spiritus Sanctus internus*). What mattered was not what the scriptures actually said, but the Holy Spirit speaking to me directly. This may or may not agree with the text of scripture, but that mattered nothing for the *Spiritus Sanctus Internus* movement. It was the Spirit speaking which was the sole authority.

Naturally, Luther was violently opposed to such groups. In fact, he considered them worse than the papists! Early communities such as the Anabaptists and later the Quakers in Britain were prime examples of such a movement. The Quakers are interesting, and perhaps another example of fading charismatics. The term 'Quaker' means one who shakes, an early phenomenon demonstrating for the Quakers that the Spirit was speaking because they quaked and shook. Eventually, however, the Quakers quietened down, and became a group in silent prayer, as they are today.

A characteristic of the development of such groups is that they are suspicious of dogma, as opposed to the Holy Spirit within. In fact, Immanuel Kant, perhaps the most influential of the philosophers of modern times, was himself a Pietist, a member of a *Spiritus Sanctus Internus* community. He claimed that we could not know reality in itself (the 'noumena'), but only things as they appeared to us (the 'phenomena'). We could not for Kant argue to the existence of God from creation, but only from our internal moral sense of absolute obligation. And Jesus too for Kant was not objectively God become Man, but a man who personified the internal Spirit in us all.

## 4.2 TRADITIONAL CHURCHES

*Christian communities which are linked to an historical tradition have survived Modernism, but cannot answer the questions raised by biblical criticism or by the contemporary world with any authoritative teaching authority.*

Biblical criticism does not seem to have affected too strongly the Orthodox Churches such as the Greek or the Russian Orthodox, since they continue to read scripture only in the light of tradition. They have been separated from Rome for a millennium. They hold to the infallibility of the Church, but in General Council. They afford to the Bishop of Rome the primacy of honour as the successor of the Apostle Peter, but they neither afford to him the executive primacy over all the bishops which was expressed explicitly by the First Vatican Council, nor his infallibility.

Such churches claim infallibility, but have not exercised any act of infallibility since the General Councils of the Church such as Nicaea or Chalcedon in the fourth and fifth centuries. The latest Council, the Second Council of Nicaea in the eighth century defended the use of icons in worship. It is not unfair to say that their exercise of the Magisterium of the Church is at present dormant. To use such a Magisterium with such a disparate group of Orthodox Churches, often disagreeing with each other, only emphasises the difficulties inherent in such a use.

Anglo-Catholics also, as we have seen, maintain the infallibility of the whole body of bishops in General Council; but, similarly to the Orthodox, have not exercised such a right. Anglo-Catholics have an additional difficulty as compared with the Orthodox in that they do not exercise any actual authority within their own church, even less now since liberal decisions have been taken of the ordination of women and acceptance of openly gay clergy under certain conditions.

In effect, I would suggest that the Anglican Church worldwide has adopted what we might call the post-modernist or liberal view, which denies that we can know with certainty the nature of the Church from the Bible or from Church Tradition, since both the Bible and Tradition have to be estimated critically. Many Anglicans, I am sure, would hold that no doctrines can be defined infallibly, since the view of the Catholic Modernist George Tyrrell, expelled from the Jesuits, and excommunicated in 1907 is described by Oliver Rafferty:

> Tyrrell argued vehemently that Christianity was primarily a religion of the heart and that no formulation of the faith, restricted as this necessarily must be by the culture in which it is expressed, could do justice to the infinity of the God in whom we believe. In the face of dogmatic propositions he believed that we should maintain a 'tempered agnosticism'. After all, in dealing with God we are dealing with ultimate mystery. [1]

A church governed by such a concept, of a non-infallible worldwide community whose decisions are a manifestation of the collective consciousness of the church, as Pius X described the Modernist consequent ecclesiology:

> For in the same way as the Church is a vital emanation of the collectivity of consciences, so too authority emanates vitally from the Church itself. Authority therefore, like the Church, has its origin in the religious conscience, and, that being so, is subject to it.[2]

I trust that it would not be inaccurate to classify the authority structure of the Lambeth Conference, the consultative body of the bishops of the worldwide Anglican Communion, as being in this way the organ of the collective consciousness of that communion. The Lambeth Conference, meeting every ten years, has grown in its importance during the past two centuries, with the increasing internationalisation of the Anglican Church.[3] It is not an infallible magisterium, but an agreed statement on matters of faith and morals by the Conference which will hopefully have some moral authority throughout the Anglican Communion.

I trust also that it would not therefore be unfair to describe the Anglican Communion in its international Lambeth Conference statements as a post-Modernist ecclesial body. It does not accept *sola scriptura* since it sees the need critically to examine the scriptures post-Enlightenment; nor does it rely upon the *Spiritus Sanctus internus* in its decisions, since it would consider itself arrogant if it claimed that the authority of the Spirit spoke directly in its Conference statements; nor finally does it claim to be an infallible magisterium, because it does not claim that its formal statements on faith or morals are protected from error as does the Catholic magisterium, which, as we shall see more clearly later, only claims such protection from error, not the direct agency of the Spirit speaking in Catholic magisterial statements.

The decrees of the Lambeth Conference are not therefore an authoritative interpretation of revelation, as in the Catholic Church. In fact, none of the systems we have briefly examined, the *Sola Scriptura* Fundamentalists, those who have more explicitly embraced the Modernist frame, the Pentecostals, the early *Spiritus Sanctus Internus* left wing Protestants, the separated Orthodox Christians, none as with the Anglicans have any authoritative body which in fact has made in the past century declarations about revelation which must be accepted by those in communion with that ecclesial body.

## 4.3 EXERCISING AUTHORITY

*Only the Catholic Church, among all the denominations of Christendom, decrees matters of faith and of morality claiming full authority over her members, and claiming full authority for the development of her doctrines.*

The Catholic view is that any solemn definitions of the Pope and of the general body of Catholic bishops united with the Pope are with the assistance of the Holy Spirit infallible. We have to examine the meaning of this doctrine, and its historical justification, during the course of the rest of this book. But to the Modernist objection that any formulations of the faith must be tentative and inadequate, and while admitting that 'the believers' act (of faith) does not terminate in the propositions, but in the realities which they express',[4] the *Catechism of the Catholic Church* insists that 'All the same, we approach these realities with the help of formulations of the faith which permit us to express the faith and to hand it on, to celebrate it in community, to assimilate and live on it more and more'.[5]

What brought Newman into the Catholic Church was the clear connection for him between infallibility and the need for development. For Newman, unless an ecclesial body saw its judgements as infallible, they could not genuinely develop. Today, looking at the various denominations in post-Modernist Christianity, just as a century and a half ago in Newman's time, there is only one which manifests both authority and developing infallibility in its decisions; the Roman Catholic Church. For Newman, there needed to be an external infallible authority in order to have such true development:

> Reasons shall be given in this Section for concluding that, in proportion to the probability of true developments of doctrine and practice in the Divine Scheme, so is also the probability of the appointment in that scheme of an external authority to decide upon them, thereby separating them from the mass of mere human speculation, extravagance, corruption, and error, in and out of which they grow. This is the doctrine of the infallibility of the Church; for by infallibility I suppose is meant the power of deciding whether this, that, and a third, and any number of theological or ethical statements are true'.[6]

There is a distinction between truths attainable by reason and those only attainable by the gift of the theological virtue of faith. Whereas we, and indeed the first Christians, (Rm 13:1) accepted that 'the powers that be are ordained of God', the Church has never, thank God, encouraged us to believe that our secular rulers are therefore infallible! Presumably that is because the truths which govern our social life are principled in natural moral law, not in revelation. A government therefore does not need an infallible gift to decide what is to be done in political and social governance. That government can, indeed can only, use the reason which God gave it to govern for the common good.

The truths of revelation, on the contrary, are beyond the power of reason. Against the Modernists, doctrines must first be revealed, and their development must also be genuine. Indeed, according to Chapter Four of the Dogmatic Constitution Dei Filius on the Catholic Faith of the First Vatican Council:

> 13. For the doctrine of the faith which God has revealed is put forward not as some philosophical discovery capable of being perfected by human intelligence, but as a divine deposit committed to the spouse of Christ to be faithfully protected and infallibly promulgated.
>
> 14. Hence, too, that meaning of the sacred dogmas is ever to be maintained which has once been declared by Holy mother Church, and there must never be any abandonment of this sense under the pretext or in the name of a more profound understanding.[7]
>
> 15. 'May understanding, knowledge and wisdom increase as ages and centuries roll along, and greatly and vigorously flourish, in each and all, in the individual and the whole Church: but this only in its own proper kind, that is to say, in the same doctrine, the same sense, and the same understanding'.[8]

Newman's very concept of the development of doctrine is a defence of this Catholic thesis, that formulations of faith can develop, but retain their essential meaning as developed. Vincent of Lerins an ancient Father of the Church gives us the analogy of the body, which retains its specific essence as human throughout the changes, whereas 'alteration' changes the essence of the thing changed:

> It is desirable then that development should take place, and that there should be a great and vigorous growth in the understanding, knowledge and wisdom of every individual as of all the people, on the part of each member as well as of the whole Church, gradually over the generations and ages. But it must be growth within the limits of its own nature that is to say within the framework of the same dogma and of the same meaning.
>
> Let religion, which is of the spirit imitate the processes of the body. For, although bodies develop over the years and their individual parts evolve, they do not change into something different. It is true that there is a great gap between the prime of youth and the maturity of later years, but the people who reach these later years are the same people who once were adolescents. So, although the size and outward appearance of any individual may change, it is still the same person, and the nature remains the same.[9]

## 4.4 NECESSARY

*Such developments are necessary in order for the Church to stay strong and to fulfil her mission.*

Some today might question whether the Church needs to develop, and whether one might remain a Christian without needing any magisterium. Particularly regarding sexual ethics, many would claim that the Church ought to keep out of the bedroom, and get on with preaching the Gospel.

But Jesus, who was unmarried, in his preaching did not keep out of the bedroom. In response to questions addressed to him, he maintained the absolute indissolubility of marriage. In the contemporary rabbinic climate where divorce and remarriage was allowed, he said 'Those whom God has joined, let not man put asunder' (Mt 19:6). Questions continued after the resurrection of Jesus. Saint Paul had to insist again on Jesus' teaching (1 Co 7:12), and to make further regulations about Christians marrying non-Christians (1 Co 7:12–15). Paul obviously speaks with authority, as we shall see in a later Chapter.

Regarding doctrinal questions, we saw in the first Chapter how the growth of relativism in the modern world evoked a response from the Vatican Congregation for the Doctrine of the Faith affirming both the full divinity of Christ as the one and only Saviour of the human race, and the affirmation that there is one visible Catholic Church. Other churches are not able to speak with such authority to their members. How can it not be good for a Church to proclaim its essential faith and morality in a world which asks questions of such a Church?

Jesus himself, the apostles after his resurrection, and the Catholic Church in her General Councils and statements of the Popes right up to today continue to speak with such authority in the name of the Church, and there is no other Church today which does so. It seems therefore reasonable that those claims should be investigated in more detail.

We will then state what those claims are from the teaching authority of the Catholic Church, and then in subsequent Chapters attempt to defend the authenticity of those claims.

## 4.5 CATHOLIC CLAIMS

*We state the claims of the Catholic Church concerning the primacy of the Bishop of Rome as the successor of the apostle Peter, and the infallibility of the Pope and of the Catholic Bishops in union with the Pope.*

## VATICAN I ON PAPAL PRIMACY AND INFALLIBILITY

*The First Vatican Council, 1870, defined the primacy, that is the supreme authority over all the bishops of the Catholic Church, of the Bishop of Rome, as based upon the promise of the Lord Jesus Christ while on earth to Simon Peter. It then defined the pope's infallibility, that is to say the pope's power to define doctrine and morals, with that same infallible authority conferred by Christ on the whole Church.*

| The Eternal Shepherd<br>Chapter 1<br>On the institution of the apostolic primacy in blessed Peter | Pastor Aternus<br>Caput Prima<br>De Apostolic Primatus in Beato Petro Institutione |
|---|---|
| We teach and declare that, according to the gospel evidence, a primacy of jurisdiction over the whole Church of God was immediately and directly promised to the blessed apostle Peter and conferred on him by Christ the Lord. | Docemus itaque et declaramus, iuxta evangelii testimonia primatum iurisdictionis in universam Dei ecclesiam immediate et directe beato Petro apostolo promissum atque collatum a Christo Domino fuisse. |

Note that the primacy of Peter in this definition, defined as a matter of faith, gives the Pope 'primacy of jurisdiction' over the whole Episcopal body; not, as is the Orthodox position, simply a 'primacy of honour'.[10] Of course, Newman would have argued in the *Development* that precisely this 'primacy of jurisdiction' in matters of faith was exercised by Pope Leo the Great at Chalcedon.

> **Chapter 4**
> **The Infallible Magisterium of the Roman Pontiff**
>
> We teach and define as a divinely revealed dogma that when the Roman Pontiff speaks EX CATHEDRA, that is, when, in the exercise of his office as shepherd and teacher of all Christians, in virtue of his supreme apostolic authority, he defines a doctrine concerning faith or morals to be held by the whole Church, he possesses, by the divine assistance promised to him in Blessed Peter, that infallibility which the divine Redeemer willed his Church to enjoy in defining the doctrine concerning faith or morals. Therefore, such definitions of the Roman Pontiff are of themselves, and not by the consent of the Church, irreformable.
>
> **Caput IV**
> **De Romani pontificis infallibili magisterio**
>
> Docemus et divinitus revelatum dogma esse definimus: Romanum pontificem, cum ex cathedra loquitur, id est, cum omnium christianorum pastoris et doctoris munere fungens, prosuprema sua apostolica auctoritatem doctrinam de fide vel moribus ab universal ecclesia tenendam definit, per assistentiam divinam, ipsi in beato Petro promissam, ea infallibilitate pollerre, qua divinus Redemptor ecclesiam suam in definienda doctrina de fine vel moribus instructam esse voluit; ideoque eiusmodi Romani pontificis definitiones ex sese, non autem ex consense ecclesiae irreformabiles esse.

The doctrine of the infallibility of the Pope is linked to the doctrine of his primacy.[11] If he has ordinary jurisdiction over the whole Episcopal body, then it follows that he must possess in himself that 'sure charism of truth' (DV 8) which the Apostolic College possesses as a collectivity. This again was manifested, as Newman demonstrated, at Chalcedon, where all the bishops were ordered to follow the decrees of the papal legates of Leo the Great.

As a result of this definition, Dr Döllinger and others left the Catholic Church to form what came to be called the 'Old Catholics' or 'The Church of Utrecht',[12] because they could not accept papal infallibility. However, as we said above, the Ultra-Montanes also were frustrated since they would have liked a much less restrictive definition of papal infallibility, which is full of conditions which have to be met before a doctrine can be said to be infallibly defined. Mr Wilfred Ward's expectation of a papal document expressing infallible truth together with his breakfast copy of *The Times* was to be disappointed! Only one decree clearly fulfilled all those conditions in the twentieth century, namely the definition of the doctrine of the Assumption of Mary.[13] You will note also how this doctrine is presented by Pope Pius XII as a prime example of the development of doctrine; indeed we can see it as an example of DV8.

## VATICAN II 1963 to 1965

*The Second Vatican Council, summoned by Pope John XXIII in 1960, redressed the balance of Vatican I by asserting the infallibility of the whole body of Catholic bishops united with the Bishop of Rome in exercising the infallible magisterium of the Church particularly in the General or Ecumenical Council.*

Since the First Vatican Council never finished its work, Paragraph 22 of the Dogmatic Constitution on the Church *Lumen Gentium* ('Light of the Nations') reiterated the doctrine of the infallibility of the magisterium of the Pope, but also of the College of the Bishops Successors of the Apostles in union with the Pope. This drew attention to the normal process by which the Church declares doctrine infallibly, namely the General or Ecumenical Council; but Vatican II expressed time and time again in the following statement that the affirmations of Vatican I on the primacy and infallibility of the Roman pontiff remain inviolate:

... one is constituted a member of the Episcopal body in virtue of sacramental consecration and hierarchical communion with the head and members of the body. But the college or body of bishops has no authority unless it is understood together with the Roman Pontiff, the successor of Peter as its head. The pope's power of primacy over all, both pastors and faithful, remains whole and intact. In virtue of his office that is as Vicar of Christ and pastor of the whole Church the Roman Pontiff has full, supreme and universal power over the Church. And he is always free to exercise this power. The order of bishops, which succeeds to the college of apostles and gives this apostolic body continued existence, is also the subject of supreme and full power over the universal Church, provided we understand this body together with its head the Roman Pontiff and never without this head. This power can be exercised only with the consent of the Roman Pontiff. For our Lord placed Simon alone as the rock and the bearer of the keys of the Church, and made him shepherd of the whole flock; it is evident, however, that the power of binding and loosing, which was given too was granted also to the college of apostles, joined with their head. This college, insofar as it is composed of many, expresses the variety and universality of the People of God, but insofar as it is assembled under one head, it expresses the unity of the flock of Christ. In it, the bishops, faithfully recognizing the primacy and pre-eminence of their head, exercise their own authority for the good of their own faithful, and indeed of the whole Church, the Holy Spirit supporting its organic structure and harmony with moderation. The supreme power in the universal Church, which this college enjoys, is exercised in a solemn way in an ecumenical council. A council is never ecumenical unless it is confirmed or at least accepted as such by the successor of Peter; and it is the prerogative of the Roman Pontiff to convoke these councils, to preside over them and to confirm them. This same collegiate power can be

> exercised together with the pope by the bishops living in all parts of the world, provided that the head of the college calls them to collegiate action, or at least approves of or freely accepts the united action of the scattered bishops, so that it is thereby made a collegiate act.

The Second Vatican Council therefore addressed an imbalance in the presentation of the primacy and infallibility of the Bishop of Rome, emphasizing the role of the whole body of bishops as together with the Pope, the Bishop of Rome, the infallible Magisterium, and granting each bishop as successor of the apostles his own right as ruler of his own diocesan church on earth.

But the Second Vatican Council was unrepentant in reiterating the teaching of the First Vatican Council that Jesus intended his church to be governed on earth by the successors of Peter as Bishops of Rome, and only further clarified the Catholic teaching that the whole body of bishops are successors to the twelve apostles, and have authority as such.

The question therefore we now have to address is the following.

## 4.6 CATHOLIC CLAIMS AND CRITICAL SCHOLARSHIP

*Critical scholarship will in general not accept that the historical Jesus made Peter the head of his church on earth after his own death and resurrection. Nor will it accept that he gave his authority to the Twelve in union with Peter. What response therefore will Catholic scholarship give to such a negative conclusion concerning the origins of its own ecclesiology?*

One immediate reaction might be to disclaim any necessity to prove that the historical Jesus had any such intention. One could argue that Catholic ecclesiology evolved after the death and resurrection of Jesus to its present beliefs in the primacy and infallibility of the Pope and the bishops in union with the Pope. It is in reality of secondary importance as to whether Jesus himself intended such a church structure and church authority.

But such a position is difficult to sustain without considerably weakening the foundations of Catholic ecclesiology. If the Catholic Church's faith in its own authority is not surely based upon Jesus' own intentions, then what authority has it? We might respond by saying that the Holy Spirit was working in the Church after the death and resurrection of Jesus. But how do we know that this *was* the working of the Holy Spirit, and not some kind of social evolution, which in such a case would surely be changeable?

For critical scholarship, it is not only that the historical Jesus had no intention of founding a church. It is rather that there was pluralism in the apostolic church, with Petrine leadership being only one model, so that we cannot appeal to the authority of the apostles any more than we can appeal to the authority of the historical Jesus himself as the basis of Catholic ecclesiology.

We might argue that the very concept of development helps us here. We might argue that the Catholic Church's authority is authenticated by the very fact that it developed out of the varied ecclesiologies of those early apostolic days. That at first sounds promising, since it is at least partly the way in which Newman argues in *The Development of Christian Doctrine*. However again, there are problems. In a post-critical age, we might ask, why should we be bound to the structures and to the concepts which eventually led to the Catholic Church with all its pomp and power? Why cannot we go back to those early apostolic days and find alternative models of church which eventually were smothered by the evolving early Catholicism (*Urkatholikizmus*)? This is in fact the objection which we find in Hans Küng's *The Church*.

On the other hand, if we could demonstrate with some reasonable certainty that the historical Jesus actually handed over the primacy of his church to Peter, and that the Twelve and Peter were in fact rulers of the church in the apostolic period, then the position of such as Küng is seriously undermined. This is precisely what the First and Second Vatican Councils proclaim, and certainly also what Newman himself maintained. Again, he would not have become a Catholic had he not believed that there was a true historical continuity between what Jesus himself intended and the Catholic Church which emerged.

## Notes

1. *The Tablet*, 4 July 2009, p. 10.
2. *Pascendi*, para 23.
3. The Lambeth Conference, 2008: 'Bishops from around the globe, joined by ecumenical participants, gathered together for worship, study, conversation, and discussion in July 2008 on the campus of the University of Kent at Canterbury, England. There was a separate Spouses Programme within the Lambeth Conference for accompanying spouses.' http://www.lambethconference.org/index.cfm [accessed 20 February 2013]
4. St Thomas Aquinas, *Summa Theologica*, IIa IIae, q.1, a.2, ad 2.
5. CCC 170.
6. DCD, pp. 78–9.
7. http:/www.ewtn.com/library/Councils/V1.htm#4 [accessed 20 February 2013], Chapter 4 paragraphs 13, 14, cf. ND **136**
8. Quotation from Vincent of Lerins, *Commonitorum primum*, 23 http:/www.ewtn.com/library/Councils/V1.htm#4 [accessed 20 February 2013], Chapter 4 paragraph 15
9. *The Divine Office; the Liturgy of the Hours according to the Roman Rite as Renewed by Decree of the Second Vatican Council Promulgated by the Authority of Pope Paul VI*. Vol. III, Weeks of the Year 6–34. London, Collins, 2006, pp. 626–7. Vincent of Lerins was a Semi-Pelagian according to the Catholic Encyclopaedia! http://www.newadvent.org/cathen/15439b.htm. [accessed 20 February 2013] But his principle of development is surely right.
10. For the English translation of the citation see ND **819**.
11. For the English translation of the citation see ND **839**.
12. See http://en.wikipedia.org/wiki/Old_Catholic_Church_of_the_Netherlands.
13. ND **715**.

# 5

# BUILDING FOUNDATIONS

In this Chapter, I rehearse in summary form some of the main arguments I introduced in *Bad, Mad or God?*, and attempt to move on to consider the implications such conclusions from BMG might have in considering the foundation of the Church by Jesus of Nazareth.

## 5.1 JESUS EXISTED

*There can be no doubt that Jesus of Nazareth existed, and that he was put to death during the Procuratorship in Jerusalem of Governor Pontius Pilate, AD 26 to 36.*

As I say in BMG Chapter 5, we could say that the existence of Jesus of Nazareth is as secure a historical fact as the existence of Julius Caesar or Shakespeare. However, it cannot be dismissed as a 'non-question', because the question is still asked. It is important to find out why it is affirmed that Jesus did actually exist, at least as a historical foundation on which to build more specific data about the Jesus of history.

Questioning Jesus' existence is less popular now than it was in nineteenth century Germany, when the dating of the Gospels was put impossibly late, into the second century AD. With acceptance today that all four Gospels including the Gospel of John, were published in their present form before the end of the first century, or latest in the first decade of the second century, the documentation about Jesus by the Christian community is only two or three generations after Jesus himself, and in the opinion of many most likely much earlier.

Scholars also today are much more favourable to the witnesses to the existence of Jesus outside of the New

Testament. It is more than possible that Josephus the Jewish historian who fought in the Jewish War defending Jerusalem in AD 70 refers to Jesus, even though some references seem to be early Christian interpolations.

More convincing still is the reference to Christians by the harshly satirical Roman historian Tacitus, writing his Roman annals between AD 115 and 117, who was certainly not in favour of the new sect. Tacitus obviously does not think that Christians were guilty of setting fire to Rome, but he has little sympathy for them:

> Therefore, to squelch the rumour, Nero created scapegoats and subjected to the most refined tortures those whom the common people called 'Christians' (a group) hated for their abominable crimes. Their name comes from Christ, who, during the reign of Tiberius, had been executed by the procurator Pontius Pilate. Suppressed for the moment, the deadly superstition broke out again, not only in Judea, the land which originated this evil, but also in the city of Rome, where all sorts of horrendous and shameful practices from every part of the world converge and are fervently cultivated.[1]

Because of the importance of references by Tacitus, it has been questioned whether he gained his information from Christian sources alone, which could have spread the myth that Jesus existed when he did not. But surely, Tacitus as a Roman historian would have known whether a prophet who achieved fame in Judea only a century earlier, and was crucified by a Roman governor, existed or not.

There is also general acceptance at least of the possibility that one text, the Babylonian Jewish Talmud tractate *Sanhedrin* 43a, does make a genuine reference to Jesus,[2] and can be dated early, in the second century.

It is impossible to demonstrate one way or the other whether or not the Talmud had a distinct source of historical information for the trial and execution of Jesus which is relayed in the text above, or whether the Talmud here is relying on Christian sources such as the Gospels for its information.

What is important, however, as with the information supplied by Tacitus above, is that the Talmud never contests the existence of Jesus. Surely, the Judean Jews of the first century would have known whether or not a famous prophet actually existed or not? If he had not existed, would not this have been the strongest of arguments against Christianity, in the early stages of the Christian movement when friction was already in evidence (Ac 13:45)? Yet never was Jesus' historical existence ever questioned. As Theissen/Merz say, 'both opponents and neutral or sympathetic observers of Christianity presuppose the historicity of Jesus and do not indicate a shadow of doubt about it'.[3] Neither should we.

## 5.2 THE CRITICAL MINIMUM

*Critical scholars have arrived at an Agreed Minimum regarding the essential points of the life of the historical Jesus, using principles developed by the 'New Quest' just after the Second World War.*

- **Jesus came from Nazareth in Galilee.**

Christ came from Nazareth. There seems no theological reason why the Christian community should have invented this. Nazareth was not highly regarded from a religious point of view. The question of a potential disciple of Jesus when told that he came from Nazareth in Galilee was "can anything good come out of Nazareth?" (Jn 1:46). That statement itself has historical credibility by virtue of the Criterion of Embarrassment.[4]

- **Jesus was linked with the preaching of John the Baptist, a popular prophet who preached in the desert of Judea, and who baptised his followers as a sign of repentance and of preparation for the coming of God.**

That Christ submitted himself to the baptism of John would seem to be a disadvantage or even embarrassment to the early Christian community, therefore it is historically admissible. (Mt 3:13).[5]

- **Around AD 30 Jesus himself emerged as a prophet, preaching the kingdom of God which he believed was near, and whose coming was related to his own ministry.**

That Jesus preached the kingdom of God through his own acts of power has no parallels in Judaism: 'But if it is by the Spirit of God that I cast out demons, then the kingdom of God has come (*ephthasen*) to you.' (Mt 12:28, Lk 11:20) The 'kingdom of God' is not a characteristic expression of the early Christian community about Jesus' ministry. The scholars accept this as part of the critical minimum using the principle of double discontinuity.[6] That Jesus began his ministry at approximately AD 30 is calculated from the date of his execution by Pilate AD 26 to 36

- **He became renowned as a worker of healing miracles, and of exorcisms. Many people acknowledged him as a prophet.**

The fact that Jesus had a reputation as a miracle worker is itself good grounds for the historicity of this particular tradition. Not every prophet had this reputation. For example John the Baptist did not. And the reaction to miracles was not necessarily Christological, betraying theological interest. Reaction to the earlier miracles was praise of God, not necessarily faith in Jesus. (Mt 15:31. The Criterion of Multiple Attestation),[7] a tradition manifested in different contexts and in different traditions, would seal the place of Jesus as a reputed miracle worker in the Critical Minimum.

- **Jesus became unpopular with the Jewish religious authorities, because he healed on the Sabbath day, and seemed to make light of some rabbinic and Old Testament regulations. He also associated himself with outcasts and sinners in society, which was against some Pharisaic thinking of the time**

Critical scholars are prepared to admit to the critical minimum that Jesus was a rebel against the strict rabbinic laws (Mk 2:25-28), since he approved of his disciples rubbing the corn between their hands on the Sabbath. It is debatable how much of Jesus' conduct which appears to provide tension with his Jewish contemporaries was in fact against Jewish law. E. P. Sanders: 'above all has put Jesus' ethics and conduct in the tradition of Jewish expectation of the Torah. Thus neither the breaches of the Sabbath nor the antitheses leave the Jewish Torah behind'.[8] The modern tendency is to emphasis Jesus' Jewish roots. Thus we might not have here the principle of discontinuity, but rather of Multiple Attestation. Jesus appears in all contexts as adopting a liberal attitude to Sabbath law, and as involving himself with 'sinners', those unacceptable within Pharisaism. (Lk 7:37) The Christian community itself would also have found Christ's ethics a challenge, and would hardly have wanted to have invented them.

- Jesus went up to Jerusalem to celebrate the Passover. He was arrested at night, being betrayed by Judas one of his disciples, in order to avoid a possible rebellion and insurrection. The Roman Prefect Pontius Pilate condemned him to death by crucifixion.

We have independent evidence from Tacitus, or at least confirmation by him as we have seen that Jesus was put to death by Pontius Pilate some time between AD 26 and 36. All four Gospels implicate Pilate in finally sending Jesus to his death by crucifixion, even if he washed his hands of it. (Mt 27:24). It does seem that he was frightened of revolution, and saw Jesus as a possible threat. Jesus' opponents played on this fact at his trial before Pilate: 'They began to accuse him, saying, 'We found this man perverting our nation, forbidding us to pay taxes to the emperor, and saying that he himself is the Messiah, a king.' (Lk 23:2) The Critical Minimum, therefore, based upon the Criterion of Coherence[9] will allow that Pilate condemned Jesus to death probably for sedition.

## 5.3 THE THREE ENIGMAS

*But the Agreed Minimum does not accept the miraculous or supernatural dimension of Jesus life and teaching. This, we maintain, is a gratuitous rejection.*

From the beginning of the Quest of the Historical Jesus, as we have seen, those who led the German Lutheran scholarly investigation all rejected *a priori* the miraculous in the life of Jesus, and above all his incarnation. In this they were influenced by the growth in the eighteenth century of the scientific age, and by Deist philosophy, which admitted a God of reason who had created the world according to fixed laws but not events transcending the laws of nature. Strauss also, as we have seen, maintained the same philosophy of the rejection of a God who worked in any way beyond secondary causes, although his philosophy was pantheistic, a God identified with the evolution of His own absolute Idea.

Thus the nineteenth-century Quest had to create a Jesus who was either an ethical teacher as Holtzmann and Harnack proposed, or a fanatical Jewish prophet looking towards the end of the world, as Schweitzer thought. The Rationalists could have accepted that Jesus had a reputation as a miracle worker, and as an exorcist. They could accept that Jesus was a genuine faith healer; although one Rationalist, Venturini, proposed that the historical Jesus carried a medicine box around with him, which caused his success as a healer! However Jesus could not, in the thinking of the nineteenth-century Quest, have performed miracles such as the walking on the water or the multiplication of the loaves, or be born of a virgin, or above all bodily rise from the dead.

But why, we must ask, must God be limited to secondary causes? If God created the world, that must have been an act of direct creation. Why could not that same God in the history of the world intervene directly as with for instance the Incarnation and the Resurrection? This might be especially the case if that God wished to indicate to the world that he was acting in a way which would reveal his plans, which we believe actually happened in the life of Jesus, God become Man.

In BMG Chapter 4, we attempted something of a demythologization of historical science. So-called 'historical science' is the attempt to verify history writing. However we are asking about the veracity of a human person or persons. The knowledge of an historical event which is not personal to our own experience has to be communicated to us by a third party. Since the person or persons communicating such knowledge might conceivably be deceiving us or be deceived, this introduces us to the concept of the human witness to such historical events.

We might put it into a formula:

## X TELLS ME THAT Y REALLY HAPPENED. I BELIEVE X.

X may be equivalent to thousands of witnesses, like the events in the Second World War. Y may be a whole sequence of events, like a flood, or a whole human life requiring thousands of witnesses. However the formula is the same. To talk about an 'historical event' is nothing other than to speak of an event witnessed by someone else, whose testimony we accept in faith. And we accept the reality, the facticity of what has been communicated to us in historical writing. To accept any reputed historical fact, we must make an act of historical faith.

## 5.4 UNANSWERED QUESTIONS

*The Agreed Minimum of historical facts about the life of Jesus leaves three important unanswered questions, answers to which challenge us to address the issue as to whether Jesus was truly the Son of God come to save us, as the Gospels maintain.*

We[10] have just outlined the 'agreed minimum', called often 'the critical minimum', of historical facts about Jesus of Nazareth which are accepted by the broad consensus of contemporary New Testament scholarship.[11] However before we become too excited about the critical minimum, it is worth noting that Wrede and Schweitzer[12] a hundred years ago, and even Reimarus two hundred years ago, as well as the *Jesus Seminar* only a decade ago, would also have been happy to agree substantially with that critical minimum, while of course disagreeing about individual points of the assessment of historical data about Jesus in the Synoptic Gospels.

In harsh reality, the Critical Minimum on its own is only a confirmation of historical Jesus studies from Reimarus onwards. Studies which seem to have all concluded, whatever the variations on the theme, that a historical Jewish prophet or sage called Jesus became a Gentile God in the view of first century Christians.

We now suggest that there are three problems,[13] three unanswered questions in critical scholarship, which we proposed to answer in BMG by the simple method of demonstrating the trustworthiness of the Gospels, and in particular the Gospel of John.

## The Enigma of Jesus

The Critical Minimum accepted Jesus as a prophet renowned for working miracles and preaching the kingdom of God. However, how did the early Christians come to see him as the divine Son of God, the Lord, in the twenty years after his death? Wilhelm Bousset's solution that the Christian community applied Greek deifying categories to one who was essentially a Jewish prophet, is the standard critical answer, which, as we have seen, is now increasingly discredited.

How could the first Christians have believed in his Resurrection if Jesus had not lived a life in some way or other, which made them think he had risen from the dead? This is precisely the argument used by Peter in his speech to the Jewish nation in Acts 2:22 that Jesus was 'a man attested to you by God with deeds of power, wonders, and signs that God did through him among you, as you yourselves know', and that the Resurrection was the vindication of the life of the just man Jesus. Somehow, then, they must have thought that his life on earth was at least an important factor in their coming to see him as divine.

## The Enigma of his Death

The Critical Minimum accepts that Jesus was put to death at the command of Pontius Pilate the Roman Prefect. But Pilate would not have put Jesus to death if there had not been some reason for it in Jesus' own message and life. Even he was not that indifferent to human life. Critical scholarship has no united answer to this question; but is this critical confusion not generated by the simple fact that historical Jesus scholarship will not accept that, as the Gospels state, Jesus was thought to be a blasphemer by his enemies because of his divine claims?

## The Enigma of his Resurrection

The third problem is the strangest of all, the phenomenon of the Christian faith in the bodily Resurrection of Jesus from the dead. We saw earlier that Reimarus considered that the disciples of Jesus, not willing to return to their fishing and viewing the attractive prospect of a clerical career, went back to an early idea that the Messiah would rise from the dead. But this begs an important question, as we will discuss more in detail later in the chapter on the Resurrection. There is no Jewish tradition for the Messiah to come back *bodily* from the dead as Jesus did after his death. What then actually happened after his death, so that the early Christians believed that he had risen in physical form from the dead? Sanders asks pertinently, 'Without the Resurrection, would (Jesus') disciples have endured longer than did John the Baptist's? We can only guess, but I would guess not'.[14] Why did they believe in his Resurrection? *What actually happened* to make them do so?

From Reimarus onwards, these have been the three main questions still to be answered by all those who accept the Critical Minimum as described above, but cannot accept the answer given by a straight reading of the Gospels, namely:

- That Jesus did himself claim during his lifetime to be the divine Son of God, and substantiated this claim by his life, teaching, and by his miracles.
- That this claim led to his being handed over for blasphemy to Pilate, and led to his death by crucifixion.
- That the first Christians found his tomb empty and he appeared bodily to them. This was the cause of their faith in him.

## 5.5 JESUS CLAIMED TO BE THE DIVINE SON OF GOD

In BMG I have attempted to demonstrate that Jesus actually claimed to be God, not only to be the expected Messiah. N. T. Wright implicitly suggests that not everyone who calls Jesus 'divine' knows what that means 'it is usually assumed that the force of this predicate is already understood'.[15] We have therefore attempted carefully to make precise what it does mean, in examining the absolute that is without a predicate, the 'I Am' sayings, in St John's Gospel:

> Unless you come to believe that I AM, you will surely die in your sins (8:24)
>
> When you lift up the Son of Man, then you will realise that I AM (8:28)
>
> Before Abraham even came into existence, I AM. (8:58)
>
> When it does happen, you may believe that I AM. (13:19)

I quote the important study of David Mark Ball[16] who refers to scholars who see the background to the 'I Am' sayings in John in Judaism contemporary with Jesus and the writing of the Fourth Gospel. He cites Dodd's *Interpretation of the Fourth Gospel*, where Dodd links *ani hu* with Rabbinic expression of the divine Name.[17] Stauffer agrees with Dodd, and links Isaiah 40–55 with the Dead Sea Sect, e.g. the *Manual of Discipline* which states in 8:13f. 'They are to be kept apart and to go into the wilderness to prepare the way of the HUAHA there....' cf. Isaiah 40:3. HUAHA is therefore the Dead Sea Sect's reference to the divine name. 'Presumably this is made up of the HUAH (HE) and A (signifying Elohim, God).'[18]

Perhaps even more significant regarding Jesus' claims to divinity is John 10:30 'I and the Father are One', which I argue in *Bad, Mad or God?* is much more than simply a declaration by Jesus of his moral unity with the will of God his Father. Rather, it is a claim by Jesus to identify himself with the One God, the *Shema* 'Hear, O Israel, the Lord your God is One Lord' (Dt 6:4).[19] This gives more than adequate reason that after the fraught conversation between Jesus and his Jewish hearers, they 'took up stones to stone him' (Jn 10:31).

It is generally accepted my modern critical scholarship that the historical Jesus was renowned as a miracle worker. That is because the evidence that Jesus did at least have the reputation of being a miracle worker is overwhelming. Also, a rationalist could accept that a man could have healing powers as yet unexplained by science. Faith healing is accepted by many as a scientific fact, whether healing is by auto-suggestion or from the subject's own inner resources. And regarding Jesus' powers of casting out devils, those could be explained in Freudian terms as release of the sub-conscious.

Meier is totally convinced that the historical Jesus was renowned as a miracle worker:

> The single most important criterion in the investigation of Jesus' miracles is the criterion of *multiple attestation of sources and forms*. As for multiple sources, the evidence is overwhelming. Every Gospel source (Mk, Q, M, L, and Jn), every evangelist in his redactional summaries, and Josephus to boot, affirm the miracle-working activity of Jesus. Indeed, each Gospel source does so more than once, and some do it repeatedly.[20]

Meier emphasises the importance of miracles in the Gospel presentation of the life of Jesus. In the reckoning of Alan Richardson, 209 verses of a total of 666 in Mark's Gospel deal with miracles directly or indirectly.[21] 'When one looks at this vast array of disparate streams of miracle traditions in the first Christian generation, some already grouped in collections, some still stray bits of material, Mark alone — writing as he does at the end of the first Christian generation

— constitutes a fair refutation of the idea that the miracle traditions were totally the creation of the early church after Jesus' death'.[22]

More controversial are what are sometimes called the 'nature miracles', the transfiguration, the walking on the water, and the miracle of the multiplication of the loaves. However it is these miracles which more precisely vindicate the divinity of Christ. They are well attested in each case at least in three out of the four Gospels. I argue to their historicity in BMG, and ask the reader to refer to that previous study for the full argumentation.

All the 'nature miracles' are authenticated by the fact that they revealed the full divine Sonship of Jesus during his life on earth. The Transfiguration revealed Jesus Christ in his glory to the disciples Peter, James and John on the holy mountain, God the Father speaking: 'This is my Son, the Beloved, Listen to him' (Mt 17:5). In the multiplication of the loaves, all four Gospels, tell us that Jesus had power like the JHWH of the Old Testament who fed his people in their desert wanderings (Mt 14:15–21 and parallels). Most of all, it is Jesus' walking on the water.

Above all, when Jesus says while walking on the water, 'It is I; do not be afraid.' (Jn 6:20) he is using the words which YHWH himself uses when announcing his saving presence in a theophany (an 'appearance of God'). In the context of his walking on the water, we could interpret 'It is I; do not be afraid' as 'Don't worry, chaps, it's only me'. However in the context of Exodus 3:14–15, where YHWH declares to Moses I AM WHO AM, the Septuagint translating as *egó eimi ho ón* (I am the One who is'),[23] and the person speaking is walking on the water in a choppy sea, then we have the combined elements of one at least like YHWH speaking in a revelation of his power and glory as the master of the element (Cf. Is 43:16).

Scholars are more cautious to admit that the plain assertions of Jesus' divinity in the Gospel of John are based upon what the historical Jesus himself asserted. Stephen T.

Davis in a fascinating recent study: *Disputed issues: contending for Christian faith in today's academic setting*,[24] does affirm that the historical Jesus claimed to be God, but 'implicitly'. In this, he uses those very texts which J. A. T. Robinson in *The Priority of John*, employed to demonstrate that the Fourth Gospel, in putting the *egó eimi* absolute statements on the lips of Jesus, is only making explicit what was implicit in the Synoptic view.[25] John's Christology is therefore not contrary to that presented in the Synoptics, as we have continually argued, particularly in Chapter 9 of BMG, where we demonstrated the authenticity and the high Christology of Mark 14:64, the Trial of Jesus, where Jesus is eventually condemned for blasphemy. Davis notes in particular that in the Synoptic presentation of the teaching of Jesus, he '"spoke with authority"' not citing sources or precedents of famous rabbis'.[26] We now turn to that condemnation of Jesus for blasphemy as another means of demonstrating the authenticity of the Gospel accounts.

## 5.6 BLASPHEMY

*That Jesus was put to death for blasphemy, and that there is no other account in the Gospels as to why Jesus was put to death, authenticates the claim of the Gospels that the historical Jesus claimed to be God during his life on earth.*

'Why did Jesus Die?'[27] Wright gives a reason at first convincing, fully in line with the biblical and historical evidence, why Jesus should not only accept his death, but even encourage it: his death would presage the destruction of the Temple and usher in a new renewed Israel community, a new Temple with himself as head and his community as members. This explains the dark shadows in Jesus' own mind; his prophecy of his own death after Peter has confessed him as Messiah in Matthew 16:21.

But the Gospels themselves go further than this. There is only one reason given in all four Gospels why Jesus' religious enemies wanted him dead. They thought he was blaspheming. Each of the four Gospels tell us that Jesus was accused of blasphemy by his enemies: Matthew 9:2–3, 26:64–66, Mark 2:5–7, 14:62–64, Luke 5:20–21, John 10:33,36. The reason why Jesus had enemies according to the Gospels is that he uttered blasphemy; and that blasphemy was regarding his own status, which was interpreted by his enemies as Jesus claiming to be God. If Jesus did not claim to be God, then he could have modified his language, or denied that he did claim to be God. However he did not.

The clearest instance was at his trial before the Jewish Sanhedrin. From Mark 14:

> And the high priest stood up in the midst, and asked Jesus, 'Have you no answer to make? What is it that these men testify against you?' But he was silent and made no answer. Again the high priest asked him, 'Are you the Christ, the Son of the Blessed?' And Jesus said, 'I am; and you will see the Son of man seated at the right hand of Power, and coming with the clouds of heaven.' And the high priest tore his garments, and said, 'Why do we still need witnesses? You have heard his blasphemy. What is your decision?' And they all condemned him as deserving death. (Mk 14:60–64)

Jesus was not condemned for claiming to be the Messiah. Such a claim did not bring the death penalty in a Jewish court. Jesus was condemned for blasphemously identifying himself with the exalted Son of Man, seated at the right hand of power, and like God himself coming in the clouds of heaven. In fact, the real blasphemy was to combine two, indeed three, texts from the Old Testament and for Jesus to apply them to himself. These texts were Daniel 7:13–14, Psalm 110:1, and finally Isaiah 14:12–15. The text in Daniel identifies the Son of Man as 'a quite specific heavenly being'.[28] In Psalm 110:1, the Lord sitting at the right hand of God is linked now with that Son of Man figure coming with the clouds of heaven. The symbolism is one of authority,[29] and finally, Isaiah 14:12–15[30] is part of a 'Taunt Song against the King of Babylon'[31], an unnamed king who seems to be a type of a wicked world ruler. Jesus, then, in speaking of 'sitting at the right hand of God and coming in the clouds of heaven' was making what was a potentially blasphemous statement for a zealous and intelligent reader of the Old Testament. He was using the same language as the idolatrous pagan king of Babylon. No wonder, then that the high priest tore his garments, 'All of them condemned him as deserving death'.

## 5.7 RESURRECTION

*That Jesus rose bodily from the dead, and appeared to his disciples before leaving them to go to his Father.*

The Resurrection was an entirely unique event. There are instances quoted of people who are ghosts appearing to terrified observers. There are horror stories of people like Frankenstein arising from the tomb. But as N. T. Wright points out, there is no other instance in history where a tomb of one who has recently died is found empty, and then within a few days that corpse appears as fully alive to his disciples; not in the same mortal coil as before, but as a risen body, able to eat fish, but able to disappear at will. This is unknown in the history of the world.

Its very uniqueness is an argument for the Resurrection. Scripture does not promise that kind of resurrection in detail. It was not invented by the Old Testament. Paganism knows nothing like it either. It was entirely a surprise to the disciples themselves, as the *Catechism of the Catholic Church* puts it. We cannot improve on its words:

> **643** Given all these testimonies, Christ's Resurrection cannot be interpreted as something outside the physical order, and it is impossible not to acknowledge it as an historical fact. It is clear from the facts that the disciples' faith was drastically put to the test by their master's Passion and death on the cross, which he had foretold (Cf. Lk 22:31–33) The shock provoked by the Passion was so great that at least some of the disciples did not at once believe in the

news of the Resurrection. Far from showing us a community seized by a mystical exaltation, the Gospels present us with disciples demoralized ('looking sad' Lk 24:17) and frightened. For they had not believed the holy women returning from the tomb and had regarded their words as an 'idle tale' (Lk 24:11) When Jesus reveals himself to the Eleven on Easter evening, 'he upbraided them for their unbelief and hardness of heart, because they had not believed those who saw him after he had risen.' (Mk 16:14)

**644** Even when faced with the reality of the risen Jesus the disciples are still doubtful, so impossible did the thing seem: they thought they were seeing a ghost. 'In their joy they were still disbelieving and still wondering.'(Lk 24:38–41) Thomas will also experience the test of doubt and St Matthew relates that during the risen Lord's last appearance in Galilee 'some doubted. (Jn 20:24–27, Mt 28:17) Therefore the hypothesis that the Resurrection was produced by the apostles' faith (or credulity) will not hold up. On the contrary their faith in the Resurrection was born, under the action of divine grace, from their direct experience of the reality of the risen Jesus.

## 5.8 BASIS OF FAITH

*This gives excellent grounds for the rapid and firm faith in the earliest church for the full divinity of Christ.*

C. F. D. Moule, the late distinguished Cambridge scholar, argues that, contrary to Bultmann, the early Christians did not call Jesus *Kurios* only as a result of Hellenisation, moving to consider Jesus as a Greek type mythical god. Rather, use of the Aramaic *mar*, Lord, for Jesus, reveals that early on in Christian thinking, 'Our Lord' and comparable phrases 'had already been applied in Semitic-speaking regions to a more than human being'.[32] After all, claims Moule, 'you do not call upon a dead Rabbi to `come'; and, since it is demonstrably possible for *mar* to signify also a divine or transcendent being, it appears that in this context it must have done so'.³³

In particular, the Semitic flavour of these affirmations of the divinity of Jesus are doubly discontinuous both with Jesus' past (no prophet before Jesus ever made such apparently preposterous claims) and with the future formulations of the post–apostolic church, which, while affirming with Ignatius of Antioch the divinity of Christ, who refers, hardly before the first century is out, to 'our God Jesus Christ'³⁴ did not use the Semitic categories which we find in St John's Gospel, but in more Hellenist terms *ho theos hémón Iésous Christos*.³⁵

Later, we shall argue that it is at least possible that Peter's idea of Messiahship before the Resurrection was less than an affirmation of the full divinity of Christ. But Peter would have reflected after the Resurrection on the miracle of the walking on the water and Jesus' statements such as 'Before Abraham was, I AM' and 'I and the Father are One', to move quickly to the affirmation of Jesus as God.

Saint Paul uses characteristically the term Christ as a title in his letters. However Paul's faith is in Jesus as *Kurios*, Lord. This term surely means more than just 'Messiah', but links with the divine name YHWH, of the burning bush episode in Exodus 3, and here it is instructive to read St Paul's Letter to the Philippians: 'Therefore God has highly exalted him and bestowed on him the name which is above every name, that at the name of Jesus every knee should bow, in heaven and on earth and under the earth, and every tongue confess that Jesus Christ is Lord, to the glory of God the Father.' (Ph 2:9–11)

We may reject Bousset's nineteenth-century theory that in using *Kurios* for Jesus, Paul is introducing Hellenistic terms. Paul was versed in Greek Philosophy as a native of Tarsus (Ac 9:11), and in using the Greek word *kurios* might well have been showing his Hellenist inculturation. But in using *Kurios*, Paul is first and foremost remembering his own encounter with the risen Lord on the Damascus Road,

(Ac 9:5), where the terrifying *Kurios* spoke to him and called him to his mission. And as a Jewish theologian, Paul would have remembered the rabbinic doctrine that when the Messiah came, he would reveal the name of YHWH. Thus for Paul, Jesus was not only Messiah, the Christ; he was the one who revealed the secret name of God.

## 5.9 BUILDING UP A CASE

*Historical arguments are never absolute, since as we have seen they depend on an act of historical faith. However we intend to build up a case which makes sense of the whole of the evidence that Jesus did reveal himself as God Incarnate, and that he came to found a Church which would fulfil his mission until he came again in glory.*

Particularly with ancient historical figures, certainty is difficult to attain. As we attempt to authenticate the historicity of Jesus being God, and intending to found a Church, we must resign ourselves that we will never have complete consensus among New Testament historians. There are a few scholars, albeit only a few, who contend that Jesus of Nazareth never existed. There are many who remain within the limited sights proposed by Reimarus, that Jesus was a Jewish prophet put to death by a cruel Roman governor, having no higher status than that.

This is not to maintain an entirely relativist position regarding historical truth. We would maintain once more that the truth can be obtained by historical investigation, but that this requires an act of historical faith, as does the acceptance of any putative historical fact.

X told me Y happened. I believe X

Why, you may well ask, should I accept this amazing set of so-called historical facts; that Jesus performed many healing miracles, walking on the water; that he claimed to be truly God to his Jewish brethren in the Temple in Jerusalem; that being put to death for blasphemy, he rose again bodily from the dead and appeared to his amazed disciples.

We would contend that if we follow a presumption, that Jesus was truly God become Man, and that he founded a Church to last to his final return at the end of time, this will rationally explain all the evidence. In fact, we would contend that unless this presumption is made, the evidence will not be sufficiently explained.

Newman would call this the verification of antecedent probability. For Newman, antecedent probability is the most important principle of verification in questions related to human life: 'He (God) may bless antecedent probabilities in ethical inquiries, who blesses experience and induction in the art of medicine'.[36] 'In all matters of human life, presumption verified by instances, is our ordinary instrument of proof, and, if the antecedent probability is great, it almost supersedes instances.'[37] I discuss Newman's concept of antecedent probability in my book: *Who Was John? The Gospel Debate After Pope Benedict XVI's 'Jesus of Nazareth'*. I submit that the Pope's hermeneutic in *Jesus of Nazareth*, that 'this Jesus—the Jesus of the Gospels—is a historically plausible and convincing figure'[38] can be justified as a hypothetical starting point for an investigation into the historical worth of the Gospels, provided it is linked with antecedent probability. In considering, therefore, the historical evidence for the truth of the Christian faith, in his final chapter of the *Grammar of Assent*, named *Revealed Religion*, Newman argues that it is antecedently probable that, if God were to provide salvation for the whole human race, he would send his Son to become man, to live and to die and to rise again to bring us into communion with himself.[39]

We will now attempt to verify this antecedently probable hypothesis that Jesus, God become Man, came to earth to found a Church, to be the sole means of the salvation of the human race.

## Notes

1. MJ1, pp. 90–91. We are grateful to Meier for all the translations from ancient sources in this section on the existence of Jesus.
2. MJ1, p. 96. names this as the view of Klausner, cf. p. 107, n.49.
3. HJCG, p. 85.
4. BMG, p. 114
5. J. H. Hughes, John the Baptist: Forerunner of God Himself. *Novum Testamentum*, 14 (1972), pp. 190–218, argues that John the Baptist was looking forward not so much to the Messiah, as to the coming of God Himself.
6. BMG, p. 115
7. *Ibid.*
8. HJ, p. 352.
9. BMG, p. 116
10. This section was copied from BMG, pages 114–121.
11. HJCG, pp. 569–572, *Retrospect: A Short Life of Jesus* presents a typical Critical Minimum in narrative form.
12. Indeed, A. Schweitzer, did not think much of this critical minimum at all: 'Those who are fond of talking about negative theology can find their account here. There is nothing more negative than the result of the critical life of Jesus' QHJ, p. 396.
13. BMG, pp. 121–123
14. E. P. Sanders, *Jesus and Judaism*, (London: SCM, 1985), p. 240.
15. JVG, p. 8.
16. D. M. Ball, *'I am' in John's Gospel: Literary Function, Background and Theological Implications.* JSNTS, p. 124, (Sheffield Academic Press, 1996). Cf. BMG, p. 244.
17. IFG, pp. 94–5.
18. E. Stauffer, *Jesus and His Story* (London: SCM, 1960), p. 145
19. BMG, pp. 247–9.
20. MJ2, p. 619.
21. Cf. MJ2, p. 636, nn. 11 and 12 regarding counting the miracles.
22. MJ2, p. 620
23. *Ibid.*, p. 918
24. S. T. Davis, *Disputed issues: contending for Christian faith in today's academic setting*, (Texas: Baylor University Press, Waco, 2009)
25. J. A. T. Robinson, *The Priority of John*, (London: SCM, 1985), pp. 388–389.
26. S. T. Davis, *et al*, editors, *The Incarnation. An Interdisciplinary Symposium on the Incarnation of the Son of God* (Oxford University Press, 2002). p. 241.
27. JVG, Chapter 12, 'The Reasons for Jesus' Crucifixion', pp. 540–611.

28. F. Hahn, *The Titles of Jesus in Christology Their History in Early Christianity* (London: Lutterworth Press, 1969), p. 17.
29. J. Fitzmyer, *Essays on the Semitic Background of the New Testament* (London: Chapman, 1971), p. 224.
30. I am grateful to A. Vanhoye, SJ, who convincingly established the link between this verse in Isaiah and Mark 14:64, in some unpublished lectures on the Passion Narratives at the Pontifical Biblical Institute, Rome, in 1970.
31. NJBC, **15:31,** p. 239. M. Black, and H. H. Rowley, *Peake's Commentary on the Bible*, Revised Edition (London: Nelson, 1962) 500, 432h.
32. OC, p. 37.
33. *Ibid.*, p. 149.
34. From Ephesians 18:2ff. See D. T. Boslooper, *The Virgin Birth* (London: SCM Press, 1962), p. 28
35. F. Dreyfus, *Jésus savait-il qu'il était Dieu?* (Paris: Editions du Cerf, 1984), p. 18. So also Bauckham, ABD, 'Jesus, worship of': 'The prevalence and centrality of the worship of Jesus in early Christianity from an early date has frequently been underestimated...' Quoted in Davis *et al*, ed., p. 234.
36. DCD, p. 112
37. *Ibid.*, pp. 113–4.
38. J. Ratzinger, Pope Benedict XVI, *Jesus of Nazareth, Volume 1, From the Baptism in the Jordan to the Transfiguration* (London: Bloomsbury, 2007), p. 22, quoted in WWJ, p. 54.
39. WWJ, p. 57; J. H. Newman, *An Essay in Aid of a Grammar of Assent*. Introduction by N. Lash (University of Notre Dame Press, 1979.)

# 6

# DID JESUS INTEND TO FOUND A CHURCH?

## 6.1 THREE STAGES

*Our method is to assume as an hypothesis the fully developed structures and authority of the Catholic Church for which we find clear evidence in the fourth and fifth centuries, and attempt to verify that hypothesis at the stages of (1) the historical Jesus (2) the apostolic age, and (3) the early post-apostolic age up to the fourth and fifth centuries.*

As we have seen Newman's aim in the *Development* was to attempt to demonstrate that the Catholic Church of his day was in genuine historical continuity with that which the Apostles left behind, that the developments which have occurred in its doctrine and practise are authentic developments, and not mediaeval corruptions.

After more than one hundred and fifty years since the *Development* was written, our testing out of the Newman hypothesis must re-focus its agenda. In the Anglicanism of his day, in particular in the Tractarian movement of which he was a leading luminary, it would not have been disputed that the sources of Christian revelation were substantially sound, and that the Apostles preached the message which the historical Jesus had intended them to preach, and founded the church which he intended to found. Again it was not questioned that the Church of the Fathers and of the Christological Councils of the fourth and fifth centuries was an authentic development from the teaching of the historical Jesus and of the Apostolic Church of the New Testament writings. It was just assumed that it was. If there were sceptical voices all over Europe and particularly in

Germany at the beginning of the nineteenth century, the Tractarians would have ignored their impiety.

However, after the rise of the critical study of the scriptures, the Quest of the Historical Jesus, and the Modernist crisis, we must test out Newman's hypothesis in reverse. Our question is this: how far is the Church of the definitions of Chalcedon, an infallible Church professing Jesus as true God become true Man, with its supreme doctrinal authority the Bishop of Rome, an authentic development, in fact the sole authentic development, from the intentions of the historical Jesus and of the doctrines and structures of the Apostolic Church?

To clarify the matter, we may set out the stages thus:

1. The stage of the historical Jesus c. AD 30
2. The stage of the Apostolic Church of the New Testament AD 30 to 100
3. The stage of the pre-Chalcedonian Church AD 100 to 451.

Our task will be to attempt to validate the teaching of Chalcedon in the light of critical-historical studies of New Testament origins and of early church history. Now if we follow Newman's methodology, I submit that it will not be quite as impossible to trace that authentic line of development as critical scholarship might at first lead us to presume.

In the science (or art)[1] of biblical scholarship certainty is not easily acquired. However, knowing the actual process of the development of doctrine as expounded by Newman, we can legitimately use the philosophical principle of coherence to authenticate the whole process from text to conciliar definitions. James D. G. Dunn is not a million miles from such a methodology in the first volume of *Jesus Remembered*, under the heading **Jesus the Founder of Christianity**:

> In fact, the obvious way forward is simply to reverse the logic. If the starting assumption of a fair degree of continuity between Jesus and his native religion has *a priori* persuasiveness, then it can hardly make

less sense to assume a fair degree of continuity between Jesus and what followed.[2]

Newman first would lead us to make a large, but in his conviction justified, presumption:

> The application which has been here of the principle (our method of proof)[3] is this - that where a doctrine comes recommended to us by strong presumptions of its truth, we are bound to receive it unsuspiciously, and use it as a key to the evidences to which it appeals, or the facts which it professes to systematize, whatever may be our eventual judgement about it.[4]

Newman is here proposing that we use a given doctrine as a presumption, and then test the hypothesis out as an example of authentic or inauthentic development. This presumption is, again, an 'antecedent probability'. 'He (God) may bless antecedent probabilities in ethical inquiries, who blesses experience and induction in the art of medicine'.[5] 'In all matters of human life, presumption verified by instances, is our ordinary instrument of proof, and, if the antecedent probability is great, it almost supersedes instances.'[6]

Regarding the authentication of a true development, Newman would surely argue, what method could we use apart from testing out the hypothesis of a given doctrine, structure or practice in the stages of its development? If, then, we discover that a given presumed teaching does seem to be validated as tested out in the original documents of that community, and we can establish a clear line of authentication, *then we do not necessarily need absolute certainty regarding the exegesis of every given text of that original document*. If such an interpretation is reasonably certain, and objections to it could be answered with at least no more than moderate difficulty, then that interpretation is authenticated not only by exegetical principles but also by the development itself, as coherent with it.

## 6.2 JESUS WAS MESSIAH

*An increasing number of scholars today would claim that the historical Jesus claimed to be the Messiah. This makes credible his desire to found a community following him.*

Obviously, the first question is as to whether the historical Jesus intended to found a church in any sense of the term. If, as Reimarus and Wrede[7] insisted, Jesus never even claimed to be the Messiah, but only to found a kingdom in Jewish religious terms, then there is no foundation in the life of the historical Jesus for any concept of a church after his death. That concept can only be discovered in the faith of the primitive community without justification in historical-critical terms.

Beare assures us correctly that today in critical scholarship it is by no means unanimously agreed that the historical Jesus claimed to be the Messiah. 'The question of authenticity does not arise at all once we reject the notion that Jesus himself professed to be the promised Messiah'. This would therefore mean that Matthew 16 'Then Simon Peter spoke up and said, "You are the Christ, the Son of the living God."' (Mt 16:16) was only an expression of the faith of the primitive church, not of Peter during the life of the historical Jesus.

On the other hand, together with N. T. Wright and other modern critical scholars, Bockmuehl has adopted a skilful and convincing explanation as to how the historical Jesus came eventually to be worshipped by Christians. His conclusions are positive. He finds that the historical Jesus' aims *'did have Messianic connotations'*,[8] that he predicted 'The Temple's destruction and reconstruction'.[9] Bockmuehl's investigations found Jesus' 'purposes to be intimately concerned with his proclamation and inauguration of the Kingdom of God, with a growing emphasis on his own death as redemptive and instrumental to the arrival of that Kingdom. In that light, his appearances to his followers after three days were seen as powerfully expressing God's vindication of those purposes'.[10]

*Did Jesus Intend to Found a Church?*

Bockmuehl concludes:

> We found that much of the early Christian reflection arose directly from convictions about the reality and significance of the resurrection of Jesus. When read against the background of Jewish monotheism and mystical reflection about God's immanence in mediator figures, the emergence of Christology can be seen as an authentic and consequential expression of the Apostolic faith in the risen Jesus.[11]

If therefore Jesus claimed to be the Messiah, and rose from the dead in vindication of those claims, then not only the early Christology finds its justification in the life, death and resurrection of the historical Jesus. The primitive Ecclesiology is also likewise vindicated. Jesus, conscious of his Messiahship, foresaw his community rebuilding the destroyed Temple and its worship after his death. This is a key element in Wright's *Jesus and the Victory of God*.[12] That primitive community saw itself therefore correctly as fulfilling the expectations of the historical Jesus in its very ecclesial life.

## 6.3 CARRY ON HIS WORK

*Clearly, if we can demonstrate, as I submit we have, that the historical Jesus was aware of himself as Messiah, then it is hardly incredible that he would wish to leave behind a community which in some way would carry on his work.*

Did Jesus intend to found a church? As Wright replies, 'Put baldly like that, it is bound to seem as out of place as the attempt to discover what sort of computer Paul used to write his letters'.[13]

What seems clear from Wright, and from any sensible discussion of the question, is that unless Jesus thought the end of the world was coming when he went to Jerusalem for the last time, which according to Wright, in *Jesus and the Victory of God* he certainly did not, he *must* have envisaged some kind of community forming with him. Even more, if there was a programme in Jesus' mind of a renewed Return of his people, and that people were to make decisions about effecting a renewal, then there must have been some kind of community with Jesus, and Jesus must have intended it. Even more, if, as Wright contends, Jesus foresaw the destruction of Jerusalem, and that destruction would be the beginning of a renewal of Israel, he would have seen his own community as leading that renewal.

## 6.4 AUTHENTIC REFERENCES

The explicit references to Jesus founding a church during his lifetime although not many are arguably authentic.

Beare notes that the word 'Church' (*ekklésia*) is used only twice in the mouth of Jesus in all four Gospels. The first is Matthew 16:14: 'So I now say to you: You are Peter and on this I will build my church' (*ekklésia*). And the gates of the underworld can never overpower it.' The second is the law which Jesus gives regarding a quarrel between the brethren. Says Jesus:

> If your brother sins against you go and tell him his fault, between you and him alone. If he listens to you, you have gained your brother. But if he does not listen, take one or two others along with you, that every word may be confirmed by the evidence of two or three witnesses. If he refuses to listen to them, tell it to the church (ekklésia); and if he refuses to listen even to the church, let him be to you as a Gentile and a tax collector. In truth I tell you, whatever you bind on earth will be bound in heaven; whatever you loose on earth will be loosed in heaven. (Mt 18:15–18).

Ekklésia translates the Hebrew qahal, the qhl jhwh. The assembly is summoned by God before God's chosen leader, as Joshua 24. It is God's muster parade! The people of God can be summoned (have a qahal) for legal purposes. As for instance Joshua 7:16, where Joshua summons the people to find the guilty party who was stealing treasures from the defeated armies. Note how entirely Semitic the text in

Matthew 16:17–19 is, as Beare admits.[14] The language is legal. 'Binding and loosing' refer to legal judgements, either releasing or binding the party in the dock.

Beare rejects the idea that Jesus could have founded a Messianic community, since 'this very argument leads into the untenable position that Jesus set out to form a sect of his own, within but separated from Israel, the people of God'.[15] However this is to deny the uniqueness of Jesus' mission, as demonstrated by Wright. Jesus' intention was not to form a sect within Judaism, but to renew Judaism by leading it back to God, a new Return from Exile.[16] Jesus therefore, in Wright's terms, saw himself as the 'new Temple'.[17]

Admittedly, Beare is correct in affirming that linguistically the universal church is referred to in the New Testament as 'the church of *God*' not 'the church of Christ'. The concept of Jesus being head of the Church 'which is his body' is clearly in texts such as Ephesians 'He has put all things under his feet, and made him, as he is above all things, the head of the Church, which is his Body, the fullness of him who is filled, all in all'. (Ep 1:22–23) The idea that Jesus could call the church 'my church' certainly therefore would have good warranty in the New Testament.[18]

However we could accept that at least initially, Jesus' references to the 'church' were not a reference to the post-resurrection church including the Gentiles, but entirely within the context of his public ministry.

Lagrange was a modern pioneer in Catholic biblical scholarship. Marie-Jean Lagrange wrote a commentary on each of the four Gospels, combining the use of the historical-critical method with a deep loyalty to the Church. He was Rector of L'École Biblique in Jerusalem, and in the climate of his time, he was accused of unorthodoxy in his biblical interpretation, and removed from his rectorship. He went personally to see Pope Pius X, protested his orthodoxy, and was reinstated as Rector. His Gospel commentaries, published during the first quarter of the twentieth century, are models of that combination of sound scholarship and Catholic faith to which we all aim.

Lagrange argues that even if we do not necessarily allude to the divinity of Christ as authority for his saying 'my church', there are Talmudic texts[19] which refer to certain rabbis being head of an assembly, equivalent to a synagogue:

> ... it was not necessarily the whole assembly of Israel (qahal or 'édah) ... One cannot determine which word Jesus has used in Aramaic, but one or the other present themselves naturally. We do not intend to diminish the grandeur of the Church in demonstrating that this word possibly designated a limited group of the faithful. The fuller meaning manifested itself in the future, just as the grain of wheat. If Jesus said 'my group', it is in that he knew the dispositions of the chiefs of the people, who reproved him and tried to nullify his teaching. Without doubt the Church was The Church of God, but not only would it not only be of Christ, but it would be truly the body of Christ. (Ep 5:23ff, 29, 32; Col 1:18, 24) The mystical deduction of Paul supposes the line manifested between the Master and his disciples. Matthew was able to write 'my church', he who spoke of the kingdom of the Son of Man (Mt 13:41) already on the lips of Jesus.[20]

Lagrange's view becomes more credible still if we consider that Jesus had a large following during the three years of his public ministry. Jesus was not just a 'marginal Jew'. We know that large crowds followed him in his Galilean mission. We know that even in Jerusalem Jesus was gaining enough followers to threaten the high priestly establishment. If he called disciples, it is utterly credible that he had a community, even with its own court if necessary, to solve disputes. Jesus' court could have been established outside, not in a specific synagogue. But being called 'Rabbi', Jesus could assume and then delegate authority among the large crowd of disciples he gathered around him. Even therefore if the term 'Church' is more a post-Resurrection term, nothing would prevent the essential concept of a community under the authority of the Rabbi Jesus being in the time of the historical Jesus.

The Catholic Church has never insisted that in the Gospels we have necessarily the *ipsissima verba* of Jesus; his very words.[21] The *Instruction of the Pontifical Biblical Commission Concerning the Historical Truth of the Gospels* makes clear that the truth of the story is not at all affected by the fact that the Evangelists relate the words and deeds of the Lord in a different order.[22] The Second Vatican Council speaks of the process of selection, synthesis and explication of the Gospels in handing on the words of Jesus in the four Gospels.[23] On the other hand, I think personally that Lagrange has made a good case above for Jesus actually using the expression 'my church' during his lifetime on earth. This is particularly since Beare himself freely admits that the texts where Jesus refers to 'my church' are Semitic in tone. It is at least just as likely that the words come from Jesus himself as in Beare's opinion 'that it originated in some debate within the Palestinian community.'[24] If it is likely, then as an interpretation, it can be part of the building up of evidence for the historical Jesus intending to found a church.

## 6.5 UNITY OF FAITH AND LIFE

*Early development manifested the Christian communities' sense of its own infallibility regarding its doctrines, and the unity of its faith and life.*

That Jesus founded a church, for Newman, is at least partly demonstrated by the very existence itself of the church as a developing body. As we have quoted earlier, 'that, as Christianity began by manifesting itself as a certain shape and bearing to all mankind, therefore it went on to manifest itself'.[25]

What we find precisely is that there is continuity between the church of the New Testament after the resurrection of Jesus and the church which emerged in the second century after the death of the Apostles. Newman describes that church as it emerged in the post-apostolic era:

> There is a religious communion claiming a divine commission, and holding all other religious bodies around it heretical or infidel; it is a well-organized, well-disciplined body; it is a sort of secret society, binding together its members by influences and by engagements which it is difficult for strangers to ascertain. It is spread over the known world; it may be weak or insignificant locally, but it is strong on the whole from its continuity; it may be smaller than all other religious bodies together, but is larger than each separately. It is a natural enemy to governments external to itself; it is intolerant and engrossing, and tends to a new modelling of society; it breaks laws, it divides families. It is a gross superstition; it is charged with the foulest crimes; it is despised by the intellect of the day; it is frightful to the imagination of the many. And there is but one communion such.[26]

No one could deny that this is an accurate profile also of the church of the New Testament. We have seen at the beginning of this work, that Ferdinand Christian Bauer thought he had detected a fundamental rift between the Petrine and the Pauline church as described in Acts on the one hand and the Pauline letters on the other. However it is beneath the surface. When we read the New Testament, whatever theories we may propose concerning hidden agendas, we are presented with one church, one visible church, and a community conscious that it is transmitting divine revelation from Jesus its risen Lord. This means that, for that church, those outside of it and denying its doctrine are at least in danger of eternal damnation. This means also that that church was persecuted by Jewish and Gentile authorities. This is to me so obvious that I simply challenge anyone who thinks otherwise to demonstrate it.

Because of the hostility it provoked, its assemblies more and more would have excluded those who were potential enemies. Thus it soon acquired the reputation of being a 'secret society', even though it was open to all who accepted Christian faith. The first century Roman historian Plinius Caecilius Secundus, man of letters, (AD 61 to c.120) refers to Christians gathering together on a Sunday to worship Christ 'as to a god' (*quasi deo dicere*). To discover information about Christians, Pliny was sent by the emperor Trajan (AD 98 to 117) with the powers of governor to the province of Bithynia and Pontus.[27] He subjected two women slaves who were Christian *ministrae* to torture to discover what Christians were about.[28] That they had to be interrogated with torture to find out whether Christians were political conspirators, which they were clearly not,[29] implies that Christians met in gatherings where non-Christians were generally not present. It was thought (quite correctly) that Christians would not pay homage to 'the statues of the gods and the image of the emperor',[30] then Romans who wished to avoid the penalties associated with being a Christian would avoid Christian meetings anyway. From the beginning, the Acts of the Apostles tells us, the first Christians: 'Each day, with one heart, they regularly went to the Temple but met in their houses for the breaking of bread; they shared their food gladly and generously (Ac 2:46). Thus from the beginning, while joining in public worship in the Temple, they had their own assemblies where only believers were participants.

We have therefore an established continuity between:

- The intention of the historical Jesus to found a church
- The church of the New Testament
- The church of the early post-apostolic age.

This in itself makes the historicity of the Fourth Gospel claims put in the mouth of Jesus that he was the I AM equivalent to the YHWH of the Hebrew scriptures that much more credible. In terms of Newman's *Development*: 'The fact, then, of such early or recurring intimations of tendencies which afterwards are fully realized, is a sort of evidence that those later and more systematic fulfilments are only in accordance with the original idea'.[31] Again, 'Another evidence, then, of the faithfulness of an ultimate development is its *definite anticipation* at an early period in the history of the idea to which it belongs'.[32]

And this for Newman would strengthen our arguments above as to the reasonableness of the interpretation of the Gospel evidence that the historical Jesus did intend to found a church. If there was compelling evidence that Jesus did not found a church, or did not have the church in any sense in his sights, that would nullify the argument. However if there are good reasons for thinking that Jesus would have had such an intention, and insufficient reasons for thinking that he did not, as we have above demonstrated, *those exegetical arguments are themselves confirmed authentically by the development of the church's life and teaching in history.*

Pierre Benoît, one of the few celebrated examples in the twentieth century who was both a Catholic exegete and a theologian of the first rank, argues similarly from the vibrant existence of the life of the early Christian community as a proof of the historical reliability of the Gospels against Bultmann who considered that the Gospels were more expressions of the faith of that community than testimonies of the words and deeds of the real Jesus. I have summarised the conclusions of Benoît's critique of *La Formgeschichtliche Methode* thus, by which he dismisses the conclusions of Rudolf Bultmann and the radical form-critics:

> The Christian religion in its early days provoked the hostility of Judaism, the hatred of paganism, the persecutions of the Roman Empire, and yet conquered the world. How can one explain this formidable movement, if one does not put at its origin Jesus, or his direct testimonies, but posits an anonymous and indefinable collectivity, which had constructed little by little its legend from the impact of inventions and creations?

Such a genesis of Christianity, insists Benoît, would be nonsense.[33] We have proposed a much more traditional but we submit a much more persuasive alternative; that the Gospels were reliable historically in presenting Jesus as one who performed miracles and drew huge crowds by his teaching, who claimed to be God and who was therefore accused of blasphemy; but who justified these claims of his by rising from the dead and giving his disciples his spirit. This is not creating nor reconstructing the evidence. It is simply accepting the evidence of the four Gospels, which gives (in the terminology of the New Quest the 'criterion of authenticity')[34] sufficient reason and a coherent explanation for the emergence of the church, itself a marvel.

## Notes

1. 'The final task of exegesis is an art'. A. Robert, and A. Feuillet, *Interpreting the Scriptures*. (New York: Desclée, 1969), p. 165, taken from the French original, *Introduction à la Bible* Volume 1, (Paris:-Tournai, Desclée, 1959).
2. J. D. G. Dunn, *Jesus Remembered Volume 1, Christianity in the Making*, (Grand Rapids: Eerdmans, 2003) 8.1, p. 174.
3. I have added this parenthesis in brackets. *Method of Proof* is the title of DCD, CHAPTER III, SECTION I, pp. 99–110.
4. DCD, pp. 109–110
5. *Ibid.*, p. 112.
6. *Ibid*, pp. 113–4.
7. BMG, p. 49.
8. MLM, p. 164.
9. *Ibid.*, p. 165.
10. *Ibid.*
11. *Ibid.*, p. 166.
12. JVG, p. 420.
13. *Ibid.*, pp. 222–3.
14. F. W. Beare in his commentary *The Gospel According to Matthew*, (Oxford, Basil Blackwell, 1981), pp. 353–5.
15. Beare, p. 353
16. BMG, pp. 126–7.
17. JVG, p. 426.
18. Whether or not we accept the authenticity of Ephesians as a genuine letter of Paul Brown, INT, pp. 620–637. Brown names Ephesians as

'deutero-Pauline'. My own view is that the case is by no means closed, and many of the objections to Pauline authorship are flimsy. Paul Kobelski notes 'Among modern scholars who defend authorship of the letter by Paul are Barth, Benoit, Bruce, Caird, Dahl....'NJBC **55.3**, p. 883. My biggest problem is, who on earth *could* have written such a great letter if not a genius such as Paul?

19  http://en.wikipedia.org/wiki/Talmud. [accessed 22 February 2013] Looking at Wikipedia is at least a start! The Talmud, compiled from the second century AD onwards, was a discussion of Jewish teaching based upon the Jewish Bible (called Taanach).

20  Lagrange, M.-J. *Évangile Selon Saint Matthieu*. (Paris: Gabalda et Fils, 4th Edition, 1927), pp. 324–5. [Lagrange *Matthew*]

21  Cf. BMG, pp. 172–175, on the controversial question of the Gospel of John and that Gospel's transmission of the words of Jesus in the evangelist's own style.

22  http://www.catholic-resources.org/ChurchDocs [accessed 10 March 2013] *Instruction of the Pontifical Biblical Commission Concerning the Historical Truth of the Gospels*, translated by J. A. Fitzmyer SJ, *Theological Studies* 1964, 9.

23  Cf. DV 19.

24  Beare, p. 354.

25  DCD, p. 5.

26  *Ibid.*, p. 208

27  HJCG, p. 80.

28  *Ibid.*, p. 81

29  *Ibid.*, p. 81 'these conjectures proved untenable, as Pliny explicitly states.' Note 52 Wlosok, *Rom*, 28, 32f.

30  *Ibid.*, p. 80.

31  DCD, p. 196.

32  *Ibid.*, p. 199.

33  P. Benoit, *Exégèse et Thèologie*, (Paris: Les Éditions du Cerf, 1961), p. 53. BMG, p. 55

34  BMG, pp. 114–118

# 7

# THE APOSTOLIC SUCCESSION, PART ONE[1]

# THE AUTHORITY OF THE APOSTLES THEMSELVES

From the viewpoint of apologetics, the question of the historical origins of authority in the Catholic Church has two parts:
1. What evidence is there that the apostles were given authority from the risen Christ to establish the Church?
2. What evidence is there that the risen Christ intended this authority to be transmitted to the apostolic college of bishops?

This Chapter deals with the authority of the apostles themselves, and the next chapter, deals with the question of the handing on of their authority to their successors the bishops of the Catholic Church.

## 7.1 IRENAEUS

*Irenaeus, a second century Father of the Church, sets out the Catholic doctrine of apostolic succession.*

Before we consider the question of the role of Simon Peter as an 'apostle', it is necessary to investigate the origins of the whole Catholic idea of 'apostolic succession' in general. It is expressed most eloquently in its fully developed form in the teaching of Irenaeus, Bishop of Lyons (AD 120 to 200). It would not be entirely inaccurate to describe Irenaeus as the Church's first systematic theologian, his *Adversus Haereses* being a prime work of apologetics, in particular against Gnosticism which was threatening the true doctrine of the Church handed down to his day from those first apostles:

> It is possible, then, for everyone in every church, who may wish to know the truth, to contemplate the tradition of the apostles which has been made known to us throughout the whole world. And we are in a position to enumerate those who were instituted bishops by the apostles and their successors down to our own times, men who neither knew nor taught anything like what these heretics rave about.[2]
>
> But since it would be too long to enumerate in such a volume as this the successions of all the churches, we shall confound all those who, in whatever manner, whether through self-satisfaction or vainglory, or through blindness and wicked opinion, assemble other than where it is proper, by pointing out here the successions of the bishops of the greatest and most ancient church known to all, founded and organized at Rome by the two most glorious apostles, Peter and Paul—that church which has the tradition and the faith with which comes down to us after having been announced to men by the apostles. For with this Church, because of its superior origin, all churches must agree, that is, all the faithful in the whole world. And it is in her that the faithful everywhere have maintained the apostolic tradition.[3]
>
> Polycarp also was not only instructed by apostles, and conversed with many who had seen Christ, but was also, by apostles in Asia, appointed bishop of the church in Smyrna, whom I also saw in my early youth, for he tarried (on earth) a very long time, and, when a very old man, gloriously and most nobly suffering martyrdom, departed this life, having always taught the things which he had learned from the apostles, and which the Church has handed down, and which alone are true. To these things all

the Asiatic churches testify, as do also those men who have succeeded Polycarp down to the present time.[4]

Since therefore we have such proofs, it is not necessary to seek the truth among others which it is easy to obtain from the Church; since the apostles, like a rich man (depositing his money) in a bank, lodged in her hands most copiously all things pertaining to the truth, so that every man, whosoever will, can draw from her the water of life.... For how stands the case? Suppose there arise a dispute relative to some important question among us, should we not have recourse to the most ancient churches with which the apostles held constant conversation, and learn from them what is certain and clear in regard to the present question?[5]

It is incumbent to obey the presbyters who are in the Church—those who, as I have shown, possess the succession from the apostles; those who, together with the succession of the episcopate, have received the infallible charism of truth, according to the good pleasure of the Father. But (it is also incumbent) to hold in suspicion others who depart from the primitive succession, and assemble themselves together in any place whatsoever, either as heretics of perverse minds, or as schismatics puffed up and self-pleasing, or again as hypocrites, acting thus for the sake of lucre and vainglory. For all these have fallen from the truth.[6]

The true knowledge is the doctrine of the apostles, and the ancient organization of the Church throughout the whole world, and the manifestation of the body of Christ according to the succession of bishops, by which succession the bishops have handed down the Church which is found everywhere.[7]

We note in particular regarding Irenaeus' doctrine of the apostolic succession:

1. He claims that the true doctrine is to be found where there is true succession from the apostles. For him, the church's *doctrine* and the *succession of its bishops from the apostles* are inextricably linked.
2. He claims to know this tradition because he knew Polycarp, who knew the apostles.
3. The present bishops of the church throughout the world are successors of the apostles.
4. Irenaeus says that, practically speaking, he cannot name the succession of all the churches stemming from the apostles. It is sufficient to name the apostolic succession of successive Bishops of Rome from Peter and Paul.

The last point is particularly important. We shall see later that there is a dispute among church historians as to whether Irenaeus gives a primacy to the Bishop of Rome as successor of Peter and Paul. We will have to consider that question later. However that does not concern us now. What is significant for us at this stage of our discussion is that Irenaeus names Peter and Paul as apostles who define what is the true teaching from 'what these heretics rave about'; and they define it because the bishops of Rome who are the successors of Peter and Paul are continuing that true teaching in their name. This is what we mean when at Sunday Mass we as Catholics today proclaim in the Nicene Creed that 'we believe in one, holy, catholic, and apostolic church'. We are in that same line of continuity of teaching and of discipline as was Irenaeus himself nineteen centuries ago.

What is also significant for us is that Irenaeus lists only two of the 'apostles', and for him that is enough, to follow 'that church which has the tradition and the faith with which comes down to us after having been announced to men by the apostles'. Other churches throughout the world, says Irenaeus, cannot go wrong if they follow the teaching of the Bishop of Rome, *because he is the successor of the apostles Peter and Paul.*

Discussion of this Irenaeus text again can be misleading if we focus only on whether Irenaeus is asserting the primacy of Peter. Rather, Irenaeus is informing us that we have the complete package of tradition if we follow that church whose bishop is the successor of *both Peter and Paul*. Peter was one of the Twelve, and Paul was especially chosen to be what we in the church call 'the apostle to the Gentiles'; as the first account of Paul's conversion puts it, when the Lord appears in a vision to the terrified Ananias 'The Lord replied, 'Go, for this man is my chosen instrument to bring my name before gentiles and kings and before the people of Israel'.[8] (Ac 9:15)

In Catholic theology, indeed in Catholic dogma, we have restricted the use of the term 'apostle' to the members of the Twelve 'chosen' by Jesus and 'sent' by him after his resurrection and ascension to preach redemption in his name and with his authority; and to Paul who never met Jesus while on earth but who received his commission directly from the risen Lord on the Damascus Road. By 'apostolic church', therefore, we have come to mean that church which is founded on the doctrine and living tradition of Jesus as handed on to us exclusively via the Twelve and Paul.

We shall soon see that the meaning of the term *apostolos* in the New Testament is complex, and is by no means limited to the Twelve and Paul. The same is true even of later church usage. Barnabas is called 'the apostle of Cyprus', and John Mark the 'apostle of Alexandria'. Neither were members of the Twelve, or given equal status by the church to Paul. The discussion has also grown in intensity in the present critical era (and not always grown in wisdom!) by the whole question of authority within the churches today. Obviously, if the Twelve and Paul do have that authority claimed by the Catholic Church as also for their successors, then 'church change' is implied. Thus the complex debate as to the use of the term 'apostle' in the earliest Christian sources is by no means purely academic.

Perhaps our most reasonable beginning would be baldly to state an argument from the text of the Gospels and other New Testament writings, at first uncritically, which seems to me to be obvious: namely that the Twelve and Paul are exclusively seen as *bearers of divine revelation from Christ*. This gives them their unique position in Christian origins, and begins to validate the doctrine of the apostolic succession of the episcopate.

## 7.2 THE COMMISSION OF THE RISEN CHRIST

*During his resurrection appearances, Jesus appeared to the Twelve, giving them specifically the power to forgive sins and to make disciples of all peoples, Jews and Gentiles.*

In all four Gospels, after the discovery of the empty tomb, the risen Christ appears bodily to his disciples. He commissions the Twelve, (or post Judas the 'Eleven') and it seems only to the Twelve, to carry his Good News with his authority to the whole world:

> **Matthew 28**: Meanwhile the eleven disciples set out for Galilee, to the mountain where Jesus had arranged to meet them. When they saw him they fell down before him, though some hesitated. Jesus came up and spoke to them. He said, 'All authority in heaven and on earth has been given to me. Go, therefore, make disciples of all nations; baptise them in the name of the Father and of the Son and of the Holy Spirit, and teach them to observe all the commands I gave you. And look, I am with you always; yes, to the end of time.'(28:16–20)
>
> **Mark 16:** Lastly, he showed himself to the Eleven themselves while they were at table. He reproached them for their incredulity and obstinacy, because they had refused to believe those who had seen him after he had risen. And he said to them, "Go out to the whole world; proclaim the gospel to all creation. Whoever believes and is baptised will be saved;

# The Apostolic Succession 1:
## The Authority of the Apostles Themselves

whoever does not believe will be condemned." (Mk 16:14–16)

**Luke 24:** and he said to them, "So it is written that the Christ would suffer and on the third day rise from the dead, and that, in his name, repentance for the forgiveness of sins would be preached to all nations, beginning from Jerusalem. You are witnesses to this. And now I am sending upon you what the Father has promised. Stay in the city, then, until you are clothed with the power from on high." Then he took them out as far as the outskirts of Bethany, and raising his hands he blessed them. Now as he blessed them, he withdrew from them and was carried up to heaven. They worshipped him and then went back to Jerusalem full of joy; and they were continually in the Temple praising God. (Lk 24:46–53)

**John 20:** In the evening of that same day, the first day of the week, the doors were closed in the room where the disciples were, for fear of the Jews. Jesus came and stood among them. He said to them, 'Peace be with you,' and, after saying this, he showed them his hands and his side. The disciples were filled with joy at seeing the Lord, and he said to them again, 'Peace be with you. As the Father sent me, so am I sending you.' After saying this he breathed on them and said: 'Receive the Holy Spirit.' (Jn 20:19–22)

We note regarding:

**Matthew:** Many would not accept that this ending of the Gospel of Matthew is historically authentic, claiming that this is a reflection of the faith of the Matthean church.[9] However it is in all the manuscripts of Matthew, and therefore was a very early ecclesiastical tradition, most likely back in the first century. He refers to 'the eleven disciples' as apparently exclusively meeting Jesus, 'going far beyond any Messianic categories in his claims for Jesus'.[10] As Jesus now claims all authority in heaven and on earth, he now sends his disciples out to the whole world, the restriction to Israel no longer applying as it did during his public ministry (Mt 10:5 ff., 15:24). The implication is that the disciples, that is the Eleven, have that same authority which Jesus now claims handed over to them for their post-resurrection mission.

**Mark:** Vincent Taylor's view, expressed in his 1952 Commentary on Mark, is that 'it is unnecessary to examine in detail the almost universally held conclusion that 16: 9–20 is not an original part of Mark'.[11] If that view is accepted, the original Gospel finishing at 16:8, then there is no commissioning of the apostles in Mark. Taylor argues that: 'The commission to preach the gospel to the whole creation is an independent version of Matthew 28:18ff. Its universalism shows that it was current in a Gentile church.'[12] But even if not canonical, Mark 16:9–20 is at least a very early ecclesiastical insertion, and thus attests to faith that the risen Jesus in appearing to his chosen disciples also commissioned them.

**Luke:** Luke is even more specific in linking Jesus' own sending from the Father to his sending of them; them in Luke being clearly the Twelve minus Judas. As Howard Marshall says, 'The links of this material with Matthew 28:16–20 and John 20:21–23 are obvious. Luke shares with Matthew the commission to go to the nations and the promise of divine power. He shares with John the promise of the Spirit and the reference to the forgiveness of sins. It cannot be doubted, therefore, that common traditions underlie these accounts, the basic nucleus being that Jesus commanded his disciples to spread the good news widely and offer forgiveness of sins and that he promised them divine power for their task.'[13] Similar themes are paralleled in the introduction of Luke's 'second volume' Ac 1:1–8, where the apostles are given the same mission from Christ who before ascending to his Father tells them to wait for the coming Spirit.

**John:** In quoting Howard Marshall regarding Luke's account of the sending by Jesus of his chosen apostles, we have advanced beyond a purely uncritical reading of the text of the four Gospels. We have also anticipated the account in John, where John repeats Luke's account in Jesus saying that he sends them (that is the 'disciples', *mathétés*) which in John means the Twelve, again minus Judas after the passion and death of Jesus; although on occasions he means the outer circle of disciples, for example Joseph of Arimathea. (Jn 19:38) We can move towards using the critical principle of 'multiple attestation' as does Howard Marshall, in verifying the historicity of these accounts that is 'a saying of Jesus in the Gospels is likely to be historically authentic if it is attested in more than one independent literary source (for example Mk, Q, Paul, Jn) and/or in more than one literary form or genre'.[14]

## 7.3 ALL NATIONS

*Jesus commissions his disciples to preach to all the nations.*

He does not have a specific command, but this is implied in the Greeks approaching Jesus before his crucifixion.

> Among those who went up to worship at the festival were some Greeks. These approached Philip, who came from Bethsaida in Galilee, and put this request to him, 'Sir, we should like to see Jesus.' Philip went to tell Andrew and Andrew and Philip together went to tell Jesus. Jesus replied to them: Now the hour has come for the Son of man to be glorified. In all truth I tell you, unless a wheat grain falls into the earth and dies, it remains only a single grain; but if it dies it yields a rich harvest. (Jn 12:20–24)

John makes clear therefore concerning the orientation of Christ's mission to the Gentiles after his death and resurrection.
- He communicates the authority he has received from his Father to them for this task. He sends them as the Father sent him.

- They will be given the power of the Holy Spirit to fulfil this commission.
- The evidence is not clear that any other followers of Jesus apart from the Eleven were given this commission.

## 7.4 EXCLUSIVITY?

*It is not clear from the evidence that only the Twelve were given such a revelation and such a commission. Others may have been included; but if they were, their contribution to the sources has disappeared.*

The evidence, on the other hand, is not absolutely clear that it was *only* the Twelve who received the commission and the authority of the risen Christ. In Matthew, it is clear that Jesus addresses only 'the eleven disciples' (Mt 28:16). In the poorly attested ending of Mark, 'Lastly he showed himself to the Eleven themselves while they were at table... Jesus says also, "Go out into the whole world; proclaim the Gospel to all creation"'. Luke does not make clear that the 'disciples' who encountered Jesus on the Road to Emmaus were among the Twelve (Lk 24:13). When Jesus appears to the disciples in Jerusalem (Lk 24:36) it does not say it was only to the Twelve that he appeared In fact, Luke says the opposite: 'They set out that instant and returned to Jerusalem. There they found the Eleven assembled together with their companions'. (Lk 24:33) Were these 'companions' also made the witnesses referred to in Jesus' commission? (Lk 24:48) Or were the 'companions' only hangers-on, not the subjects given authority by the risen Christ? Elsewhere in his Gospel, Luke is most definite among the evangelists that the Twelve, and only the Twelve, were *apostoloi*. (Lk 6:13). Therefore we can assume that the commission of the risen Christ applied only to those same *apostoloi*: particularly because in his 'second volume', the Christ about to ascend into heaven, addresses his commission to his *apostoloi* (Ac

# The Apostolic Succession 1:
## The Authority of the Apostles Themselves

1:2), after the casting of lots Matthias making up the number 'twelve apostles' again (Ac 1:26).

Similarly, in John the question is also complicated. As Barratt says, 'It is often impossible to say whether, by *mathētai*, 'disciples', John means the inner or outer circle of the followers of Jesus...'[15] Barrett quotes with approval F. J. A. Hort's *The Christian Ecclesia*, 1914:

> In such a matter the mere fact that doubt is possible is a striking one. It is in truth difficult to separate these cases [after the resurrection] from the frequent omission of the evangelists to distinguish the Twelve from other disciples... Granting that it was probably to the Eleven that our Lord directly and principally spoke on both these occasions [in John and Matthew]... yet it still has to be considered in what capacity they were addressed by him. If at the Last Supper, and during the discourses which followed, when the Twelve or Eleven were most completely secluded from all other disciples as well as from the unbelieving Jews, they represented the whole Ecclesia of the future, it is but natural to suppose that it was likewise as representatives of the whole Ecclesia of the future, whether associated with other disciples or not, that they had given to them those two assurances and charges of our Lord, about the receiving of the Holy Spirit and the remitting or retaining of sins..., and about his universal authority in heaven and on earth.[16]

Hort's conclusion is most reasonable. At the Last Supper in all four Gospels, and at the conclusion of the risen Jesus' appearances to his disciples, the Twelve figured so prominently as a special group addressed that it is reasonable to assume that they alone were the recipients of the authority conferred upon them by Jesus sent by the Father. If there were others given similar authority, we do not know who they were, nor did they figure in any way in the accounts we have of the primitive church. The case is almost similar to the problem of canonicity. We cannot be sure that there were no books which the church accepted as canonical but which have disappeared. The fact that the church does not proclaim other books as canonical gives us reasonable, if not absolute, certainty, that there were none. But now the question arises, precisely what authority were the Twelve given?

## 7.5 THE CLASSICAL PROTESTANT OBJECTION

*Against the classical Protestant objection, it appears from the evidence that the apostles were not only given a power from the risen Christ to preach the Gospel, but were given personal authority to reconcile sinners.*

The classical Protestant objection to considering the Catholic view that the Twelve (the Eleven were made up again to Twelve by the election of Matthias, Ac 2:23) is that the apostles were commissioned to preach, and they had no more authority than that of preachers of the Gospel.

The Catholic response is that, on the contrary, Jesus conferred a personal authority on the Twelve, an authority that the history of the earliest church in the Acts of the Apostles demonstrates they used. Jesus says in John's account of the commission, 'After saying this he breathed on them and said: Receive the Holy Spirit. If you forgive anyone's sins, they are forgiven; if you retain anyone's sins, they are retained.' (Jn 20:22–23). This is equivalent to a legal binding and loosing. It is not simply a declaration of forgiveness. Brown quotes a discussion between J. R. Mantey, who attempts to show that 'the theological implication that no more is involved than declaring the forgiveness of sins which has already taken place', with H. J. Cadbury who is not a Catholic, but who argues on the contrary that 'When you forgive men's sins, at that moment God forgives those sins and they remain forgiven.'[17] Brown also sees a parallel with Matthew 16:19, 'whatever you bind on earth will be bound in heaven'.[18] This exegesis would justify the Catholic interpretation as referring to the Sacrament of Reconciliation, as expressed in *The Catechism of the Catholic Church*:

> **1444** In imparting to his apostles his own power to forgive sins the Lord also gives them the authority to reconcile sinners with the Church. This ecclesial dimension of their task is expressed most notably in Christ's solemn words to Simon Peter: 'I will give you the keys of the kingdom of heaven, and whatever you bind on earth shall be bound in heaven, and whatever you loose on earth shall be loosed in heaven.' 'The office of binding and loosing which was given to Peter was also assigned to the college of the apostles united to its head.'
>
> **1445** The words *bind and loose* mean: whomever you exclude from your communion, will be excluded from communion with God; whomever you receive anew into your communion, God will welcome back into his. *Reconciliation with the Church is inseparable from reconciliation with God*.

And Barrett, a Methodist, concludes. 'This joint work, of Christ in sending the Holy Spirit and of the Holy Spirit in bearing witness to Christ, is exercised in and through the church as represented by the disciples, *aphienai* (literally 'to release', 'let go') is used here (that is in Jn 20:23) only in John with the meaning 'to remit', *kratein* signifies the opposite: 'to hold fast', 'to retain'. Brown's long and admirable discussion (II, 1039–45) leads to a conclusion similar to that adopted here'.[19]

## 7.6 THE FIRST EXERCISE OF APOSTOLIC AUTHORITY

*This power they exercised immediately from Pentecost onwards, with the authority of Christ setting up the infant church with their teaching, the breaking of bread, the common life of the Church, and daily worship.*

A classical Protestant version of the church immediately after Pentecost would be a preacher expounding the scriptures, obviously charismatically as did Peter.

In fact, however, what we see is Simon Peter asserting the authority which Christ gave him by forming the first Christian community. Luke asserts that it is the twelve *apostoloi* (Ac 1:26) who were assembled in Jerusalem waiting at the command of the ascended Christ for the gift of the Spirit. When, after Peter's inspiring first sermon proclaiming Jesus risen from the dead and now at the right hand of the Father, we see that the beginning was focussed on the authority of the *apostles*, not upon a reading of scripture:

> He (i.e. Peter the apostle) spoke to them for a long time using many other arguments, and he urged them, 'Save yourselves from this perverse generation.' They accepted what he said and were baptised. That very day about three thousand were added to their number. These remained faithful to the teaching of the apostles, to the brotherhood, to the breaking of bread and to the prayers. And everyone was filled with awe; the apostles worked many signs and miracles. And all who shared the faith owned everything in common; they sold their goods and possessions and distributed the proceeds among themselves according to what each one needed. Each day, with one heart, they regularly went to the Temple but met in their houses for the breaking of bread; they shared their food gladly and generously; they praised God and were looked up to by everyone. Day by day the Lord added to their community those destined to be saved. (Ac 2:40–47)

Far from scripture reading being the centre of their activity, they had to attend to the *teaching of the apostles*, not then recognized as canonical scripture. That teaching included of course the teaching of Jesus while on earth, but presented with their authority, without having any doubts as to its veracity; and that before, as far as we are aware, nothing being yet written down. This teaching was reinforced by miracles, performed we see above *exclusively by the apostles.* This surely was to validate their authority, and not only to testify to the truth of the Resurrection of Jesus. They celebrated what we call the Eucharist, that rite again not in the scriptures which they possessed, but the tradition handed on by Jesus on the night of his betrayal, which, as Hort has explained to us earlier, *Jesus celebrated exclusively with the Twelve.* They practiced community of goods, no doubt following the example of Jesus himself, who as Son of Man had nowhere to lay his head (Mt 8:20), and who lived day by day with his disciples on provisions from their common fund (Jn 13:29). Again, there is no suggestion in the Old Testament, their scriptures, that God's people should practice community of goods. Their authority was Jesus, who had sent them just as the Father sent him. Scholars question the historicity of Acts; but no one has suggested an alternative scenario for the beginning of the church, directed by the apostles; nor is there any other alternative scenario in the New Testament or in the earliest sources.

Again not averting to Peter as necessarily primate of the apostles, what is important here is that the apostles as a group, led by Peter, are aware of the revelation, both of doctrine and of practice, which the risen Christ had given them, either during his life on earth, or just before ascending to his Father. And they promoted that teaching and that practice with full authority, not asking for others to verify from the scriptures that what they said was the correct interpretation. There are all the signs that they were aware of their own infallibility!

Even more, as time went on, the apostles acted authoritatively in allowing male Gentiles to become Christians without being circumcised (Ac 15). There is no record in the four Gospels of Jesus discussing the issue of circumcision; which presumably he would have done if the Gospels were according to the Bultmann tradition, the Christ of faith and not the historical Jesus! Peter had received a vision which contradicted much of what the rabbis said; to the effect that nothing which God called clean was unclean. Peter, due to meet a Gentile called Cornelius, had a vision where he saw animals, presumably pigs, forbidden to be eaten by the Torah. A voice then said to him, 'Now, Peter, kill and eat!' (Ac 10:13) The Council of Jerusalem ratified the Apostle Peter's vision, (Ac 15) and decided to allow male Gentiles to become members of the Church without circumcision.

## 7.7 THE HISTORICAL EXISTENCE OF THE TWELVE

*It can be persuasively argued from critical scholarship that the historical Jesus founded the Twelve as a group during his lifetime to represent the twelve tribes of Israel, and so to renew the people of God.*

Walter Schmithals, in *The Office of Apostle in the Early Church*. Transl. J. E. Steely. (London, S.P.C.K., 1971) dismisses completely the historicity of the Twelve as post-resurrection:

> As regards the circle of the *dódeka*, generally, in my opinion it does not reach at all back into the time before the resurrection ... In Mark, *dódeka* is found only ten times, and those ten passages belong collectively to the more recent traditions of Mark's Gospel.[20]

For Schmithals, Judas was not part of the original tradition. He was one of the Twelve who saw the resurrection, since 'the old tradition speaks of an appearance of Jesus before the Twelve'. 'What the book of Acts knows about them — selection of Matthias, Acts 1:15–26; further, their appearance, Acts 2:14, 6:2 — is legend. Even Paul mentions the twelve only in the formula taken over from the primitive community (1 Co 15:5). Otherwise he does not know them.[21]

Schmithals' view is that the twelve were formed after the resurrection:

*The Apostolic Succession 1:*
*The Authority of the Apostles Themselves*

> ... as the representatives of the eschatological community of salvation. A resurrection vision was shared with them. Very soon, then–probably with the slackening of the eschatological expectation upon which it lived–this circle of the twelve must have fallen apart; at the latest after the death of James the son of Zebedee, and perhaps already after the "betrayal" of Judas, it was scattered. The primitive community accommodated itself to the new situation, began with the (Jewish) mission, and had men at its head who indeed had belonged to the circle of the twelve, but who gained the leading positions not as members of this circle but on the ground of their achievement, and who later could be supplanted by the Lord's brother, James.[22]

On the contrary, John P. Meier, with typical rigour, argues that the historical Jesus during his public ministry called the Twelve from the large group of his disciples to be representative of the twelve tribes of Israel. He first demonstrates that Jesus the preacher attracted large crowds. This is attested both by the multiple attestation of sources and from the fact that Jesus being crucified is best explained by the fact that large crowds were following him.[23] He then demonstrates that the fact that Jesus called 'disciples' is also authenticated historically:

> It would appear that the massive use of *mathétés* for the disciples of Jesus in the four Gospels is not a projection of a usage found in the OT (MT or LXX), intertestamental literature, and Qumran, nor a retrojection of a designation for Christian believers commonly used in the 1st century A.D. It may well be that, during the public ministry, either Jesus himself or his immediate followers selected the word 'disciple' (in Aramaic, *talmida*), which was not yet a technical term in the later rabbinic sense. The word was chosen to designate the unusual type of relationship that existed between the Elijah-like prophet and teacher (a 'rabbi', also in the non-technical sense) and those he had called to follow him literally. In

adopting this (at least for Jewish Palestine) relatively recent terminology for a specific movement, Jesus and his disciples may reflect the Hellenistic milieu that had come to influence Palestine from the days of Alexander the Great onwards. But for Jesus, a more immediate influence and model would have been supplied by the Baptist and his group of disciples, to which Jesus may have for a while belonged.[24]

In the Gospels, the characteristic expression was 'The Twelve' to indicate those who later were called 'the twelve apostles':

> I use the phrase 'The Twelve' to indicate a special group of twelve men who were not only disciples of Jesus but also formed an inner circle around him. In this I imitate the usage of Mark and John, who always speak of 'the Twelve' absolutely (e.g. Mark 6:7, John 6:67). They never used phrases like 'the twelve disciples' or 'the twelve apostles'.[25]

Next, Meier examines the disputed question as to whether 'the group called the Twelve existed during the ministry of the historical Jesus. Once the existence of the group is established, we can proceed to inquire about its characteristics and function'.[26] Meier gives a positive answer to that question. He agrees with Wolfgang Trilling that 'while many of the Marcan references to the Twelve may well be redactional, at least two references seem firmly embedded in the pre-Marcan tradition'.[27]

Similarly regarding the lists of the Twelve (Mk 3:16–19, Mt 10:2–4, Lk 6:14–16, Ac 1:13): 'Far from the variations in the lists of the Twelve disproving the group's existence during Jesus' lifetime, the Synoptists' disagreements within the basic agreement of their lists argue for a primitive oral tradition that underwent some changes before the Gospels were written'.[28] Bauckham in his fine study *Jesus and the Eyewitnesses: The Gospels as Eyewitness Testimony* adds significantly: 'The lists show, not carelessness about the precise membership of the Twelve, but quite the opposite: great care to preserve precisely the way they were known in their own milieu during the ministry of Jesus and in the early Jerusalem church.'[29]

Furthermore, it is remarkable for Meier that 'the Twelve are hardly mentioned outside of the Gospels.'[30] They are mentioned in 1 Corinthians 15:5, never after Acts 6:2. The conclusion for Meier is obvious:

> The only reasonable conclusion one can draw to explain the creating and ebbing of references to the Twelve in the NT is the commonsense one: the Twelve are prominent in the story of Jesus because that is where they actually played a significant role. On the basis of their close relationship with Jesus, which they claimed had been restored and confirmed by a resurrection appearance, the role of the Twelve continued into the earliest days of the church but it declined and disappeared with surprising rapidity.[31]

Why did the historical Jesus institute the Twelve? Meier is equally clear and positive:

> The basic intention of Jesus in creating the Twelve seems to have been more wide-ranging than simply providing a permanent example of discipleship. His intention apparently corresponded to the core of his proclamation to Israel: the coming of the kingdom of God, who would establish his rule definitively over a restored Israel...[32]

> From the major and minor prophets to the late narrative and wisdom literature, from what became the canonical Old Testament to pseudepigraphic and Qumranite literature close to the time of Jesus, all sorts of literary forms representing various streams of postexilic Judaism testify to the lively and ongoing hope of the regathering of God's scattered people, the reassembling of the twelve tribes in the promised land.'[33]

Jesus did, according to Meier, send his disciples out on a mission during his lifetime.[34] Mark 6:7, Luke 9:1 tells us that the Twelve performed the same exorcisms and miracles as Jesus, because they had his 'power' (*exousia*). 'If the very existence of the Twelve was meant to symbolize the beginning of the eschatological regathering of Israel, who else would b e better suited for a mission to Israel that would initiate, however symbolically, such a regathering?'[35]

## 7.8 CONFERRED AUTHORITY NECESSARY

*That the risen Jesus would wish the Twelve to have his specific authority to found the church can be argued from the principle of sufficient reason, namely that if Jesus was truly God become man, then he would either give them a Bible and expect them to preach the Good News with all Christians being equal, or he would give a group of people the same authority as he had to create the new community. The evidence clearly suggests the latter actually happened.*

Meier therefore has demonstrated the existence of the Twelve as disciples of special importance during the public ministry of the historical Jesus. But how can we jump from an historical argument as to the existence of the Twelve pre-resurrection to that authority which the end of each of the four Gospels gives to them of being sent by Jesus, just as he was sent by the Father?

The relatively simple answer, it seems to me, lies in the principle of authenticity called 'sufficient reason' (that is 'A saying of Jesus in the Gospels is likely to be authentic if it coheres with other sayings and deeds of Jesus').[36] If Jesus was truly God, and claimed such during his life on earth, then he would wish a group of his disciples to continue his work with his authority. He would in fact need such a group with such authority in order for his work to continue, unless he gave them a set of Bibles and commissioned them to preach from those Bibles. Jesus on the contrary would want his work to continue as he had begun it.

The clearest example of this apostolic authority is to be found in the life and letters of Saint Paul, Apostle of the Gentiles.

## 7.9 PAUL

*We argue that Paul after his conversion became convinced that the risen Lord had given him authority from divine revelation to bring Gentiles into the Church. He seemed to act with infallible authority, for example regarding the admission of Gentiles into the church without the need for circumcision.*

By this time in the history of the infant church, the lone addition to the Twelve had already appeared. Saul of Tarsus was of the tribe of Benjamin, (Rm 11:1) a zealous Pharisee (Ph 3:5) and a native of Tarsus (Ac 9:11), a city in the south of Asia Minor, today on the south coast of Turkey. Saul had studied rabbinic theology at Jerusalem, as he said, under Gamaliel, (Ac 22:3) a member of the Sanhedrin who had counselled tolerance regarding the new sect of The Way, later to be called Christianity (Ac 5:34). Saul was also a Roman citizen (Ac 22:25), which gave privileges such as the right to claim due process of law, no doubt obtained through his father, a successful burger of Tarsus.

Luke is quite clear in Acts, when recounting the story of Saul's conversion on the Damascus Road, that Saul had a unique vocation. After he had been blinded by the light of his encounter with the Lord, and heard the divine voice asking him why he was persecuting Christians:

> For three days he was without his sight and took neither food nor drink. There was a disciple in Damascus called Ananias, and he had a vision in which the Lord said to him, 'Ananias!' When he replied, 'Here I am, Lord,' the Lord said, 'Get up and go to Straight Street and ask at the house of Judas for someone called Saul, who comes from Tarsus. At this moment he is praying, and has seen a man called Ananias coming in and laying hands on him to give

> him back his sight.' But in response, Ananias said, 'Lord, I have heard from many people about this man and all the harm he has been doing to your holy people in Jerusalem. He has come here with a warrant from the chief priests to arrest everybody who invokes your name.' The Lord replied, 'Go, for this man is my chosen instrument to bring my name before gentiles and kings and before the people of Israel.' (Ac 9:10–15)

We note that in the vision to Ananias the terrified Christian disciple at Damascus, the Lord explains to Ananias that Saul is his 'chosen instrument', singular (*skeuos*[37] *eklogé*). Saul therefore has a singular role, guaranteed by divine vision. He is himself aware of this role, which gives him the authority to know what Christ's revelation is, and gives him the authority to anathematise those who do not accept that revelation. This is what he says to the Galatian Jewish Christians, who refuse to allow Gentile and Jewish Christians to eat together:

> Now I want to make it quite clear to you, brothers, about the gospel that was preached by me, that it was no human message. It was not from any human being that I received it, and I was not taught it, but it came to me through a revelation of Jesus Christ. (Ga 1:11–12)

Anyone who departs from this Gospel, Saul says, is anathema. (Ga 1:9) Saul insists 'But even if we ourselves or an angel from heaven preaches to you a gospel other than the one we preached to you, let God's curse be on him.' (Ga 1:8) No other Christian in the New Testament or after it claims such authority. Saul, whose other name is Paul (Ac 13:9), even insists that he did not receive it from Peter, or those others who were 'apostles before me' (Ga 1:15–17). Rather, he did not go up to Jerusalem until three years after his conversion and spent fifteen days with Peter (Ga 1:18), presumably to guarantee with the leader of the Twelve that his own 'gospel' meshed with theirs.

Schmithals, for his part, completely denies that Paul's concept of being an 'apostle' gives him any authority consequent upon that revelation. Schmithals, whose complex but to me fantastic view of the evolution of the concept of 'apostle' in the primitive church we will have to examine more carefully, takes on the other hand the classical Lutheran view that the 'apostle' has no authority except that of the message itself, sharing that authority with the rest of the Christian community, and having no more authority than any other member of that community:

> The fact that he is an *apostle* who has been called by Christ himself becomes, by comparison, a matter of indifference, and in fact the corresponding assertion has, even in the Galatian letter, only the purpose of substantiating the message as such, not of attesting the messenger's preferential place.... Thus Paul himself confirms the evidence which we have already seen that an apostle possesses no function which *only he* of all the primitive Christian missionaries can exercise. In spite of his well-known special position which is grounded in the form of his call, his service is the same as that performed by the other missionaries who are not called apostles.[38]

We will have to examine Schmithals' arguments more closely shortly. But surely, even a preliminary look at Galatians 1 surely contradicts such an assertion. Paul is prepared actively to anathematise those who oppose his 'gospel', which he has received by divine revelation. Could any other Christian in the community exercise such authority? If so, then why does Paul take the trouble to insist upon the fact that his threat of anathema is dependant upon his revelation given specially to him by the Lord? It is clear that not every other Christian has received such a revelation, otherwise again Paul could not insist upon the singularity of that revelation.

We have here from Schmithals, at the beginning of the discussion about apostleship at least, simply a gratuitous assertion of classical Protestant theology that no Christian has any special authority from the Lord himself in matters of doctrine or discipline.[39] On the contrary, this Galatians text rather confirms the Catholic position, that Paul as a unique apostle was given divine authority to excommunicate those who do not accept 'his gospel'. This therefore presumes that Paul knows what that gospel is, and also that he considers that he has been given divine authority to separate from communion those who do not accept it. And there is no other record either in the New Testament literature or in the earliest oral tradition that anyone else in the primitive church apart from the Twelve shared such authority with Paul.

## 7.10 THE APOSTLES INFALLIBLE?

*Paul speaks and acts as if he could never be wrong regarding the revelation of Christ and its essential corollaries in terms of church doctrine and practice. The conclusion is therefore more and more generated that Paul did not simply know the truths of revelation, but even more that he was infallible in this understanding*

This only seems to confirm as we have seen the view of the Tractarians that the apostles, that is the Twelve and Paul, were infallible.

However we need to pause and initially consider this question of infallibility. What we have clearly seen is that Paul is certain of the truth of the Gospel he proclaims, because it comes from divine revelation. But certainty is not necessarily infallible certainty. I can be certain that I am right today, but does that guarantee that I will always be right? Paul was certain of the Gospel in writing to the Galatians; but does that guarantee that he could always be certain of the truth that he was proclaiming, to the extent that he *could not ever be wrong regarding the Christian revelation*?

We would have to say as Catholics that there is no statement to that effect in the New Testament scriptures.

There is no explicit text which says 'the apostles were infallible'. However, if a person is always certain that he is right, and refuses even to countenance the possibility that he might be wrong, excommunicating all those who oppose his view, then the use of this *anathema* generates the conclusion more and more that this person is not just certain of what he defines as to be true. He just *cannot be wrong*. Certainly, Paul gives the impression that he cannot ever be wrong regarding revelation!

The case is even clearer if we consider, as we have discussed earlier, that the doctrines of the Church go beyond reason. If that is so, how could one be certain that one is always right without divine revelation? The logical conclusion would be that Paul's gift of being certain leads quite naturally to consider that he could never be wrong as an apostle; otherwise, how could he be certain *now* concerning divine revelation? Might he be wrong now? That doubt will always be there unless he were infallible in teaching the true doctrine of revelation.

## 7.11 THE APOSTLES: EXECUTIVE AUTHORITY?

*The evidence suggests clearly that Paul exercised executive authority in excommunicating the incestuous Corinthian, and regarding another person, restoring a sinner to communion. This was a fulfilment of the Lord's command, 'Whosoever sins you forgive, they are forgiven. Whosoever sins you retain, they are retained'.*

The other question is as to whether Paul saw his authority simply as that of a preacher, proclaiming what is right according to his gospel; or whether he considered himself as having executive power to carry out the excommunications he declared on those who do not follow his gospel. Here, it seems to me, the answer comes from the text of the New Testament:

> It is widely reported that there is sexual immorality among you, immorality of a kind that is not found

even among gentiles: that one of you is living with his stepmother. And you so filled with your own self-importance! It would have been better if you had been grieving bitterly, so that the man who has done this thing were turned out of the community. For my part, however distant I am physically, I am present in spirit and have already condemned the man who behaved in this way, just as though I were present in person. When you have gathered together in the name of our Lord Jesus, with the presence of my spirit, and in the power of our Lord Jesus, hand such a man over to Satan, to be destroyed as far as natural life is concerned, so that on the Day of the Lord his spirit may be saved. (1Co 5:1–5)

Paul is quite clear at this point:
- A man has committed incest among the Corinthian Christian community.
- Paul says that he should be excommunicated (lit. 'expelled from your midst')
- Paul insists that although he is a long way away, he has already condemned the man.
- Therefore, when the community meets again, that man is to be 'handed over to Satan' by that community, of which Paul himself is a part, his own spirit being present.
- This is a clear executive order from Paul, to excommunicate this incestuous Corinthian.

As H. L. Goudge says in his commentary on 5:4:

> Saint Paul has already passed judgment by his Apostolic authority, but he calls upon the Corinthian church to associate itself with, and carry out his sentence. Cf. Acts 15:22, 23, and 2 Corinthians 2:6 But the action of Saint Paul and the Church is not simply their own; it is 'in the name of the Lord Jesus'. By His authority and with His power will the sentence be pronounced. Cf. Matthew 28:18–20, where we find our Lord authorising the Church to act in His name. See fuller note at the end of this chapter (that is pp.41–42). [40]

*The Apostolic Succession 1:*
*The Authority of the Apostles Themselves*

In the second letter to the Corinthians, Paul refers to another excommunicated man,[41] and urges his restoration to the community:

> If anyone did cause distress, he caused it not to me, but—not to exaggerate—in some degree to all of you. The punishment already imposed by the majority was quite enough for such a person; and now by contrast you should forgive and encourage him all the more, or he may be overwhelmed by the extent of his distress. That is why I urge you to give your love towards him definite expression. This was in fact my reason for writing, to test your quality and whether you are completely obedient. But if you forgive anybody, then I too forgive that person; and whatever I have forgiven, if there is anything I have forgiven, I have done it for your sake in Christ's presence, to avoid being outwitted by Satan, whose scheming we know only too well. (2 Co 2:5–11)

This too is an executive act on the part of Paul:
- The community had obeyed Paul and punished the man.
- He now urges the man's restoration, the man having served his punishment, to test as to whether 'you are completely obedient'. (Literally 'whether you are obedient in everything'), that is obedient to his, Paul's authority.
- Paul in effect passes down his authority, that if the community forgives the person, Paul forgives him. The community therefore is acting in Paul's name.

To my mind, there is hardly possible a more manifest example of executive apostolic authority, which of course eventually became expressed in its sacramental form in the Sacrament of Penance or Reconciliation.

## 7.12 'APOSTLE' IN THE NEW TESTAMENT

*We argue that the term apostolos in the New Testament and later in the early history of the Church had a wider meaning than a reference to the Twelve and to Paul; but that it always meant one who was sent, either by Christ himself or by the prophetic spirit in the Church, to found first generation apostolic churches.*

So far, we have demonstrated that those whom tradition now calls 'apostles', that is the Twelve and Paul exclusively, exercised doctrinal and disciplinary authority in the infant church; and they exercised that authority claiming that it came from the risen Jesus himself.

However we have argued to this conclusion without analysing what the word *apostolos* meant in the New Testament where it occurs 79 times and of these 68 instances are in Luke, Acts, and the Pauline corpus.[42] The word only occurs once in John (13:16), and rarely in Matthew and Mark. Matthew 10:2, 'These are the names of the twelve apostles...', and Mark 3:14 'and he appointed twelve; they were to be his companions and to be sent out to proclaim the message....' Curiously, the New Jerusalem Bible translates *apostolous*, 'apostles' as 'companions'. The New International Version provides a much better translation: 'He appointed twelve—designating them apostles—that they might be with him and that he might send them out (*apostellé* ) to preach and have authority to drive out demons'. You will note the use of the noun 'apostle' and the verb 'send out' in Mark in the same sentence, a significant connection, as I will attempt to demonstrate.

All scholars note that the word *apostolos* is never used on the lips of Jesus in the Gospels, but only in the evangelists' narration. Thus it seems a fairly obvious conclusion that the word *apostolos* was a term used by the first Christians, not by the historical Jesus himself. As we have attempted to demonstrate, Jesus called his chosen inner circle 'The Twelve', not 'apostles'. It was only after the Resurrection

## The Apostolic Succession 1:
## The Authority of the Apostles Themselves

most likely that they were called 'apostles', and, as we have already said, the term 'apostle' in the infant church was not always restricted to the Twelve and Paul.

What, therefore, was the origin of the term 'apostle' as used in the first days, indeed the first decades, of the church? The question is important, because the word 'apostle' was obviously used by the church to indicate their function, also their authority. There is still a debate of some intensity in the world of biblical scholarship, precisely because at stake could be a crucial understanding or misunderstanding of authority in the primitive Christian community. The meaning of *apostolos* could be significant for the discovery of the historical church.

The classical study of *apostolos* in the New Testament, published at the end of the nineteenth century,[43] but by no means past its sell-by date, was by J. B. Lightfoot in his commentary on the *Epistle to the Galatians*. Lightfoot defines the word as follows:

> The word *apostolos* in the first instance is an adjective signifying 'despatched' or 'sent forth'. Applied to a person, it denotes more than *angelos*. The 'Apostle' is not only the messenger, but the delegate of the person who sends him. He is entrusted with a mission, has powers conferred upon him. Beyond this, the classical usage of the term gives no aid towards understanding the meaning of the Christian apostolate.[44]

In the Old Testament Greek LXX, *apostolos* is a translation of *shaliah*, for example 1 Kings 14:6 'And it was so, when Ahijah heard the sound of her feet, as she came in at the door, that he said, "Come in, thou wife of Jeroboam; why feignest thou thyself to be another? I am sent (*shaliah*) to thee with heavy tidings." As Lightfoot says, 'where it has the general sense of a messenger, though with reference to a commission from God'.[45]

However, Lightfoot considers that the meaning of *apostolos* which was the origin of the term in early Christianity was more specific. The Jewish *apostolos*, or in Hebrew *shaliaḥ*, was one given 'a highly responsible mission':

> With the later Jews, however, and it would appear also with the Jews of the Christian era, the word was in common use. It was the title borne by those who were despatched from the mother city by the rulers of the race on any foreign mission, especially such as were charged with collecting the tribute paid to the temple service. After the destruction of Jerusalem, the 'Apostles' formed a sort of council about the Jewish patriarch, assisting him in his deliberations at home, and executing his orders abroad. Thus in designating His immediate and most favoured disciples 'Apostles', our Lord was not introducing a new term but adopting one which from its current usage would suggest to His hearers the idea of a highly responsible mission.[46]

Lightfoot seems to infer that Jesus did call his chosen Twelve 'apostles', but does not develop this argument in his article. To me, there is no evidence that Jesus actually used the word 'apostle', presumably in its Semitic term *shaliaḥ*, to describe the Twelve during his lifetime on earth. But a greater difficulty with considering the *apostolos* in the early Christian decades as a fully-fledged Jewish *shaliaḥ* is that evidence is lacking that the *shaliaḥ* as an office pre-dated the Fall of Jerusalem in AD 70. As Schmithals concludes, countering the view of Adolf Harnack, who thought with Lightfoot that *apostolos* did find its origin in the Hebrew *shaliaḥ*: 'A special exemplification of the *Shaliach*, to which Harnack turned his attention, is represented by those of the apostle whom the Palestinian patriarchate used to send forth.' Harnack quotes as his source the early church historian Eusebius: a certain Joseph from Tiberias, who 'had received the blessed activity *tés apostolós*, and thereupon was sent with the corresponding pieces of writing to Cilicia, in order to bring the tithes and the first fruits from the Jews of each city to Jerusalem'.[47]

Schmithals admits that 'These passages are clear, and in their decisive points, unequivocal. There were Jewish apostles who were sent out by the Jerusalem patriarchate, whose most important task it was to take up the offerings for the central authorities, but who were at the same time authorized to attend to the supervisory powers of Jerusalem... But can the above-mentioned apostolate of the central authorities have been the prototype of the primitive Christian apostolate? That is ruled out because before A.D. 70 it did not exist, at least in this form'.[48] Only after the destruction of the Temple, Schmithals claims, would the Jewish authorities, with the number of pilgrims decreasing, need to ask for love offerings.[49]

We would have to conclude therefore that, with Schmithals, there is not actual and positive evidence that the role of *shaliah* was used in the time before the Fall of Jerusalem AD 70. We would therefore conclude further with Schmithals that the origin of the term *apostolos* cannot demonstrably be found in the bringing by a *shaliah* of the tithes and first-fruits from the Jews of each city to Jerusalem, even though such a possibility cannot be ruled out.

## 7.13 THE APOSTLES AND THE GNOSTICS

*The origin of the term* **apostolos** *is not to be found in early Christian Gnosticism.*

Lightfoot, even though sure that the origin of the term *apostolos* is to be found in the Jewish *shaliah*, yet does not use this firm conclusion of his to secure any clear meaning of what *apostolos* means in the New Testament, or even in early Christian writings. In his immaculately researched article, *The Name and Office of Apostle*, Lightfoot cannot find any criterion which acts to limit with any certainty the qualifications of an *apostolos* in the New Testament usage. For instance, Lightfoot argues that the criterion of a personal call of Jesus was not verified in the case of Matthias who was chosen by lot to replace Judas.[50] (Ac 1:26) Likewise, the criterion of possession of the gifts of the Spirit (for example 2 Co 12:12) also fails to justify exclusively the calling of one an 'apostle', 'these gifts are given to those who were not necessarily apostles'.[51]

This agnosticism of Lightfoot after so much study as to finding any final criterion whereby one in the primitive church was called an *apostolos* led in the twentieth century to a spate of writings attempting to find the origin of the term. One of the more recent, and certainly one of the most imaginative, attempts to sketch the evolution of the term *apostolos* is in Walter Schmithals' *The Office of the Apostle in the Early Church*.

As a disciple of Bultmann, Schmithals is equally skeptical of the New Testament evidence while equally credulous regarding the Gnostic writings. Bultmann had proposed the fantastic theory that the Fourth Gospel idea of the *logos* becoming flesh has its roots in the Mandaean idea of the Gnostic redeemer. Not surprisingly, Pope Benedict in his *Jesus of Nazareth* describes Bultmann's view as 'breathtaking'.[52] How could Bultmann give credence to a form of Gnosticism as the first century origin of the Johannine *logos* when we have no actual manuscript evidence for Gnosticism before AD 700?[53] As I argue in *Who Was John?*, it is because Bultmann cannot accept that the historical Jesus was actually God become flesh in human form that he has to find the origin of John's view of the *logos* in late Gnostic literature that would be adjudged in any other circumstances to be itself rather a Gnostic re-writing of the Gospel and dependant on it, rather than the origin of the Gospel idea.

Similarly, I submit, it is because Schmithals cannot accept that the historical Jesus was God become man, and handed on his authority to his chosen apostles, that he has to invent an equally fantastic source of origin for the idea of *apostolos* in the New Testament.

As we saw earlier, having rejected the historicity of the origin of the Twelve in the earthly life of Jesus, Schmithals now has freed himself up to completely detach the idea of the Twelve from the idea of the Apostle. For him, the idea of the Apostle in the New Testament does not have its origin of the sending by Jesus, but rather in a mixture of the Gnostic myth of the primal man with the historical figure of Jesus of Nazareth. Its origin is in another type of Gnosticism, where the Gnostic is the privileged communicator of the primeval revelation. Mani, the Gnostic recipient of revelation, understood himself to be an apostle in this sense, even though later he was honoured as an 'historical emissary':

> In that certain year of the reign of Ardaschir the 'living Paraclete' came down to me and spoke to me. He revealed to me the hidden mystery which was concealed from the world and the generations.... He taught me the mystery of the tree of knowledge from which Adam ate, whereby his eyes were opened, the mystery of the apostles who are sent into the world.
>
> Then this present revelation descended and this present prophecy resulted in the present and most recent age through me, Mani, the apostle of the true God, in the land of Babel.[54]

Schmithals claims that 'The Gnostic, who has received Gnosis from the heavenly emissary, himself becomes an emissary, who has Gnosis to communicate'.[55] But even more, Schmithals claims that this form of Gnosticism was there from the beginning in the primitive Christian community. He finds evidence of this origin in Paul's Hymn to the humiliated and exalted Christ in the letter to the Philippians: (c. AD 60)[56]

> The Christ hymn in Philippians 2:6–11 already shows the connection of the historical figure of Jesus of Nazareth with the Gnostic presentation of the descent of the primal man. Either Christ was first fitted out in Gnostic circles with the traits of the primal man or primal emissary, or the significance of the person of Jesus was first expressed in the forms of the Gnostic myth within the ecclesiastical communities.[57]

You will note that even Schmithals cannot claim that the actual text of the Hymn is Gnostic as it stands. On the contrary, it speaks of one who being in the *morphé theou*, divine in origin, takes on the *morphé doulou*, the 'form of a servant'. It is clearly incarnational, not Gnostic. As Brendan Byrne says, whether we consider that Paul actually wrote this hymn himself as part of the letter to the Philippians, or is a quotation by Paul of a pre-existing hymn, 'In its original form the hymn theologically situates the "story" of Jesus within the overall framework of God's eschatological design to reclaim the universe for himself, seeing the selfless obedience of Christ foreshadowed in his pre-temporal "career"'[58] A Gnostic redeemer, on the contrary, simply descends to earth to grant knowledge to the initiate. He does not act in human history to redeem.

Schmithals can only argue therefore that this early Gnosticism is concealed within the Philippian Hymn. But, we must insist, this can in no way count as *evidence* for the existence of such Gnosticism in the early Christian community. It is simply an unsubstantiated hypothesis. There is no positive evidence whatsoever of this 'Gnostic myth' in the early ecclesiastical communities. Schmithals has to invent such a Gnostic community within Semitic culture; thus he produces Syrian Gnosticism as its source, geographically convenient for the location of this secret Gnosticism in the early church.

## THE ACTS OF THOMAS AND THE GOSPEL OF THOMAS

Schmithals quotes from the Apocryphal Gospel: *The Acts of Thomas*. Geoff Trowbridge says that this is also the only apocryphal book of Acts claiming apostolic authorship, though it is difficult to fathom how Thomas could have recorded his own martyrdom. Most believe that the author wrote in the early third century, though links to the Gospel of Thomas may place it earlier, as we will discuss.[59]

Regarding *The Acts of Thomas*,[60] Schmithals claims that they 'are witnesses to a Syrian Gnosticism of a Christian variety, even to the mythologizing of the narrative material. The church's influence is particularly inescapable in the fact that Christ takes the role of the redeemer. But he is not the only redeemer'.[61] Thomas is called an apostle. 'But Thomas is not an "apostle of Jesus Christ", but a twin brother of Christ and an apostle of God in the sense in which the Gnostic redeemer in general and even Christ can be called "apostle"; more precisely, in the sense in which Simon, as part of the "great power", was called an apostle.'[62] 'In the Acts of Andrew also, the apostle himself is basically the redeemer'.[63]

If Schmithals is right, therefore, the origin of the term *apostolos* in the New Testament is that of a Gnostic emissary who considers himself to be equal to the one who sent him in that he has had a mystical experience. He is not one who has been sent by the historical Jesus now ascended into heaven to be *his* emissary. But where is the evidence that this primitive form of Gnosticism was earlier than the third century? We cannot date the *Acts of Thomas* earlier than the third century; unless there are traces of *The Gospel of Thomas* in *The Acts of Thomas*, in which case we must take this theory just a little more seriously.

As to the *Gospel of Thomas*, part of the find at Nag Hammadi, scholars take it most seriously of all the Apocryphal Gospels. Scholars have been divided on the nature and sources of this work almost from the time of its publication in 1959.[64] It is a collection of 114 sayings purportedly by Jesus. Meier argues that *The Gospel of Thomas* 'is usually dated c. AD 200. 'It is somewhere in the 2nd century that the composition we know as the Gospel of Thomas took shape as one expression of second-century Gnostic Christianity.'[65]

As documentary testimony, therefore, we cannot take *The Gospel of Thomas* back to the first century, as opposed to the four Gospels, which are all dated within the first century, apart from John, which is given its latest date 110, and Luke, which Schmithals wishes to date well into the second century. We will consider his view of Luke later. However, regarding *The Gospel of Thomas*, some scholars argue that some of the sayings of Jesus in it are genuine. Of all the apocryphal Gospels, Meier gives the longest consideration in the first volume of his *Marginal Jew* to *The Gospel of Thomas*.[66]

Among the 'sayings of Jesus' in *The Gospel of Thomas*, there are sayings 'similar to sayings in the Synoptic Gospels. Taken by themselves, or, *a fortiori*, taken in their Synoptic context, such sayings would never strike one as Gnostic. Yet in *The Gospel of Thomas* such Synoptic-like sayings are juxtaposed to sayings with a definite Gnostic tinge and seem at times to have been reworked to convey a Gnostic message.'[67]

Jesus in this Gnostic Gospel of Thomas 'comes into this world to wake these spirits up, to remind them of their true origin and destiny, to free them from the illusion that they belong to this material world of death.'[68] 'Sex is seen as evil, and the female role in bearing new spirits imprisoned in bodies is especially deprecated....'[69] 'Jesus said, "It is I who am the All; it is from me that the All has come, and to me that the All goes. Split a piece of wood: I am there. Lift a stone, and you will find me there" (Saying 77). Jesus said, "Whoever drinks from my mouth will become like me; I, too, will become that person" (Saying 108). 'Simon Peter said to them, "Mary should leave us, for females are not worthy of life."...' (Saying 114)[70]

Meier goes thoroughly into the debate among the Nag Hammadi scholars as to whether the Synoptic-like sayings are in fact possibly genuine sayings of the historical Jesus; or as to whether these Synoptic-like Sayings in *The Gospel of Thomas* are dependant on the Synoptic Gospels. Meier concludes to the latter,[71] but after considerable discussion. However what of those statements such as quoted above, which are alien not only to the Synoptic style but even more to the Synoptic doctrine of Jesus? Meier concludes that *'the other (Gnostic) sayings stem from 2nd century Christian Gnosticism'*[72]

However, would not Schmithals (whose book was written before the full scholarly debate on the Nag Hammadi finds had begun) have claimed that this second century Gnosticism was close in time to the first Christian century? Would he not therefore had concluded that it was even more plausible than he had at first thought that the New Testament concept of *apostle* had originated in a form of Syriac Gnosticism, from thence to become part of that historical Christianity which eventually dominated the Great Church barely a hundred years before *The Gospel of Thomas* was written?

## FIRST CENTURY GNOSTICISM?

We have no sure documentary evidence for first century Gnosticism. But I think that it is quite possible that Gnostic ideas were countering the orthodox Christian faith almost from the day of Pentecost onwards, and certainly by the end of the first century. The Second Epistle of John is dated by most scholars about AD 100, and it already counters Doceticism, close to Gnosticism. 'There are many deceivers at large in the world, refusing to acknowledge Jesus Christ as coming in human nature *(Greek en sarki, 'in flesh')*. They are the Deceiver; they are the Antichrist.'(2 Jn 1:7). As Pheme Perkins notes, 'Writing at around AD 110, Ignatius of Antioch opposes Christians in Asia Minor who deny the importance of Jesus as a human being by advocating a docetic Christology, one which denies that the divine Savior really took on humanity.'[73]

Perhaps Gnosticism was there at the beginning, in various Jewish, Syrian, and Hellenistic forms, side by side with Christianity. Paul was able to develop his Christology based upon the Damascus vision, together with his immersion in the Jesus tradition of genuine incarnation. He, and indeed John, could have used the variant synchretistic forms of Gnosticism, and forged their theology using some Gnostic concepts, just as the early Fathers used an equally alien philosophical tradition, and 'spoiled the Egyptians'. Doceticism, in this view, would have been an attempt by Gnostics to accommodate Christianity to Gnosticism. There one could find some agreement with Schmithals.[74] Gnosticism here makes use of a motif widely employed in the history of religions, according to which the god disguises himself so that he can be perceived by human eyes, or so that he is not recognized by the demons as god. [75] Paul, for his part, perhaps accommodated some Gnostic ideas, just as he accommodated Hellenistic philosophy, to genuine incarnational faith.

What is without grounds for persuasive argumentation to me, however, is to consider either that the origin of the New Testament doctrine of Jesus is to be found in the Hellenistic Divine Man, as we have argued in BMG, but rather in the historical Jesus' understanding of his own being and mission. Equally, now considering the origin of the concept of *apostolos* in the New Testament, we reject the view that the understanding of *apostolos* arose from primitive Gnosticism within the Christian community. Rather, we shall now argue that the origin of *apostolos* in the New Testament is linked essentially with the idea of the historical and bodily risen Jesus sending out the Twelve with a special mission and authority, which is then applied most of all to Paul's apostolate, but also to the first missionaries of the Church, sent out by the Holy Spirit.

## 7.14 FROM 'SENT' TO 'APOSTLES'

*Rather, the origin of the term apostolos in the New Testament came from simply the fact that one who was sent either by Christ or by the Holy Spirit in the Church went with the full authority either of the risen Christ himself or of the Church. In post-apostolic Christianity, the term apostolos came more and more to be applied solely to the*

***Twelve and to Paul, because they were the known recipients and authoritative communicators of divine revelation.***

If we assume, as I submit we have proved in BMG, that the historical Jesus knew and demonstrated that he was God become Man, then, as we have already stated, it would be hardly difficult to conclude that he would wish to continue his mission after his bodily Resurrection and Ascension into heaven. Thus it is credible that he gave his authority to the Twelve, whom, as we have seen, he called precisely to represent the twelve tribes of Israel. They would go out from Pentecost onwards to baptise all nations, and to bring them into the community of the Church. This is precisely what we see in Acts, Peter representing and leading the Twelve. This is to fulfil the commission of the risen Jesus 'As the Father sent me, so am I sending you'. (Jn 20:21.)

The Twelve were conscious of this 'sending' by the risen Jesus, as was Paul, who was always conscious of himself as an *apostolos*. 1 Corinthians 9:1 'Am I not free? Am I not an apostle? Have I not seen Jesus our Lord? Are you not my work in the Lord?' Paul was conscious of having 'seen the Lord', presumably on the Damascus Road. Thus his qualification as an 'apostle' was that the risen Jesus had 'sent' him. Therefore it is easy to see how the concept of 'sending' could change to the concept of an 'apostle', that is one who is sent. In fact, Luke uses the verb *exapostelló*: 'And behold, I send the promise of my Father upon you; but stay in the city, until you are clothed with power from on high.'(Lk 24:49), rather than John's 'Just as the Father apostled *(apestalken)* me, so I send *(pempó)* you'.

Thus the origin of the New Testament concept of *apostolos* is not in Gnostic redeemer ecstasy, but simply in the consciousness of the first Christian preachers of their being sent by the risen Christ to bring in Jew and Gentile to the kingdom by baptism.

It is then not difficult to explain how the term *apostolos* evolved as evidenced in the New Testament literature. We may find Lightfoot's *shaliah* useful here. Early on in the use of the term *apostolos*, the idea of special commissioning would have taken shape, and thus the *apostolos* would be given a special status in the church.

> In the church at Antioch the following were prophets and teachers: Barnabas, Simeon called Niger, and Lucius of Cyrene, Manaen, who had been brought up with Herod the tetrarch, and Saul. One day while they were offering worship to the Lord and keeping a fast, the Holy Spirit said, 'I want Barnabas and Saul set apart for the work to which I have called them.' So it was that after fasting and prayer they laid their hands on them and sent them off. So these two, sent on their mission by the Holy Spirit, went down to Seleucia and from there set sail for Cyprus. (Ac 13:1–4)

The scenario here is not that the risen Christ but the charismatic Holy Spirit in the early church gives out a message that Barnabas and Saul have to go out on a mission. They are therefore *apostoloi*, in the sense that they are divinely sent, but not by the risen Christ as were the Twelve. Various verbs can be used for 'sent' (Ac 13:3 *apelusan*, Ac 13:4 *ekpempthentes*), but we can easily see how the various verbs for 'sent' or 'sent out' could coalesce in the more static noun *apostolos*, with its special sense of commissioning from the Holy Spirit in the Church or from the risen Christ. It is usual also that the *apostolos* was related to *church founding*, (1 Co 9:2ff.), which is why presumably the office of *apostolos* was linked with miraculous signs of the mission (2 Co 12:12). Churches were founded in those early days by people who had the special gift of the Holy Spirit sending them out for that purpose. In that sense Barnabas, though not one of the Twelve and not commissioned by the risen Lord as was Paul, was an *apostolos* both because he was sent out on his mission by a special charismatic act of the Spirit, and because he was the founder of the Church of Cyprus, and of other churches in Asia Minor with Paul on the first missionary journey.

Thus in Romans 1:1, Paul claims a unique apostleship as a 'servant of Jesus Christ'; Paul is 'an apostle of Jesus Christ' or of 'Christ Jesus' (1 Co 1:1, 2 Co 1:1, Ga 1:1) 'Paul, an apostle; sent not from men nor by man, but by Jesus Christ and God the Father, who raised him from the dead', (Col 1:1, Ep 1:1, 1 Tm 1:1, Tt 1:1). Note that Paul claims to be 'apostle of Jesus Christ' or of 'Christ Jesus', but does not attribute that title to Timothy or Titus his successors.[76]

Lightfoot notes that in the apostolic fathers, the term apostolos is used 'indeed vaguely and inconsistently, sometimes in a narrower, sometimes in a wider sense, than the New Testament writings would seem to warrant....'[77] Moreover, Lightfoot goes on, 'Writers of the subsequent ages are more obviously lax in their use of the title'.[78]

Yet, on the other hand, Lightfoot is equally clear that the Apostolic Fathers such as Clement of Rome and Ignatius 'all look upon themselves as distinct from the Apostles.'[79] We can conclude therefore that, while the term *apostolos* could have a wider application than the Twelve and Paul, in early church writings as in the New Testament, it was a term used to describe those who held their office of *apostolos* in the first days of the Church. They were specially 'sent' either by Christ himself or by the Holy Spirit to found the Church.

The singular case of Matthias, who replaced Judas to complete the number Twelve of the apostles, perhaps did not have a specific revelation and commission from the risen Christ himself. Matthias' qualification was, according to Acts 1 'Out of the men who have been with us the whole time that the Lord Jesus was living with us, from the time when John was baptising until the day when he was taken up from us, one must be appointed to serve with us as a witness to his resurrection.' (Ac 1:21–22) Matthias therefore was both a witness to the public life of Jesus whom he followed as a disciple, and was one of the witnesses of the resurrection listed by Paul in 1 Corinthians 15. Presumably, therefore, in this unique case the Eleven were able to add the commissioning of Christ himself by the use of casting lots, the ancient Old Testament method of divining the divine will (for example Lv 16:8).

Granted this meaning of *apostolos*, as one who was 'sent' by Christ himself or by the Holy Spirit, it is not difficult to see now how eventually the term became exclusively reserved in the theology of the Church to the Twelve and to Paul, since it was only they who have left in the documents of Christian origin and in Christian tradition clear traces of their apostolic activity and of their apostolic authority. We will finally explore the significance of this fact.

## 7.15 SUPERNATURAL SELECTION

*It is possible that others than the Twelve and Paul, for example James, were given a special revelation from Christ; but they, with the majority of the Twelve, faded out of the picture, and left us with Peter, Paul, and John as the transmitters of the apostolic tradition; and they are sufficient for the needs of divine revelation.*

We have discussed at length the role of the Twelve and Paul as unique 'apostles' in the scriptures and in the earliest records of the church. But as Lightfoot points out in his extended Excursus III, *St Paul and the Three*,[80] in reality both in scripture and in tradition, only James, Peter and John of the Twelve have any significant mention after the Ascension of Christ:

> Three and three only of the personal disciples and immediate followers of our Lord hold any prominent place in the Apostolic records—James, Peter, and John; the first the Lord's brother, the two latter the foremost members of the Twelve. Apart from an incidental reference to the death of James the son of Zebedee, which is dismissed in a single sentence, the rest of the Twelve are mentioned by name for the last time on the day of the Lord's

> Ascension. Thenceforward they disappear wholly from the canonical writings.
>
> And this silence also extends to the traditions of succeeding ages. We read indeed of St Thomas in India, of St Andrew in Scythia: but such scanty notices, even if we accept them as trustworthy, show only the more plainly how little the Church could tell of her earliest teachers. Doubtless they laboured zealously and effectively in the spread of the Gospel; but, so far as we know, they have left no impress of their individual mind and character on the Church at large. Occupying the foreground, and indeed covering the whole canvas of early ecclesiastical history, appear four figures alone, St Paul and the three Apostles of the Circumcision.[81]

This makes the importance of Paul even greater, since in the New Testament his profile is larger even than that of Peter; although, as we shall see later, the role of Peter is highly significant in the Gospels and in the rest of the New Testament.

Strangely enough, the situation is not dissimilar to the history of the twelve tribes of Israel itself. Beginning with twelve tribes, all occupy their place in the geography of the settlement in the Holy Land, cf. Jos 13:1–21:45[82] (apart from the tribe of Levi, who were given towns from the other tribes as a kind of collection for sacristancs! Jos 21:1ff). Eventually there is only one tribe of any real prominence left, namely Judah, from which we derive the term 'Jew'. From this tribe, the tribe of King David came the Messiah.

Likewise, of the twelve apostles, after the death of Judas replaced by Matthias and the martyrdom of James the Son of Zebedee (Ac 12:2) at the order of Herod, we have only Peter and John left active. They are mentioned as being together fourteen times in the New Testament (Once in Lk 22:8 and Ga 2:9, and twelve times in Ac). Thus John the Son of Zebedee was prominent in the early mission as Peter's companion in the early preaching of the Church, if you like his co-apostle. Since James Son of Zebedee was martyred, of the three intimate disciples of Jesus, Peter, James and John who went up the mountain of Transfiguration (Mt 17:1, Mk 9:2) two only therefore remained. It is perhaps also significant that we are told in Acts 13:13 that 'From Paphos, Paul and his companions sailed to Perga in Pamphylia, where John left them to return to Jerusalem.' John the Son of Zebedee saw himself as part of the Jerusalem mission, and returned there rather than go on the mission to the Gentiles with Paul.

There is persuasive evidence that both Peter and Paul went to Rome, and were martyred there. The tradition handed on by Irenaeus is that John the Son of Zebedee, together with Mary the mother of Jesus, went to Ephesus. This evidence is controverted,[83] but we could say that, wherever in fact John died, his apostleship was continued through the transmission of his Gospel.

However of the rest of the Twelve, as Lightfoot says, we know next to nothing with certainty. Like the majority of the tribes of Israel merged into the race of Judah, they have been swallowed up in the unique apostleship of Paul and Peter in Rome as the 'apostolic see'.

Yet as Bauckham says, 'On the orthodox side, Clement of Alexandria (died c. AD 215)[84] believed that the risen Jesus "gave the tradition of knowledge to James the Just and John and Peter, these gave it to the other Apostles, to the seventy, of whom Barnabas also was one" (*apud* Eusebius, *Hist. Eccl.* 2.1.4.)'.[85] Thus the tradition as late as the third century was wider in its application of the term *apostolos* than the Twelve and Paul.

In fact, we do at least know one who was not one of the Twelve who would certainly have been a candidate for this special 'knowledge' Clement speaks about, namely James 'the brother of the Lord'. Jerome thought that this James, who is given some prominence in the New Testament, was James the Son of Alphaeus, and so one of the Twelve (Mt 10:3, Mk 2:14, Mk 3:18, Lk 6:15). This was mainly because Jerome was attempting to argue that this 'James the brother of the Lord' was in fact a close relative (hence in the wider sense 'brother') because he was son of Alphaeus, and so not a biological son of Joseph and Mary.[86]

However, Acts 1:13 lists the apostles including 'James Son of Alphaeus', but elsewhere in Acts he is just 'James': Peter says after his miraculous release from prison: '"Tell James and the brothers about this," he said, and then he left for another place.' (Ac 12:17) It is Paul in Galatians 1:15 who calls him 'James the Lord's brother', not naming him explicitly as an apostle, but clearly 'James, Peter and John reputed to be pillars'[87] (Ga 2:9) that is a source of wisdom in the community. Thus Paul sees James as important, and indeed elsewhere (1 Co 15:7) Paul says that the risen Jesus appeared to him. In Acts 15:13, James plays a decision making role. James of course could have been a 'relative' of Jesus and not his blood brother even if he had not been Son of Alphaeus.[88]

James is therefore perhaps the best candidate of all to be qualified as an *apostolos* in the sense of having a specific revelation from the risen Christ, when it is at least not clear that he was one of the Twelve. As we shall see, he was the first leader of the Church in Jerusalem. We have to take account of the possibility, therefore, that not only James, but others also had a key role in the first generation Church, having seen the Lord and perhaps having had a commission from the risen Christ, who were not either one of the Twelve or Paul. However like the tribes of Israel, they are lost to us, and so are not part of the revelation of God through the apostles. The essence of 'revelation' is that it is revealed in some way or other. Thus, if there were canonical books of the New Testament which now are lost to us, or if there was some *apostolos* of the infant church whose teaching we no longer possess, then that simply is by default not part of the revelation handed down to us in Scripture and in Tradition. We are stuck with Peter and Paul, with what we have got! And what God has handed on is sufficient for us.

## Notes

1. In my book *What is Catholicism? Hard Questions, Straight Answers*, (Huntingdon, Indiana: Our Sunday Visitor Publishing Division, 1997), I ask Q. 17, p. 86, What evidence is there in the primitive Church that the apostles were convinced of their infallibility in questions of faith or morals? On pp. 86–89 I give a brief answer to that question, which is of course considerably expanded in this chapter.
2. St Irenaeus, Against Heresies 3:3:1. The English translation of this text from AD 189 was found in http://www.catholic.com/library/Apostolic_Succession.asp [accessed 21 February 2013].
3. *Ibid.*, 3:3:2.
4. *Ibid.*, 3:3:4.
5. *Ibid.*, 3:4:1.
6. *Ibid.*, 4:26:2.
7. *Ibid.*, 4:33:8.
8. This is a text we must look at more in detail later. Paul says in Galatians 2:7: 'On the contrary, once they saw that the gospel for the uncircumcised had been entrusted to me, just as to Peter the gospel for the circumcised...' But, as we shall see later, it is clear that Paul preached to the 'circumcised' as well as the 'uncircumcised'; and Peter preached to the Gentiles, e.g. Cornelius. I personally interpret Galatians 2:7 as meaning that when the church began, Peter preached entirely to the Jews; and when Paul was converted on the Damascus Road, it was with the particular aim of converting the Gentiles.
9. Cf. Brown, INT, p. 203. Brown simply assumes that 'the baptismal formula in the name of three divine agents was presumably in use in the Matthean church at this period, having replaced an earlier custom of baptizing in the name of Jesus (Acts 2:38, 8:16 etc.)'. Also Vincent Taylor, *Mark*, p. 612.
10. Beare, *Matthew*, p. 544.
11. V. Taylor, *The Gospel According to Mark*, Second Edition (London: MacMillan St Martin's Press, 1966) p. 610.
12. *Ibid.*, p. 612.
13. I. H. Marshall, *The Gospel of Luke: A Commentary on the Greek Text*. (Exeter: Paternoster Press, 1978) pp. 903–4
14. BMG, p. 115.
15. C. K. Barrett, *The Gospel According to John: An Introduction with Commentary and Notes on the Greek Text*, Second Edition (London: SPCK, 1978) p. 568.
16. J. F. A. Hort, p. 33. quoted in C. K. Barrett, *John*
17. Brown II, p. 1024.
18. *Ibid.*, p. 1039.

19. Barrett, p. 571.
20. Schmithals, W. *The Office of Apostle in the Early Church*. Trans. J. E. Steely. (London: SPCK, 1971) pp. 68–69.
21. *Ibid.*. p. 70.
22. *Ibid.*, pp. 70–71.
23. MJ3, p. 22.
24. *Ibid.*, pp. 44–5.
25. *Ibid.*, p. 125.
26. *Ibid.*, p. 128.
27. *Ibid.*
28. *Ibid.*, p. 130.
29. Bauckham, R. *Jesus and the Eye-Witnesses: The Gospels as Eye-Witness Testimony*, (Cambridge, Eerdmans, 2006), p. 108.
30. MJ3, p. 146.
31. *Ibid.*, p. 147.
32. *Ibid.*, p. 148
33. *Ibid.*, p. 152.
34. *Ibid.*, p. 154.
35. *Ibid.*, p. 158.
36. BMG, p. 116.
37. The expression *skeuos*: for example 'a jar (*skeuos*) full of sour wine…' John 19:26. For New Testament references, cf. Abbott-Smith, *A Manual Greek Lexicon of the New Testament* (Edinburgh: T. and T. Clark, third edition 1937), p. 408.
38. Schmithals, *op.cit.*, p. 35.
39. Another post-Bultmannian Lutheran scholar, Cullman, does think that a unique authority is implied for the apostles. We will be examining his view later when we consider the early history of testimonies to papal primacy.
40. H. L. Goudge, *The First Epistle to the Corinthians*, Westminster Commentaries. Revised Edition, (London: Methuen, 1926).
41. Goudge is convinced that 'The offender spoken of in 2 Corinthians 2:5–11 cannot be the same as the offender of 1 Corinthians 5…' *Op. cit.* p. 41. Murphy-O'Connor agrees: 'Most ancient and a few modern commentators wrongly identify the offender with the man condemned in 1 Corinthians 5:1–5. The differences are highlighted by Furnish, *II Corinthians*, 164–66.' NJBC, **50:11,** 819.
42. J. B. Lightfoot, *Saint Paul's Epistle to the Galatians: A Revised Text with Introduction, Notes and Dissertations*. Ninth Edition, (London: MacMillan, 1887), p. 94, n. 5.
43. *Ibid.*, Excursus The Name and Office of an Apostle, pp. 92–101.
44. *Ibid.*, pp. 92 93.
45. *Ibid.*, p. 93.

[46] *Ibid.*, pp. 93–4.
[47] Schmithals, pp. 98–99.
[48] *Ibid.*, p. 100
[49] *Ibid.*, p. 101.
[50] Lightfoot, p. 98.
[51] *Ibid.*, p. 99.
[52] JN p. 220.
[53] *Who Was John?* p. 125.
[54] n. 227, 149. 'preserved in Al-Biruni's chronology; cited following G. P. Wetter, *Der Sohn Gottes*, FRLANT NF, IX (1916), p.16. Cf. G. Widengren, *The Ascension of the Apostle and the Heavenly Book*, 1950, p. 59.
[55] Schmithals, p. 150.
[56] Brendan Byrne in NJBC dates Philippians from AD 54–58, presupposing that the letter in fact contains more than one letter from Paul to the Philippians. NJBC, **48:10**, 792.
[57] Schmithals, p. 134.
[58] NJBC, **48:22**, 795.
[59] http://www.maple.net/trowbridge/actsthom.htm
[60] Text of *The Acts of Thomas,* Ed. http://www.earlychristianwritings.com/text/actsthomas.html [accessed 21.02.2013] James, M. R. *The Apocryphal New Testament*, translation and Notes, Oxford: Clarendon Press, 1924
[61] Schmithals, p. 187, Refers to G. Bornkamm, *Mythos und Legende in den apokryphen Thomasakten*, FRLANT NF, XXXI.
[62] Schmithals, p. 188.
[63] Schmithals, p. 189.
[64] See MJ1, p. 124.
[65] *Ibid,*, p. 127.
[66] *Ibid.*, pp. 124–139.
[67] *Ibid.*, p. 125.
[68] *Ibid.*, p. 126.
[69] *Ibid.*
[70] *Ibid.*, p. 127.
[71] *Ibid*, p. 139.
[72] Ibid.
[73] NJBC, **62:3–5**. p. 987.
[74] Schmithals p. 133, n.149.
[75] Cf. Bultmann, *John*, p. 61, n.1.
[76] You will note that Ephesians, Colossians, and 1 Timothy and Titus are disputed as to Pauline authorship. Cf. Brown, INT, NJBC for the introductions to each of these New Testament books. A sizeable minority of scholars, including myself, consider that scepticism

# The Apostolic Succession 1:
## The Authority of the Apostles Themselves

concerning Pauline authorship of these books is not justified, and is to some extent the result of the refusal to admit an 'early Catholicism' in Paul and in the infant church in general. But, for the purposes of our present apologetic, even if Paul did not write these letters attributed to him, they are still evidence of the meaning of *apostolos* in the earliest sources.

[77] Lightfoot, *Galatians*, p. 99.

[78] *Ibid.*

[79] *Ibid.*

[80] *Ibid.*, p. 293-374.

[81] *Ibid.*, p. 293

[82] There is predictably a continuing debate as to how far this allocation of the twelve tribes is what happened in the history of the conquering tribes at the time of Joshua, and how far it reflects the statement of a claim based upon theological interest. Cf. NJBC, **7:62,** p. 125. Coogan avers 'The primacy given to Judah is an indication of the general origin of the material, i.e. in the Judean monarchy, probably after the fall of Samaria'.

[83] Cf. WWJ, pp. 160-161

[84] http://www.newadvent.org/cathen/04045a.htm [accessed 21.02.2013]

[85] Bauckham, R. *Jesus and the Eyewitnesses: The Gospels as Eyewitness Testimony* (Cambridge, Eerdmans, 2006).

[86] Cf. *Hastings Dictionary of the Bible*, Volume 1, (Edinburgh, T and T Clarke, 1898), p. 321.

[87] See Lightfoot, *Galatians*, p. 109, col.2 on *stuloi*: 'commonly used by the Jews in speaking of the great teachers of the Law'. Is Paul being sarcastic here in calling James, Peter and John 'pillars', since he is violently disagreeing with them? Perhaps there is an element not of sarcasm but more likely of bitterness. He is certainly not questioning the reality of their authority, or of their being actually *stuloi*.

[88] CCC 500 states the Catholic faith that Mary was a perpetual virgin. 'In fact James and Joseph, brothers of Jesus, are the sons of another Mary. They are close relations of Jesus, according to an Old Testament expression.' BV, 21. Cf. Gn 13:8, 14:16, 29:15 etc.

# 8

# THE APOSTOLIC SUCCESSION, PART TWO

# THE MONARCHICAL EPISCOPACY

## 8.1 PROGRESS TOWARDS THE MONARCHICAL EPISCOPATE[1]

*The progress from the apostolic age to the age of the Catholic Church and its Monarchical Episcopate seems to have taken place in three stages*:

Stage One, AD 40 to 80. The rule of the apostles themselves
Stage Two, 80 to 120. The apostles hand over their authority to their successors
Stage Three, 120 to 200. The threefold ministry becomes the unswerving norm

### Stage One AD 40 to 80

The apostles founded churches and often governed them themselves; although Acts tells us that Paul and his missionary companions left 'elders', that is *presbyteroi*. Acts 14:23, 'In each of these churches they appointed elders, and with prayer and fasting they commended them to the Lord in whom they had come to believe.' It is not clear what function these elders had except as with a Jewish council to make key decisions to rule the community. Acts 4:5, 'It happened that the next day the rulers, elders and scribes held a meeting in Jerusalem.'

## Stage Two AD 80 to 120

The apostles began to hand over rule to those whom they saw as their successors. We see this evidenced in the Pastoral Letters, I and II Timothy and Titus; and in I and II Peter. Important evidence we see also in the letters of Ignatius of Antioch, where he foresees one bishop in each church community, head of the body of presbyters, and also together with the third order, deacons.

## Stage Three 120 to 200

The threefold ministry of bishop, presbyter and deacon became the unswerving norm throughout the Catholic Church. As Brown concludes: 'If at an earlier period there was in many churches a twofold order consisting of presbyter-bishops (plural) and deacons, by Ignatius' time in some churches in Asia Minor the bishop had emerged as the highest authority with the presbyters and the deacons under him—the famous threefold order that for all practical purposes became universal by 200.'[2]

## HYPOTHESIS VERIFIED

In fact, we will argue in this Chapter that the complexity of the early evidence of church order, and its uni-directional outcome in the universal threefold ministry of bishop, presbyter, and deacon, is explained as the verification of the hypothesis of apostolic succession.

**Stage One:** In the early days of the Church, the apostles were themselves the Church leaders, or Church founders, as we demonstrated earlier. This explains the fact that even if there were elders in the churches, they were directly under the authority of the Church founding apostle, for example Paul.

**Stage Two:** The fact that with Ignatius of Antioch, some churches evidenced monarchical episcopacy is explained by the hypothesis that these churches had already a successor to the apostle who was the monarchical head of that church. The tradition is that Ignatius himself was the successor of Peter the first *episcopos* of the Church of Syrian Antioch.³ On the other hand, where the apostle was still alive, as for instance regarding the Pastoral Epistles and the Epistles of Peter, the apostle himself still exercised authority, and thus monarchical episcopacy had not yet emerged as the sole church structure.

**Stage Three**: In the second century, with the apostles passed to their eternal reward, all the churches were ruled by a single authority, an *episcopos*, who was, in Irenaeus' terms, a true successor of an apostle, the *episcopos*, with priests, *presbyteroi*, and *diaconoi*. These corresponded with the three Old Testament orders of High Priest (*cóhén har rósh*), priests (*haccóhén* Lv 1:13), and Levites *halléwyyim*, (2 Ch 8:15).⁴ This threefold order remained the sole ministerial structure throughout the Church until the sixteenth century Protestant Reformation.

# 8.2 THE CHALLENGE OF HANS KÜNG

*Küng rejects the Catholic dogma of the infallibility of the Church, which for him cannot give a normative interpretation of scripture.*

Hans Küng in his book: *The Church*,⁵ and later in: *Infallible? An Enquiry*,⁶ rejected the doctrine of the infallibility of the Church, which doctrine, he insists, is 'man-made'. We must examine more in detail later the whole question of the infallibility of the Pope and of the Church in the context of the 1968 debate on *Humanae Vitae*. At this point, our concern is simply to state that in denying the infallibility of the Pope and the Church Küng is obviously denying a dogma of the Church, but then to point out that Küng even more radically is at fault in denying the Church's teaching on the roots of divine revelation in scripture and in tradition. His complaint against the 'Inquisition' that declared him not a Catholic theologian is therefore gratuitous. Every Christian denomination has a right to defend its beliefs against those who attack those beliefs, within or without the Church community.

Our apologetic in this chapter is the defence of the Catholic faith against one of its own famous scholars, the Swiss Professor Hans Küng. In the history of the Church, it is by no means unusual that those who oppose its teaching come from among its own ranks; for example Arius was an Alexandrian Catholic priest, Luther an Augustinian Friar. What is surprising regarding Küng is that many Catholics today, even those in quite high positions in the Church, after nearly fifty years do not seem to understand the reasons why he has been officially excluded from his 'canonical mission' as a priest and is not recognized as a Catholic theologian. The Wikipedia entry describes his present situation thus:

> In the late 1960s Küng became the first major Roman Catholic theologian after the late 19th century Old Catholic Church schism to reject the doctrine of papal infallibility in particular in his book *Infallible? An Inquiry* (1971). Consequently, on December 18, 1979 he was stripped of his *missio canonica*, his licence to teach as a Roman Catholic theologian, but carried on teaching as a tenured professor of ecumenical theology at the University of Tübingen until his retirement (Emeritierung) in 1996. To this day he remains a persistent critic of papal infallibility, which he claims is man-made (and thus reversible) rather than instituted by God. He was not excommunicated *ferendae sententiae*.[7]

Perhaps one reason for the confusion is that Küng has not been excommunicated for heresy, while having his canonical mission as a Catholic theologian removed. There is no doubt, according to the principles of Catholic ecclesiology, that his teaching is heretical, against a defined dogma of the Church, as the online Encyclopaedia states.

This is the way in which Küng describes his own relationship with the Catholic Church:

In 1979 I then had personal experience of the Inquisition under another pope (that is John Paul II). My permission to teach was withdrawn by the church, but nevertheless I retained my chair and my institute (which was separated from the Catholic faculty). For two further decades I remained unswervingly faithful to my church in critical loyalty, and to the present day I have remained professor of ecumenical theology and a Catholic priest in good standing. I affirm the papacy for the Catholic Church, but at the same time indefatigably call for a radical reform of it in accordance with the criterion of the gospel.[8]

We must wonder how one who promotes dissent from a dogma of the Church, that is the infallibility of the Church, can be a 'Catholic priest in good standing'? Has not a Catholic priest the obligation to teach the Catholic faith, not to oppose it? If there is misunderstanding, then one reason may be that Hans Küng's situation *vis à vis* the law of the Church which has remained so for fifty years is itself ambiguous.

Küng claims that he has remained in 'critical loyalty' to the Church. Again, can one be 'loyal' to the Church even 'critically' if one persistently rejects a doctrine of the Church? He claims that the doctrine of the infallibility of the Church is 'man-made'. On the contrary, the First Vatican Council affirmed that the Pope rejoiced 'in that infallibility which the divine Redeemer wished his church to enjoy in defining doctrine concerning faith or morals'.[9] Vatican IIs *Lumen Gentium* repeats and further explains the church's faith in the Pope's infallibility, adding that the Pope's 'definitions are said to be irreformable of themselves, and not from the consent of the church, since they are delivered with the assistance of the Holy Spirit which was promised to him in blessed Peter...'[10] LG then adds that 'The infallibility promised to the church exists also in the body of bishops when, along with the successor of Peter, it exercises the supreme teaching office'.[11]

Importantly, therefore, Küng does not only deny the infallibility of the Pope, but much more the infallibility of the Church, in which according to the Church the Pope shares in certain defined instances. He argues that because the Church is not infallible, it is quite possible that it made an error concerning the apostolic succession of ministry, which for him could have been otherwise, not only historically but also now in the present-day Church. To give an appraisal therefore of Küng's critique of the apostolic succession of ministry in the church, we must begin where Küng begins, namely with his fundamental concept of Scripture, Tradition, and Magisterium.

## 8.3 KÜNG'S ECCLESIOLOGY

*Küng rejects the Catholic dogma that the apostles handed over their authority to their successors, the apostolic college of bishops led by the successor of the Bishop of Rome. The successors to the apostles rather are 'the whole church'.*

In his book on *The Church*, Küng first denies that the Catholic Church can authoritatively interpret scripture because, as he says, the relationship between the Church and scripture is one of *norma normata*, but never *norma normans*. This means that he must deny the authority of the living tradition of the Church, as affirmed by Trent, Vatican I, and Vatican II. Küng can in his own eyes justify this theologically because for him the 'apostolic succession' does not imply that certain individuals called 'apostles' had the divine gift to hand on this authority to their successors the bishops of the Catholic Church. Rather, the whole Church is 'apostolic' in that these apostles handed on their authority to the whole Church, no one having authority over another member of the Church. This clearly contradicts the teaching of the Catholic Church on divine revelation.

Küng adopts a position regarding revelation which is difficult to distinguish from Luther's sola scriptura. Küng states: 'All commentaries and interpretations, all explanations and applications must always be measured against and legitimized by the message contained in scripture with its original force, concentrated actuality, and supreme relevance. Sacred Scripture is thus the *norma normans* of the Church's tradition, and tradition must be seen as the *norma normata*'.[12]

That is the first fundamental difference between Küng's theology of revelation and that of the Catholic Church. This is the teaching of the Catholic Church which asserts both scripture and tradition to be equally the Word of God:

> Hence there exists a close connection and communication between sacred tradition and Sacred Scripture. For both of them, flowing from the same divine wellspring, in a certain way merge into a unity and tend toward the same end. For Sacred Scripture is the word of God inasmuch as it is consigned to writing under the inspiration of the divine Spirit, while sacred tradition takes the word of God entrusted by Christ the Lord and the Holy Spirit to the Apostles, and hands it on to their successors in its full purity, so that led by the light of the Spirit of truth, they may in proclaiming it preserve this word of God faithfully, explain it, and make it more widely known. Consequently it is not from Sacred Scripture alone that the Church draws her certainty about everything which has been revealed. Therefore both sacred tradition and Sacred Scripture are to be accepted and venerated with the same sense of loyalty and reverence.[13]

The teaching of Vatican II only develops the teaching of the Council of Trent on tradition, which Council 'clearly perceives that this truth and rule are contained in written books and in unwritten traditions which were received by the apostles from the mouth of Christ himself, or else have come down to us, handed on as it were by the apostles themselves at the inspiration of the Holy Spirit'.[14] Thus tradition cannot be, as Küng claims, only *norma normata*, a 'normed norm', that is to say only conforming to what is demonstrably in scripture. That would be effectively a *sola scriptura* position. Tradition in Catholic theology is itself the Word of God, and thus has an authority equivalent to that of scripture, precisely because Tradition is equally from the apostles, albeit unwritten.

Küng has no problem whatsoever in claiming that Vatican II was wrong in its view of tradition, precisely because he does not admit that the apostles handed on their authority to define doctrine, so giving those who succeeded them a *norma normans*. Both Trent and Vatican II therefore could be mistaken! He does admit that 'Without the witness and ministry of these first public witnesses authorized by Christ, without the witness and ministry of Peter and the twelve ... and of all the other apostles down to the last, Paul, the Church could not exist.'[15] He is in agreement also with Catholic theology when he says 'The apostolic office as a whole is unique and unrepeatable',[16] and when he says 'What remain is a task and a commission. The apostolic commission is not finished, but will remain until the end of time. The apostolic task is not completed; it embraces all peoples to the ends of the earth'.[17]

However, according to Küng, what succeeds the apostles? 'There can only be one basic answer: the Church. The whole Church, and not just a few individuals, is the follower of the apostles.'[18] There is no mention in Küng of a group of those who authoritatively follow the apostles as their successors in authority. 'Apostolicity can never mean power through which the Church might rule. It is not a question of others submitting to the Church; the Church must itself submit by accepting the authority of the apostles and of the Church's and the apostles' Lord.' [19]

So, for Küng, the apostles did not hand over their authority to specific successors. He admits that the apostles themselves had authority to preach and teach the Word of God. But he does not admit that the apostles handed on their authority to specific successors. That would make them bearers of unwritten tradition, giving them the author-

## 8.4 STAGE ONE: DIRECT RULE FROM THE APOSTLES

*Küng claims that, while in the primitive Jerusalem churches elders were appointed, in Gentile churches such as Corinth a more freely structured or 'charismatic' church was implied. I respond that precisely in Corinth, Paul exercised personal apostolic authority for example in excommunicating the incestuous Corinthian. This coheres with Paul's conviction of his own infallibility as apostolic recipient of revelation, as we have argued earlier.*

Küng, as we have seen, admits that the apostles had special authority in the earliest church. But his view is that the New Testament presents evidence of two types of church rule in the earliest days: the 'Jewish' type of rule in the infant churches, which followed the Old Testament system of elders, and the 'Gentile' type or rule, particularly manifest in the church at Corinth. 'There is no evidence anywhere of a monarchic episcopate existing in the primitive period, not even in Acts (on the contrary, cf. Ac 20:28).'[20]

> The remarkable thing is that neither of the two basic systems we find in the primitive Churches can be regarded as *the* original one. Both kinds, in outline at least, seem to have co-existed from the very beginning. While bishops and deacons probably originated in the Gentile Christian communities, the office of elder comes from a Judaeo-Christian, indeed from Jewish tradition.[21]

Luke tells us that, during their first missionary journey, in each church they had founded, Paul and Barnabas 'appointed elders, and with prayer and fasting they commended them to the Lord in whom they had come to believe'. (Ac 14:23) But Küng maintains that in this case, '... Luke is making an unhistorical addition—either theologically conditioned, or based upon a tradition which had developed in the meantime...'[22] Küng is convinced that only in primitive churches of Jewish foundation, such as in Jerusalem, would such elders have been appointed, not in the Gentile churches which were founded by Paul and Barnabas. In those churches, Küng maintains, a more freely structured or 'charismatic' church structure would have applied. 'There appears to be no monarchical episcopate in the Pauline communities at all....'[23]

But Küng is surely misguided in considering that one would expect to see monarchical episcopate in churches where the apostles in those first days themselves were ruling the churches directly. Our contention in this chapter is that this only becomes a unified form of church order ultimately after the death of the respective apostle. We have freely admitted earlier that the term 'apostle' in the New Testament is complex in its meaning. It is quite possible that in those early days the rule of every church was by an 'apostle', whether that 'apostle' was one of the Twelve or Paul, or another church founder closely related to the apostolic witness such as Barnabas. This would not negate the historicity of the claim in Acts that Paul and Barnabas elected elders in each church community. Rather, it would simply mean that the rule of these elders was subject to the apostle who had founded that particular church. It was only after the apostle died that the 'elders' (in Greek *presbyteroi*, from which the word *priest* eventually came down to us from the Old English *prēost)*[24] assumed more authority as successors of that apostle. A single successor of the apostles, an *episcopos*, became the monarchical leader of that church, as at Antioch with Ignatius being the *episcopos*.

Küng is correct in seeing the Jewish origin of the *presbyteroi*. Moses appointed 'elders', Exodus 24:9, Hebrew *zākén*, ('an old man') to assist him in his rule of God's people. Luke refers to the 'chief priests and elders' (Ac 4:23), denoting the important place that the $z^e k\acute{e}nim$ held in the Sanhedrin rule of Jerusalem. The first Jewish Christians simply took over that word and that role for those who they saw as the government of each church. Much is made in Protestant apologetic of the fact that the word 'priest' is not used to refer to Christian leaders in the New Testament. But the first Christians would not have called the member of the governing group a *hieros*, because that would have confused him with the hereditary Jewish *cóhén*, many of whom in the early days became members of the Way: 'The word of the Lord continued to spread: the number of disciples in Jerusalem was greatly increased, and a large group of priests *(hiereón)* made their submission to the faith.' (Ac 6:7) It was not until the second century, when the split with Judaism was tragically complete, and when there was no longer the sacrificial system operating from the Temple in Jerusalem destroyed after AD 70 that sacrificial language became more and more applied to the Christian episcopate and presbyterate.

Küng argues that the church at Corinth, with two letters from Paul whose authenticity is unquestioned by modern scholarship,[25] is a prime example of a Gentile church in the earliest days which did not have any structure of elders in charge. Küng insists, 'We know from Paul's lists exactly how many different kinds of ministries there were at Corinth—apostles, prophets, teachers, and so on. But there were no "bishops", deacons or elders. Moreover, when it is a question of restoring order in matters of preaching, the Lord's Supper and Church discipline, Paul never addresses himself to a single official or a single group of officials, responsible for all the community. He addresses himself throughout to all and at the same time to each individual.'[26] Küng concludes that 'All this is much more than an *argumentum e silentio*. The burden of proof lies with those who wish to assert that there existed in the Corinth community, in Paul's time, an office of leadership, whether elders or the later monarchic kind of episcopate.'[27]

My contention here, however, is that Küng is anachronistic, applying to a situation which existed only after the apostles' death to a situation existing in the church at a time when the apostles were actively ruling the churches as church founders. Regarding the situation at Corinth, Küng sees a clear proof of his thesis:

> And with regard to the incestuous man, where the writer of the pastoral letter might have said something like: "The elders are to exclude him from the community" (or even perhaps: "Let the bishop excommunicate him"?), what Paul actually says, addressing himself to the whole community is: "When you are assembled, and my spirit is present, with the power of our Lord Jesus, you are to deliver this man to Satan.... Drive out the wicked person from among you." (5:4 f. and 13)[28]

However this case proves contrary to Küng that Paul himself is taking personal authority as an apostle in excommunicating from a distance the incestuous man. We have already seen how in Galatians, Paul acts as the bearer of revelation. It is precisely he, and he alone, who acts to maintain church discipline. It is not necessary for him to mention the elders, if such exist. It may even be that he is ignoring them because they are ineffective in excommunicating the immoral Corinthian Christian. Paul does not need a successor, any bishop representing his authority, to exercise his authority. He is quite capable of exercising that authority himself, as indeed he does!

Certainly, by AD 96, when Clement of Rome is writing his letter to the Corinthians, who are again in trouble, he expects those Christians of Corinth to obey their presbyters:

> You, therefore, the prime movers of the schism, submit to the presbyters, and, bending the knees of your hearts, accept correction and change your minds. Learn submissiveness, and rid yourselves of

your boastful and proud incorrigibility of tongue. Surely, it is better for you to be little and honorable within the flock of Christ than to be esteemed above your deserts and forfeit the hope which He holds out. For thus the excellent Wisdom says: Behold, I will speak out the words of my spirit; I will teach you my message. Since I called you and you did not listen, and since I put forth my message and you paid no attention, but set my counsels at naught and disobeyed my warnings: therefore will I in turn laugh at your destruction; and I will exult when ruin overtakes you, and when you are seized suddenly by dismay, and the catastrophe is at hand like a squall, or when distress and siege come upon you. Yes, when you call upon me for help, I will not listen to you. Seek me the wicked will, but they will not find me. For they hated wisdom and did not choose the fear of the Lord, and they refused to attend to my counsels and sneered at my reproofs. Therefore they shall eat the fruits of their own way, and be glutted with their own impiousness. Because they wronged the little ones, they shall be slaughtered; and a searching inquiry shall destroy the impious. But he who listens to me will find shelter in hope and confidence and will rest secure from every ill.[29]

Our thesis is quite simple; that there is no clear evidence of monarchical episcopacy, nor does there need to be, as successor of the apostles while the apostles themselves exercise that authority personally. There is a problem perhaps as to who presided over the Eucharist in those early days. But presumably anyone commissioned by an apostle could do so, however he was commissioned, or by whatever title he was called.

## 8.5 THE FIRST SUCCESSORS OF THE APOSTLES

*Admittedly, the threefold ministry is not clear in the Pastoral Letters of Paul and in I and II Peter. But these ancient letters represent Stage Two, where the apostles are still in overall control of the churches under their authority, but where they are gradually handing over that authority to their successors. Even where the authenticity of these letters is doubtful, they still represent that stage of intermediate apostolic rule.*

The Second Stage, that of a situation where the apostles were still alive, but beginning to appoint successors, we find evidenced in the Pastoral Epistles of Paul, I and II Timothy and Titus, and in I and II Peter. We recognise the critical problems of the authenticity of these letters, while contending that sometimes these critical problems have been exaggerated by anti-ecclesiastical bias. But there is no reason to doubt that these letters date not later than the early second century, and manifest a situation where their writers and their readership accept that Peter and Paul had authority to appoint successors, who themselves would represent the apostles in their authority and ministry. At this early stage, the distinction between *episcopoi* and *presbyteroi* was not absolute, since again it was assumed that the apostles were still exercising their actual authority in the churches.

The main evidence for the apostles handing on their authority immediately to successors is to be found in the so-called Pastoral Letters of Paul, that is, 1 and 2 Timothy and Titus, and 1 and 2 Peter. Regarding the later books of the New Testament, Hebrews is no longer accepted as Pauline, even in the liturgy of the Church (we refer now to 'the Letter to the Hebrews', not to 'St Paul's Letter to the Hebrews').[30] The Book of Revelation could have been written by the apostle John,[31] but also could have been written by a Christian prophet now not known to us.[32] Who the 'James' was, that wrote the Letter bearing his name is again disputed, apparently he is not conscious of handing his message on to any successor.[33] Likewise, the three Letters of John do not indicate that there is imagined any successor to the one writing those Letters. 'Jude' could have been an apostle, although that again is disputed,[34] and Jude does not give us any evidence that he was handing on his authority to a successor.

## 8.6 THE AUTHENTICITY OF THE PASTORALS AND I AND II PETER

*We accept that a Catholic could hold to the pseudonymity of the Pastorals and I Peter. But in any case, whether the authorship is pseudonymous or not, we have a Church in Stage Two, that of the handing over of direct apostolic rule to successors.*

The significant evidence of such apostolic succession, therefore, is contained in the Pauline Pastorals and 1 and 2 Peter. Our first task, however, is to discuss the authenticity of these apostolic letters. Before the Second Vatican Council, Catholic biblical scholars would tend strenuously to defend the authenticity of these letters, against what was seen as Protestant critical attack; although the best Catholic commentators would acknowledge difficulties in demonstrating apostolic authorship.

For example, Alfred Wickenhauser's *New Testament Introduction*, first published 1958,[35] recommended by Joseph Fitzmyer as a 'Vade mecum for all seminarians', argued for the authenticity of the Pastoral letters, even though recognizing and respecting those who had difficulties with authenticity. His arguments are detailed, well reasoned, and to me are certainly worth considering.[36] Wickenhauser argues that 'Many of the peculiarities can be explained by the special nature and purpose of these Epistles, which are directions to the leaders of the communities.'[37] Regarding the First Letter of Peter, Wickenhauser acknowledges difficulties regarding Petrine authorship, but concludes that Peter used an amanuensis, 'as distinct from a secretary who wrote to dictation'.[38] Regarding 2 Peter, Wickenhauser concludes that arguments against authenticity are strong, and 'if pseudonymous, was probably written about AD 90–95 by an unknown author'.[39]

Even well before the Second Vatican Council, therefore, Catholic scholars such as Wickenhauser were prepared to acknowledge genuine difficulties regarding the authenticity of the Pastoral Letters and Peter, and to admit that the authorship by the Big Fisherman of II Peter could well be denied by a loyal Catholic. The momentous Encyclical on biblical studies by Pope Pius XII, 1943 *Divino Afflante Spiritu* ('By the breath of the Holy Spirit'), authored it is said by the Rector of the Pontifical Biblical Institute Augustine Bea, later Cardinal, commends the Catholic commentator to pay serious attention to the literary genres of the sacred text:

> Hence the Catholic commentator, in order to comply with the present needs of biblical studies, in explaining the Sacred Scripture and in demonstrating and proving its immunity from all error, should also make a prudent use of this means, determine, that is, to what extent the manner of expression or the literary mode adopted by the sacred writer may lead to a correct and genuine interpretation; and let him be convinced that this part of his office cannot be neglected without serious detriment to Catholic exegesis.[40]

Already, in 1958, Wickenhauser had accepted the opinion at least as not against Catholic faith that 'Paul made use of some intimate assistant, such as Luke, as amanuensis for the writing of these (i.e. the Pastoral) Epistles.'[41] This amanuensis would have had a much more active role in the writing of the letters than simply that of a scribe.

But general critical opinion today would go much further than the proposal of an amanuensis in writing the Pastoral Epistles and Peter, and Catholic scholars would have no scruple to concur. We may take the conclusions of Raymond E. Brown, in his *Introduction to the New Testament*[42] as a typical modern viewpoint, a Catholic biblical scholar in full agreement with modern critical conclusions.

Brown concludes his lengthy investigation by selecting the third of four possibilities:

> All three Pastorals are pseudonymous, but II Timothy was written not long after Paul's death as a farewell testament by someone who knew Paul's last days, so that the biographical details therein would be largely historical, even if dramatized with some license. Titus and I Timothy were written pseudonymously later, most likely toward the end of the first century, partly in imitation of II Timothy. A 'second career' was created (i.e. after Paul's imprisonment in Rome).[43]

My own view is that Wickenhauser's careful arguments in defence of the Pastorals as being genuinely from St Paul are, as I have said, worthy of careful consideration. These arguments become even more credible if we think of them as analogous to bishop's pastoral letters having official status. Such letters are often written by his office staff, or by a designated theologian. We have already seen this operating in the case of the papal encyclical *Divino Afflante Spiritu*. This would explain the differences in style so frequently mentioned. Is there also a bias among biblical scholars against the institutional Church, which becomes more and more evident in the Pastorals? Do many find it really difficult to believe that Paul could have been a Catholic? The same applies to the First Letter of Peter. We have no other writings of the Big Fisherman, so we have nothing else with which to compare that letter. Is it impossible that Peter did acquire a skill in writing (he had forty years and more after the Resurrection to develop those literary skills)? Or is it not possible again that he employed a literary assistant to write for him, as we would say a 'ghost writer'?

What is clear from the viewpoint of evidence is that in the Pastorals and in I Peter (accepting for the moment the pseudonymity of II Peter) we have the picture of a Church in an intermediate stage. The apostles, in this case Paul and

Peter, are viewed as still in charge of the churches under their authority. Thus again it is anachronistic to conclude that here we have an instance of a church without a monarchical episcopate. On the contrary, the 'monarchical episcopos', the 'single overseer', is the apostle himself, Peter or Paul. This would be true even if we accepted that the epistles were pseudonymous, since the writers whoever they might be claim to be acting with the authority of the apostles.

Thus we are not surprised that there does not always seem a clear distinction between 'elder' (*presbyteros*) I Timothy 5:19–20, and 'presiding elder' or 'bishop' (*episkopos*), I Timothy 3:1.[44] In terms of an evolutionary or developmental methodology, the evidence would clearly be accounted for by the hypothesis that this precisely was an intermediate stage between the direct rule of an apostle and, after the apostles' death, the single *episkopos* representing the apostle in the monarchical episcopate.

We shall now briefly examine in turn the Pauline and the Petrine epistles, to verify the mid-point characteristic of these letters.

## 8.7 THE PASTORAL LETTERS OF PAUL

*Regarding the Pastoral Letters of Paul, unless one holds implausibly to a late date into the second century, they represent a powerful argument for the transmission of the ministry and authority of Paul soon after his death AD 80 to 100.*

Even if, considering first the Pauline Pastorals, we accepted the critical view that they were pseudonymous, Brown argues that this would not necessarily deny either their divine inspiration or that this was a legitimate process on the way towards the monarchical episcopate. This would be a case of disciples of Paul and of Peter were writing with their authority to maintain the apostolic tradition. If this happened some time between AD 80 and 100 then this would fit into the evolutionary framework of a mid-stage in the process towards the monarchical episcopate. Brown first correctly rejects as hyper-critical the view that the Pastorals were written well into the second century, then justifies a date of 80 to 100 in terms of its conformity with biblical inspiration:

> If the Pastorals are the creations of a pseudepigrapher, why did he choose as his pattern letters addressed to individuals (of which there is only one undisputed Pauline instance: Phlm) instead of the much more common pattern of letters addressed to communities? Why did he not shape letters of Paul to Crete and to Ephesus instead of Titus and I Tim? If the Pastorals were written in the 2d century and the biographical details reported in them are fictional, why has their fate (acceptance into the biblical canon) differed so sharply from other fictional compositions by or about Paul, e.g., III Corinthians, Letter to the Laodiceans, Acts of Paul and Thecla, which were not accepted?
>
> Those who do not believe in inspiration and those who do but without a literalist understanding of the divine communication do not find the notion of pseudepigraphy an obstacle in itself when it is understood in terms of disciples continuing the Pauline tradition and assuming the mantle of the apostle to speak loyally in his name to new problems facing a later generation. It is hard to see, however, how a proposal that the writer of the Pastorals was intentionally deceptive and consciously desired to counteract Paul's genuine heritage can be fitted into any notion of inspiration, even a sophisticated one.
>
> In varying ways the factors just listed have contributed to a situation where about 80 to 90 percent of modern scholars would agree that the Pastorals were written after Paul's lifetime, and of those the majority would accept the period between 80 and 100 as the most plausible context for their composition. The majority would also interpret them as having some continuity with Paul's own ministry and thought,

but not so close a continuity as manifested in Col and Eph and even II Thess.[45]

If the Pastorals therefore were written just after Paul's death, 80 to 100, then they present a powerful argument for the intermediate stage between personal apostolic rule, and apostolic rule after the death of the apostle. Even if they are pseudonymous, continuing Paul's authority, this is in a way at least as strong an argument for the transmission of the tradition of ministry as if they were genuine.

If they were authentic, however, then they would be dated earlier, 60 to 80. I personally think that this is the preferred solution. I would accept Wickenhauser's argument that there is no *discontinuity* between the theology of the letters accepted by scholars as genuine (for example Romans, Galatians and 1 and 2 Corinthians) and the Pastorals. Such an argument only has force if one thinks that the accepted letters of Paul betray an anti-ecclesiastical, and anti-structural bias, which I would argue is a misreading through Protestant eyes! In this case, therefore, they are proof of that intermediate stage between direct apostolic rule and the rule of a monarchical successor of the apostles. They would be also a demonstration of the incipient early catholicism of Paul if they are genuinely, as I would argue, consistent with the development of his thought. As the Christian Church becomes more developed, it needs the structures that Paul, through his amanuensis, imposes on the primitive church in those Pastoral letters.

## 8.8 I AND II PETER

*Regarding I and II Peter, I Peter is most plausibly authentic, and represents clearly the handing over by Peter of his authority to the churches under his mandate. II Peter, considered almost unanimously inauthentic, is not relevant to this discussion, regarding church order, even though it is important doctrinally.*

Regarding the two letters of Peter, they are both called traditionally 'Catholic or General Epistles' along with James, I, II, and III John, and Jude. This was, as Brown says, since Eusebius the Church historian of the fourth century, '... a designation that (at least in Eastern Christianity), was deemed appropriate for works addressed to the church universal...'[46] as distinct from the Pauline letters which were addressed to early church communities or to individuals.

There is an immense difference of critical judgement regarding their authenticity. As Brown concludes, 'Of all the Catholic Epistles I Peter has the best chance of being written by the figure to whom it is attributed.'[47] On the contrary, regarding II Peter, Brown asserts 'Indeed, the pseudonymity of II Peter is more certain than that of any other New Testament work.'[48]

Regarding canonicity, 1 Peter was never questioned as to its place in the New Testament canon. 'It has been an undisputed part of the New Testament Canon since the end of the second century.'[49] Regarding 2 Peter, however, its canonicity was disputed right up to the fourth century.[50] Brown argues that 2 Peter was written early in the second century,[51] 'by someone desiring to present a final message with advice from Peter'.[52] However, 2 Peter is not in itself relevant to our discussion of the monarchical episcopate, since ministry by *presbyteroi* or *episkopoi* is not mentioned. The author is too concerned about false doctrine even to mention the orders in the church. This silence may indicate that the monarchical episcopate and the threefold ministry were already established by the writing of II Peter at about 130; but its silence could not be considered real evidence either for or against such an established order.

On the other hand, 1 Peter gives us evidence equal to that of the Pauline Pastorals of the mid-point between direct and personal apostolic rule and the monarchical episcopate. This argument would apply whether, as with the Pastorals, the author was genuinely Peter, writing the epistle perhaps through his amanuensis Silvanus (1 Pt 5:12), identical with Silas, 'who for many years was a fellow worker of Paul's',[53] in which case 1 Peter was written most likely before AD 64,[54] or even if 1 Peter was pseudonymous, as with the Pastorals it must have been written before the end of the first century, it is known to the earliest second century testimonies of Polycarp and Papias.[55]

Regarding church order, 1 Peter explicitly mentions the 'elders':

> I urge the elders (*presbuterous*) among you, as a fellow-elder myself and a witness to the sufferings of Christ, and as one who is to have a share in the glory that is to be revealed: give a shepherd's care to the flock of God that is entrusted to you: watch over it, not simply as a duty but gladly, as God wants; not for sordid money, but because you are eager to do it. (1 Pt 5:1-2)

Brown quotes the view that 'the church organization implied in 5:1 with established presbyters, seemingly appointed and salaried, fits the last one third of the century better than Peter's lifetime (n. 21 above). That may be true; but the reference to varied charisms in 4:10–11 suggests a transitional period, earlier, for instance, than that envisioned by 1 Timothy...' [56] 1 Peter therefore could have been written any time from the 60s until the end of the first century; precisely that interim period we are discussing between direct and personal apostolic rule, and the post-apostolic monarchical episcopate established at the very latest by the end of the second century as testified by Irenaeus.

## 8.9 STAGE THREE: THE THREEFOLD MINISTRY OF BISHOP, PRIEST, AND DEACON

*The Threefold Ministry of Bishop, Priest and Deacon is clearly evidenced in the writings of Ignatius of Antioch, c.*

## AD 50 to 117. From Ignatius onwards, there is no evidence of any other model of authority and ministry in the early church.

Ignatius of Antioch, also called Theophorus (*ho Theophoros*) was born in Syria around the year AD 50. He died at Rome between 98 and 117. Thus Ignatius of Antioch was a truly sub-apostolic Father. We may reject as legend that Ignatius was the child taken up in the arms of the Lord described in Mark 9:35. But it is more than credible that Ignatius was an auditor of John the Beloved Disciple, and that he was the second bishop of Antioch appointed by Peter himself.

Ignatius was martyred during the reign of the Emperor Trajan (98 to 117) a vigorous and enterprising ruler of the Roman Empire.[57] This gives us the dating for Ignatius, the historical fact of his journey to Rome for martyrdom is not questioned by scholars. Ignatius was actually tried for refusing to worship the pagan gods before the Emperor himself, who was visiting Antioch at the time. Ignatius was then sent to Rome under guard and with great privations, there to become the food of wild beasts and a spectacle for the people. At several places along the road his fellow-Christians greeted him with words of comfort and reverential homage. He wrote to the Christians of Rome, pleading with them not to prevent his martyrdom, which he desired beyond everything else. This desire was fulfilled when he was mauled to death in the Flavian amphitheatre.

The Catholic Encyclopaedia summarises the importance of Ignatius of Antioch:

> It is scarcely possible to exaggerate the importance of the testimony which the Ignatian letters offer to the dogmatic character of Apostolic Christianity. The martyred Bishop of Antioch constitutes a most important link between the Apostles and the Fathers of the early Church. Receiving from the Apostles themselves, whose auditor he was, not only the substance of revelation, but also their own inspired interpretation of it; dwelling, as it were, at the very

fountain-head of Gospel truth, his testimony must necessarily carry with it the greatest weight and demand the most serious consideration. Cardinal Newman did not exaggerate the matter when he said ('The Theology of the Seven Epistles of St Ignatius', in *Historical Sketches*, I, London, 1890) that 'the whole system of Catholic doctrine may be discovered, at least in outline, not to say in parts filled up, in the course of his seven epistles'.[58]

## 8.10 IGNATIUS' WRITINGS

*The seven letters of Ignatius quoted by the church historian Eusebius, written to churches as Ignatius was on his way to martyrdom in Rome, under the persecution of the Emperor Trajan, c. AD 98 to 117, are now considered substantially authentic. These testify to the existence of the threefold ministry at the beginning of the second century. We have no evidence of any other ministerial structure in the post-apostolic church.*

The oldest collection of the writings of St Ignatius known to have existed was used by the historian Eusebius in the first half of the fourth century, but unfortunately it is no longer extant. It was made up of the seven letters written by Ignatius whilst on his way to Rome, addressed to the Christians of Ephesus (*Pros Ephesious*); of Magnesis (*Magnesieusin*); of Tralles (*Trallianois*); of Rome (*pros Romaious*) of Philadelphia (*Philadelpheusin*); of Smyrna (*Smyrnaiois*); and to Polycarp (*Pros Polykarpon*).

There are also other letters purportedly from Ignatius addressed mainly to persons, for example to Mary of Cassabola, six of which are certainly spurious, and one genuine, to the Philippians. Even the genuine letters may have added redactions; but the support of nineteenth century scholars such as the Catholic Denzinger, the Anglican Bishop Lightfoot, and the Liberal Protestant Harnack have led in the twentieth century to the acceptance of these seven letters in Eusebius being accepted as substantially genuine. A reference in Irenaeus, and a mention of Ignatius' letters in The romance of Lucian of Samosata '*De morte peregrini*', written in 167, for Harnack puts the genuiness of the Ignatian letters beyond question.[59]

Radical German historical criticism of the early and middle nineteenth century was dismissive of the genuiness of all the Ignatian letters, notably Baur,[60] who also posited the four Gospels as late second century as well as Ignatius. Baur was a Hegelian, and the existence of a Catholic orthodoxy of the late first and early second century did not fit in with his philosophy of evolutionary history. However we can be confident concerning the genuineness of the Ignatian letters contained in Eusebius not from an abstract philosophy of development, but by a simple explanation; that Ignatius was already the second bishop to succeed Peter at Antioch. He was a successor of the apostles, and thus the threefold ministry was itself fully developed at Antioch. The Pastoral Letters of Paul, and I and II Peter, even if we grant their pseudonymity as late in the first century or early in the second, do not have a consistent concept of the threefold ministry precisely because the apostles who were at least purportedly authors of those epistles were alive, or again were conceived of as alive.

In the letter to the Magnesians, one of those authentic letters, Ignatius mentions explicitly the orders of bishop, priest, and deacon, to which order he commends the Christians in the name of church unity. This model became unvarying and normative from Ignatius onwards.

> Since therefore I have, in the persons before mentioned, beheld the whole multitude of you in faith and love, I exhort you to study to do all things with a divine harmony, while your bishop presides in the place of God, and your presbyters in the place of the assembly of the apostles, along with your deacons, who are most dear to me, and are entrusted with the ministry of Jesus Christ, who was with the Father before the beginning of time, and in the end was revealed. Do all then, imitating the same divine

> conduct, pay respect to one another, and let no one look upon his neighbour after the flesh, but continually love each other in Jesus Christ. Let nothing exist among you that may divide you; but be united with your bishop, and those that preside over you, as a type and evidence of your immortality.[61]

In the same vein, Ignatius writes to the Trallians:

> Equally, it is for the rest of you to hold the deacons in as great respect as Jesus Christ; just as you should also look to the bishop as a type of the Father, and the clergy as the apostolic circle forming his council; for without these three orders no church has any right to the name. I am sure these are your own feelings too, for I have had with me, and still have, an example of your affection in the person of the bishop himself, whose grave demeanour is a notable lesson in itself, and whose very gentleness is power.[62]

In his letter to the Ephesians, Ignatius clearly assumes that the monarchical episcopate is universal:

> For we can have no life apart from Jesus Christ; and as he represents the mind of the Father, so our bishop, even those who are stationed in the remotest parts of the world, represent the mind of Jesus Christ. That is why it is proper for your conduct and your practices to correspond closely with the mind of the bishop. And this, indeed, they are doing; your justly respected clergy, who are a credit to God, are attuned to their bishop like the strings of a harp, and the result is a hymn of praise to Jesus Christ from minds that are in unison, and affections that are in harmony.[63]

Ignatius writes as if all over the world there is no other model of leadership, the single bishop united with his presbyterate, the clergy. From Ignatius on, there is no evidence for any other model for church ministry other than the threefold ministry of bishop, presbyter, and deacon, right up to the Reformation. Ignatius obviously expects that the bishop will be obeyed in all matters, and he cannot conceive of the bishop teaching false doctrine. Ignatius has a clear concept of the infallibility of the Church as expressed in the person of the bishop. What is not so explicit in Ignatius is the succession of the bishop from an apostle. That Ignatius was the second bishop to succeed Peter in Antioch may explain his silence in this regard. He took for granted that he was the successor of an apostle. We must also say that implicitly Ignatius follows apostolic authority in the totality of his presentation of Catholic doctrine. As Philip Hughes states:

> The next stage in the development begins when death removes the Apostles. Their office, status, power was unique. No one ever put in a claim to be an Apostle of the second generation. Because of the fact which constituted them Apostles they were necessarily irreplaceable. To their authority succeeded the new hierarchy of episcopoi and presbyteroi, and as it took their place this new hierarchy itself underwent a change. The college of episcopoi or presbyteroi who, under the Apostles, had ruled the local Church gave place to an arrangement where in each local Church there was but one episcopos whom a number of subordinates, now termed presbyteroi, assisted. By the time of St Ignatius of Antioch (i.e. the end of the first century, within from thirty to forty years of the death of St Paul) the new system—the so-called 'monarchical episcopate'—is so universal that he takes it for granted as the basis of his exhortations.
>
> The change took place with so little disturbance that it has left no trace at all in history. It passed with so general an agreement that one can only infer that it had behind it what alone could sanction so great a change, what alone could secure it so smooth a passage, the consciousness of all concerned that this was part of the Founder's plan wrought out in detail by the Apostles He had commissioned.[64]

Some historians are sceptical of Hugh's clear delineation of monarchical episcopacy from Ignatius onwards, for example Uhlhorne:

> There is, indeed, no reason to abandon the oldest tradition of the Church, according to which, Clement was the third bishop of Rome after Peter; only it must be remembered that he was not a bishop in that sense of the word which the monarchical tendency of a later period developed. He was simply one of the most prominent presbyters of the Roman (493) congregation immediately after the post-apostolical age.[65]

Likewise, Kelly asserts regarding Pope Clement (c. AD 91 to 101):

> While Clement's position as a leading presbyter and spokesman of the Christian community at Rome is assured, his letter suggests that the monarchical episcopate had not yet emerged there, and it is therefore impossible to form any precise conception of his constitutional role.[66]

However, in reply, Hughes would be asking where was the evidence that there was ever more than one leader of the Church of Rome, even if the constitutional implications of the episcopate were still developing during the second century? There is evidence, as we have discussed, in the New Testament, a lack of clear distinction between the episcopate and the presbyterate; but, as we have argued, this appertains for the period prior to the death of the apostles. After the death of the apostles, we have no evidence contrary to the Ignatian monarchical episcopate. Ignatius clearly speaks as if the monarchical episcopate is universal. Failing such contrary evidence, we may accept the testimony of Ignatius that from his time onwards the rule of a single bishop as successor of the relevant apostle was universal, even if the full expression of that rule was nuanced. Clement may well have been cautious, playing down his own authority as 'low key' in order to unite the varied church communities of Rome as ruled respectively by the 'glorious apostles Peter and Paul'. What we do not have is any contradiction of monarchical episcopacy in the post-apostolic era by evidence of another model of church government.

## 8.11 WHAT WAS THE ORIGIN OF THE THREEFOLD MINISTRY IN IGNATIUS?

*I propose that the source of that threefold ministry is nothing other than the threefold order of High Priest, Priest, and Levite in the Old Testament.*

In my adult catechetical question and answer book: *What is Catholicism?*[67] I answer the question as to the origin of the threefold ministry thus:

> My own suggestion is that the pattern of ministry was eventually decided most likely by the close of the first century, by analogy with the orders that developed in the Old Testament. These were the High Priest (*cohen harosh*, 2 Ch 24:11), Priests (*haccohen*, Lv 1:13), and Levites (*hallewiyyim*, 2 Ch 8:14), assigned 'to their tasks of praise and of assisting the priests in accordance with day-to-day requirements'. These three Old Testament orders corresponded to the bishop, priests, and deacons of the Church respectively. Many, even within the Catholic theological community, have argued that, with the New Testament, there came an end of the cult of the Old Testament with its cultic orders. But the new Catechism argues that, on the contrary, the orders of the New Testament are a fulfilment of the orders of the Old Testament: 'The liturgy of the Church, however, sees in the priesthood of Aaron and the service of the Levites, as in the institution of the seventy elders, a prefiguring of the ordained ministry of the New Covenant' (CCC 1541).

Our own deeper studies in compiling this book have if anything upgraded this suggestion into at least a most plausible theory. Antioch, indeed Syria in general, was closely related to Judaism in that many in that region were Jewish Christian converts, the southern borders of Syria touching upon 'Galilee of the Gentiles', from whence came Jesus and his apostles. Syria was truly the cradle of Christianity. Küng, in this I believe quite rightly, sees the origin of the institution of the elders as emanating from the Old Testament. The sacrificial role of the priests (the *cóhénim*) would not have been uppermost, since up to the sacking of Jerusalem AD 70 the Old Testament sacrificial system was still in place. Ignatius is firm in his belief in the Catholic doctrine of the Real Presence as heretics were condemned 'who confess not the Eucharist to be the flesh of our Saviour Jesus Christ, which suffered for our sins, and which the Father, of His goodness, raised up again'.[68] But he does not emphasise the sacrificial nature of the Eucharist as an act of worship. This is a doctrine drawn out later to become more explicit.

Thus the elders in the theology of orders of Ignatius are principally collaborators with the bishop, the 'high priest' in the Sanhedrin. Even in the Jerusalem of the pre-70 hierarchy, the principle role of the high priest would be that of the religious leader of the Jewish community, even if he also had an important liturgical role in the sacrificial liturgy. The role of the deacons likewise would have been as assistants of the priests. As the Old Testament sacrificial system based in Jerusalem became more and more of a memory, even during the lifetime of Ignatius, the sacrificial aspects of the threefold order of bishop, presbyter and deacon came more and more to the fore. Christianity became self-contained as a liturgical system, in fulfilment of the Old Law.

Similarly, Ignatius would have seen no need to stress his links with the apostle Peter, since they would have been obvious to everyone, granted that he was the second

Episcopal successor to Peter at Antioch. A century later, however, such a link would need to be stressed. It is therefore not at all surprising that it is Irenaeus of Lyons who gives us the clearest concept of succession from apostles. If Ignatius gives us the earliest testimony to the threefold ministry, it is to Irenaeus that we look for the origins of apostolic succession; and Irenaeus, we repeat, claims a direct link to the apostles themselves through Polycarp of Smyrna and so linked up with John the Son of Zebedee. So now we must return to Irenaeus and church history before and subsequent to him, to examine the concept of apostolic authority in more depth, and in particular the primacy of Rome.

## Notes

1   On this whole question of apostolic succession and the succession of the threefold ministry of bishop, priest, and deacon, I recommend first as a catechetical summary a reading of my *What is Catholicism: Hard Questions—Straight Answers*. (Huntingdon, Indiana: Our Sunday Visitor Publishing Division, 1997), in answer to the question No. 26, p. 117, It is clear from historical studies that there is no evidence of the universal practice of 'monarchical episcopacy' (i.e. one bishop over each local church) before the middle of the second century. How, then, can the Roman Catholic Church claim that the bishops are, as a college, the successors of the apostles?

2   INT, note 19, p. 63.

3   'More than one of the earliest ecclesiastical writers have given credence, though apparently without good reason, to the legend that Ignatius was the child whom the Savior took up in His arms, as described in Mark 9:35. It is also believed, and with great probability, that, with his friend Polycarp, he was among the auditors of the Apostle St. John. If we include St. Peter, Ignatius was the third Bishop of Antioch and the immediate successor of Evodius (Eusebius, Church History, II.3.22). Theodoret (*Dial. Immutab.*, I, iv, 33a, Paris, 1642) is the authority for the statement that St. Peter appointed Ignatius to the See of Antioch. St. John Chrysostom lays special emphasis on the honour conferred upon the martyr in receiving his episcopal consecration at the hands of the Apostles themselves (*Hom. in St. Ig.*, IV. 587). Natalis Alexander quotes Theodoret to the same effect (III, xii, art. xvi, p. 53).' Art. Ignatius of Antioch, *Catholic*

Encyclopaedia, http://www.newadvent.org/cathen/07644a.htm [accessed 21.02.2013].

4   J. Redford, *What is Catholicism?: Hard Questions, Straight Answers*, (Huntingdon, Indiana: Our Sunday Visitor Publishing Division, 1997), p. 119.
5   H. Küng, *The Church*, (London, Burns and Oates, 1968). This book was given the *nihil obstat* and the *imprimatur* by the Westminster archdiocese, cf. the page after the title page. One wonders whether the one appointed as diocesan censor of this book could have read it, since, as we shall clearly see, it denies a defined dogma of the Church!
6   Küng, *Infallible? An Enquiry*. Trans. E. Mosbacher. (London, Collins, 1971). The *imprimatur* was not given to this book, whether such ecclesastical approval was sought or not.
7   http://en.wikipedia.org/wiki/Hans_K%C3%BCng [accessed 21.02.2013]
8   Küng, *The Catholic Church: A Short History* (2002), Introduction, p. xviii.
9   Vatican I, Session 4, Chapter 4. Tanner, II, p. *816.
10  LG 25, Tanner II, p. *869.
11  *Ibid.*, p. *870.
12  Kung, *The Church*, 16.
13  Vatican II, *Dei Verbum*, 9.
14  Trent, Session 4, 1546, Acceptance of the sacred books and apostolic traditions. Tanner, II, p. *663.
15  Kung, *The Church*, p. 353.
16  *Ibid.*, p. 354.
17  *Ibid.*, p. 355.
18  *Ibid.*
19  *Ibid.*, p. 358.
20  *Ibid.*, p. 404.
21  *Ibid.*
22  *Ibid.*, p. 405.
23  *Ibid.*, p. 402.
24  *Concise Oxford Dictionary* (Oxford, Clarendon Press, 1990, p. 946, entry *Priest*.
25  Regarding 1 Corinthians, 'AUTHENTICITY: Not seriously disputed'. Brown, INT, p. 512. Regarding 2 Corinthians, 'Although there is no doubt that Paul wrote II Cor, transitions from one part of the letter to the other have been judged so abrupt that many scholars would chop it up into once-independent pieces.' Brown, INT, p. 539.
26  Kung, *The Church*, p. 403.
27  *Ibid.*

28. Ibid.
29. Pope Clement I, *Letter to the Corinthians*, 57 as found on http://www.catholic-forum.com/saints/stc14001.htm [accessed 21.02.2013]
30. NJBC, **60:2**, p. 920, 'the identity of the author of Hebrews is unknown...'
31. Authorship by the apostle John was accepted by Irenaeus, Justin Martyr, Hyppolytus and Tertullian. *Ibid*, **63:7**, p. 997.
32. *Ibid.*, 'In the prologue of Rev (1:1–3) the author is simply referred to as God's servant (v.1). He does not call himself an apostle or a disciple of Jesus. He does not even claim the title prophet, although he is closely associated with prophets and prophecy in the text (**10:11**, 229). He authorizes his message by describing its heavenly origin.'
33. *Ibid.*, **58:2, p.** 909: '...Who is this James? Is he actually the author of the epistle?...'
34. INT, pp. 748–750.
35. NTI.
36. *Ibid.*, pp. 445–452.
37. *Ibid.*, p. 448.
38. *Ibid*, p. 506.
39. *Ibid*, p. 519.
40. Pope Pius XII, *Divino Afflante Spiritu*, 38.
41. NTI, p. 448.
42. New York, Doubleday, 1997. Note that this book has been given the *imprimatur*; i.e. 'it may be printed', it has passed the diocesan censor and been given episcopal approval, that nothing is in it contrary to Catholic faith or morals.
43. Brown, INT, p. 675.
44. Cf. discussion in INT, pp. 645–648.
45. *Ibid.*, pp. 667–8.
46. *Ibid.*, p. 705.
47. *Ibid.*, p. 718.
48. *Ibid.*, p. 767.
49. *Ibid.*, p. 509.
50. *Ibid.*, p. 514. Eusebius of Caesarea considered it spurious, while Cyril of Jerusalem and Jerome considered it canonical and authentic.
51. *Ibid.*, p. 767. 'Thus a date of 130, give or take a decade, would best fit the evidence'.
52. *Ibid.*, p. 762.
53. *Ibid.*, p. 506.
54. *Ibid.*, p. 508.
55. *Ibid.*, p. 721. 'If the letter was pseudonymous, written by a disciple, its range would be 70 100'.
56. *Ibid.*, p. 719.

57. http://en.wikipedia.org/wiki/Trajan [accessed 21.02.2013].
58. http://www.newadvent.org/cathen/07644a.htm Ignatius. [accessed 21.02.2013].
59. http://www.newadvent.org/cathen/07644a.htm Ignatius. [accessed 21.02.2013].
60. http://www.earlychurch.org.uk/ignatius.php [accessed 21.02.2013].
61. http://www.newadvent.org/fathers/0105.htm Epistle of Ignatius. [accessed 21.02.2013].
62. Saint Ignatius of Antioch, *Letter to the Trallians*.
63. St Ignatius of Antioch, *Letter to the Ephesians*, 2.2.–5.2. *The Divine Office*, Volume I, London, Collins, 1974, 410.
64. P. Hughes, *A History of the Church. Volume 1, The World in which the Church Was Founded*. (London: Sheed and Ward, 1979), p. 50.
65. *http://www.earlychurch.org.uk/clemrome.php [accessed 21.02.2013]* G. Uhlhorn, 'CLEMENS ROMANUS,' P. Schaff, ed., *A Religious Encyclopaedia or Dictionary of Biblical, Historical, Doctrinal, and Practical Theology*, 3rd ed., Vol. 1. (Toronto, New York & London: Funk & Wagnalls Company, 1894). pp. 492–494.
66. ODP, p. 8.
67. J. Redford, *What is Catholicism? Hard Questions–Straight Answers*, (Huntingdon, Indiana: Our Sunday Visitor Publishing Division, 1997), p. 119.
68. http://www.newadvent.org/fathers/0109.htm Epistle of Ignatius. [accessed 21.02.2013].

# 9

# THE PRIMACY OF PETER

## PART ONE:
## THE NEW TESTAMENT EVIDENCE

### 9.1 THE TEXTS

*The First Vatican Council defined the dogma that Jesus handed on the primacy of the universal church to Simon Peter.*[1]

> The First Vatican Council, Session 4: 18 July 1870
> First Dogmatic Constitution on the Church of Christ
> Chapter 1
> On the institution of the apostolic primacy
> in blessed Peter
>
> 1. We teach and declare that, according to the gospel evidence, a primacy of jurisdiction over the whole Church of God was immediately and directly promised to the apostle Peter and conferred on him by Christ the Lord.
> *Docemus itaque et declaramus, iuxta evangelii testimonia primatum iurisdictionis in universam Dei ecclesiam immediate et directe beato Petro apostolo promissum atque collatum a Christo domino fuisse.*
> 2. It was to Simon alone, to whom he had already said You shall be called Cephas, that the Lord, after his confession, You are the Christ, the son of the living God, spoke these words: Blessed are you, Simon Bar-Jona. For flesh and blood has not revealed this to you, but my Father who is in heaven. And I tell you, you are Peter, and on this rock I will build my Church,

> and the gates of the underworld shall not prevail against it. I will give you the keys of the kingdom of heaven, and whatever you bind on earth shall be bound in heaven, and whatever you loose on earth shall be loosed in heaven.
>
> 3. And it was to Peter alone that Jesus, after his resurrection, confided the jurisdiction of Supreme Pastor and ruler of his whole fold, saying: Feed my lambs, feed my sheep.
>
> 4. To this absolutely manifest teaching of the Sacred Scriptures, as it has always been understood by the Catholic Church, are clearly opposed the distorted opinions of those who misrepresent the form of government which Christ the Lord established in his Church and deny that Peter, in preference to the rest of the apostles, taken singly or collectively, was endowed by Christ with a true and proper primacy of jurisdiction.
>
> 5. The same may be said of those who assert that this primacy was not conferred immediately and directly on blessed Peter himself, but rather on the Church, and that it was through the Church that it was transmitted to him in his capacity as her minister.
>
> 6. Therefore, if anyone says that blessed Peter the apostle was not appointed by Christ the Lord as prince of all the apostles and visible head of the whole Church militant; or that it was a primacy of honour only and not one of true and proper jurisdiction that he directly and immediately received from our Lord Jesus Christ himself: let him be anathema.

## 9.2 INTRODUCTION

*We cannot exclude at least the possibility from the outset of our investigation that the conferring by the historical Jesus of the primacy upon the historical Peter is the actual meaning of Matthew 16:17–19.*

In one sense, the above definition of the First Vatican Council is the most important statement about the role of Peter, and then subsequently by implication as later affirmed by the same Council about his successor the Bishop of Rome, that the Magisterium has ever made. Later, that same Council was to define that the Pope was infallible, a definition which was much more controversial. However it could well be argued that the doctrine of the primacy of the Pope is more important than the doctrine of his infallibility. First, it could be argued that the Pope only has such infallibility because, having primacy over the infallible Magisterium of the bishops as successors of the apostles, he can under certain conditions exercise that role without their explicit agreement. Secondly, and perhaps more important, the exercise of his ordinary primacy over the whole church is ongoing and daily, whereas the occasions where the Pope will exercise the prerogative of infallible decisions are severely limited (so far, only twice in the past one hundred and sixty years, with the defined dogmas of the Immaculate Conception 1854,[2] and the Assumption 1950).[3]

At the time of the definition, the primacy of the Pope was less politically controversial. The secular rulers of Europe saw the doctrine of the infallibility of the Pope as an attack on democracy, restricting freedom of thought. However perhaps they could sleep more easily concerning the doctrine of the primacy of the Pope, since this more obviously gave him authority to govern the Roman Catholic Church, and need not have too many political implications concerning his authority outside the confines of the Church.

During the twentieth century, with the ecumenical movement, the primacy of the Pope became more of an issue. Anglicans and the Orthodox would grant the Bishop of Rome primacy of honour because of his historic role as Bishop of the Apostolic See of Rome, but only as the 'first among equals' within the college of bishops. They would not grant him primacy of authority in matters of church doctrine and discipline.[4]

After the controversial papal encyclical *Humanae Vitae*, promulgated by Pope Paul VI in 1968[5] the whole question of dissent from the teaching of the Church, especially its moral teaching, was much more openly debated within the

Church. Today, there are those within the Catholic Church who consider it their right publicly to dissent from teaching clearly promulgated by the Magisterium of the Bishop of Rome on the grounds of religious liberty.[6] Pope Paul VI, in *Humanae Vitae*, on the contrary, claims that:

> This kind of question requires from the teaching authority of the Church a new and deeper reflection on the principles of the moral teaching on marriage —a teaching which is based on the natural law as illuminated and enriched by divine Revelation.[7]

Since the Pope is not claiming infallibility here (and, all agree, for a statement itself to be considered infallible by the Pope there must be an explicit statement declaring such, for example in the statement of the dogma of the Assumption)[8] then in this case it follows that the Pope is demanding obedience from Catholics for a matter concerning their salvation not from his infallible Magisterium, but from his ordinary jurisdiction as the Successor of Peter. Such obedience to the teaching of the Pope comes under the definition of 'religious submission of mind and will', as Vatican IIs Dogmatic Constitution on the Church affirms:

> This religious submission of mind and will must be shown in a special way to the authentic Magisterium of the Roman Pontiff, even when he is not speaking *ex cathedra*... [9]

This therefore brings to the fore the importance of the teaching of the Church that the Bishop of Rome as the successor of Peter has ordinary jurisdiction over the bishops of the Catholic Church and over all the faithful. This teaching Vatican I states infallibly comes directly from Jesus himself. The Council relates this teaching as the authentic interpretation of Matthew 16:12–20, as the Vatican I text we have quoted above explicitly affirms. The First Vatican Council would therefore seem clearly to have defined that the historical Jesus while on earth made Simon Peter head of the Church on earth, which primacy Peter would assume after Jesus rose from the dead and returned in glory to his Father in heaven.

Of course, classical Protestantism has always conducted a vigorous apologetic against this interpretation of the Petrine text in Matthew. The most general objection has been that Jesus did not give Peter jurisdiction over the church, but that Peter's faith was to be the rock on which the Church was to be built. Peter's faith was a type of belief which was to be the foundation of the church. Others such as Cullmann argued that Jesus gave Peter jurisdiction over the church after his death and resurrection, but this jurisdiction was not given to successors of Peter as Bishops of Rome. Such a view we must discuss later when we consider the Petrine succession. For the moment, the question is this; is there exegetical evidence that the historical Jesus gave primacy of jurisdiction to Peter over all the other apostles?

## 9.3 PETER IN THE NEW TESTAMENT

*We will use as our starting-point for examination the ecumenical study Peter in the New Testament. While admiring the competence of the study, we do question whether it is impossible to demonstrate that the Petrine text originally did mean that the primacy in Matthew was given to Peter.*

Our text for discussion of this question will be *Peter in the New Testament: A Collaborative Assessment by Protestant and Roman Catholic Scholars* edited by R. E. Brown, K. P. Donfried, and J. Reumann, Minneapolis: Augsburg Publishing House, 1973. Without doubt, this study was of the greatest importance both as an expression of common views among critical scholars about the role of Peter in the New Testament, and as relevant for the study of ecclesiology. The fact that agreement was reached concerning important issues was significant ecumenically and in terms of biblical studies. We will note those agreements where relevant to our purpose.

However, at the same time, we must also note the limitations of that study, and indeed possible disagreements with it. The biggest disagreement we must immediately note is concerning possible conclusions of the study of *Peter in the New Testament* (hence PNT). The participants in the study immediately assert: 'The whole tone of the theological discussion in this National Dialogue has been set by an effort to see in a *new* light the old problems that have separated the churches'.[10] To this end, 'The norm was not total agreement, but a consensus about the reasonable limits of plausibility'.[11]

This seems to be a reasonable methodology for an ecumenical study of biblical texts. We shall see later one or two examples where the Group have reached conclusions which do indeed put the person and role of Peter in a new light, helpful for all the churches. But one must register disagreement with the fact that the group have it seems excluded even the possibility that the New Testament, and particularly Matthew 16, see Jesus giving the primacy to Peter:

> No matter what one may think about the justification offered by the New Testament for the emergency of the papacy, this papacy in its developed form cannot be read back into the New Testament; and it will help neither papal opponents nor papal supporters to have the model of the later papacy before their eyes when discussing the role of Peter. For that very reason we have tended to avoid 'loaded' terminology in reference to Peter, e.g. primacy, jurisdiction. Too often in the past, arguments about whether or not Peter had a "universal primacy" have blinded scholars to a more practical agreement about such things as the widely accepted importance of Peter in the New Testament and his diversified image.[12]

That may be true. However is it *a priori* impossible that the historical Jesus actually gave to the historical Peter the 'universal primacy' that is rule over his church? Could that not be precisely what the historical Jesus actually intended for his church? We quote the wise words of the Anglican N. T. Wright '... we should not be thrown out of gear by the anti-ecclesiastical mood of some contemporary writers, who have amused themselves by creating a straw man ('Jesus came to found the church, complete with buildings, bishops, cardinals and candlesticks') and then knocking it down with a supposedly neutral and disinterested enquiry.'[13] We are not arguing for cardinal's birettas in the New Testament. It may well be also that it would have been impossible in any case for a group of Lutheran scholars to agree with Catholic scholars as to the Petrine primacy, which would have implied church change for them. However surely it is not true necessarily that belief in the Petrine primacy, of Peter's universal jurisdiction, is 'read back into the New Testament' if that is in fact what the text means, and even if the text does not use specific Latin ecclesiastical legal terms customary in a later generation.

We must also note at the beginning the limitations of biblical exegesis itself. The Second Vatican Council clearly states 'Consequently it is not from Sacred Scripture alone that the Church draws her certainty about everything which has been revealed.'[14] From this flows the need, according to Vatican II on revelation, for Sacred Tradition. It would be difficult to find any text of the Bible where scholars have reached unanimous agreement as to its meaning. Our purpose will be therefore to discover the most plausible interpretation of a passage, and, where that interpretation is the most plausible, to call tradition to our aid, in the sense that text has been lived out in the history of the Church.

## 9.4 THE PRIMACY TEXTS IN THE SYNOPTIC GOSPELS

*Since our primary concern is the exegetical testing of the affirmation of the primacy of Peter in the First Vatican Council, we will first set out the text in Matthew 16:13–23, together with its parallels in Mark 8:27–33 and Luke 9:18–23:*

| Matthew 16:13-23 | Mark 8:27-33 | Luke 9:18-23 |
|---|---|---|
| Now when Jesus came into the district of Caesarea Philippi, he asked his disciples, 'Who do men say that the Son of man is?' And they said, 'Some say John the Baptist, others say Elijah, and others Jeremiah or one of the prophets.' He said to them, 'But who do you say that I am?' Simon Peter replied, 'You are the Christ, the Son of the living God.' And Jesus answered him, 'Blessed are you, Simon Barjona! For flesh and blood has not revealed this to you, but my Father who is in heaven. And I tell you, you are Peter, and on this rock I will build my church, and the powers of death shall not prevail against it. I will give you the keys of the kingdom of heaven, and whatever you bind on earth shall be bound in heaven, and whatever you loose on earth shall be loosed in heaven.' Then he strictly charged the disciples to tell no one that he was the Christ. From that time Jesus began to show his disciples that he must go to Jerusalem and suffer many things from the elders and chief priests and scribes, and be killed, and on the third day be raised. And Peter took him and began to rebuke him, saying, 'God forbid, Lord! This shall never happen to you.' But he turned and said to Peter, 'Get behind me, Satan! You are a hindrance to me; for you are not on the side of God, but of men.' | And Jesus went on with his disciples, to the villages of Caesarea Philippi; and on the way he asked his disciples, 'Who do men say that I am?' And they told him, 'John the Baptist; and others say, Elijah; and others one of the prophets.' And he asked them, 'But who do you say that I am?' Peter answered him, 'You are the Christ.' And he charged them to tell no one about him. And he began to teach them that the Son of man must suffer many things, and be rejected by the elders and the chief priests and the scribes, and be killed, and after three days rise again. And he said this plainly. And Peter took him, and began to rebuke him. But turning and seeing his disciples, he rebuked Peter, and said, 'Get behind me, Satan! For you are not on the side of God, but of men.' | Now it happened that as he was praying alone the disciples were with him; and he asked them, 'Who do the people say that I am?' And they answered, 'John the Baptist; but others say, Elijah; and others, that one of the old prophets has risen.' And he said to them, 'But who do you say that I am?' And Peter answered, 'The Christ of God.' But he charged and commanded them to tell this to no one, saying, 'The Son of man must suffer many things, and be rejected by the elders and chief priests and scribes, and be killed, and on the third day be raised.' And he said to all, 'If any man would come after me, let him deny himself and take up his cross daily and follow me. |

## 9.5 MATTHEW'S ADDED RESPONSE

*Matthew's added response, 16:17–19, as an Aramaic addition, clearly pre-dates the written Gospel, and reflects at least one section of the early Palestinian Christian community which held that Peter had a special role in the Church given to him by the Lord Jesus*

Matthew has added the response of Jesus to Peter, making Peter the 'Rock' after Peter confesses Jesus as the Son of the living God:

> And Jesus answered him, 'Blessed are you, Simon Barjona! For flesh and blood has not revealed this to you, but my Father who is in heaven. And I tell you, you are Peter, and on this rock I will build my church, and the powers of death shall not prevail against it. I will give you the keys of the kingdom of heaven, and whatever you bind on earth shall be bound in heaven, and whatever you loose on earth shall be loosed in heaven.' (Mt 16:17–19)

Matthew also adds with Mark Peter's refusal to accept the suffering Son of Man: 'But he turned and said to Peter, "Get behind me, Satan! You are a hindrance to me; for you are not on the side of God, but of men."' (Mk 8:33). As PNT says, 'It is significant that, despite the way Matthew has magnified Peter in the special material he has inserted into the Marcan scene of Peter's confession, he has also kept and indeed heightened the rebuke of Peter at the end of the scene (Mt 16:23=Mk 9:33).'[15]

PNT concludes from this that 'in 16:17 Matthew has redactionally brought together elements that came to him from an earlier tradition. In so doing he has produced a verse that gives Peter a special distinction: he is the only disciple in the Gospels who is the named recipient of a dominical blessing, and his insight about Jesus is confirmed as being a revelation from Jesus' Father.'[16] As we have seen,

Beare does not consider that this text comes from the historical Jesus; but he does at least have to admit that 'The language of these verses (17—19) is entirely Semitic in tone; it cannot be doubted that it has been drawn by Matthew from an Aramaic source, and that it originated in some debate within the Palestinian community.'[17]

The Matthean pericope about Peter being named by Jesus as 'the Rock', therefore, pre-dates the written Gospel of Matthew, published in its first edition towards the end of the first century AD. If, as Beare says, this is evidence of a 'debate within the Palestinian community', then we have no record in any of the Gospels or in the New Testament itself, or indeed in the tradition of the Church, of Jesus naming anyone else, more specifically among the Twelve, as being the 'Rock'. Peter, and Peter alone, has been given this unique title.

PNT points out that the theological view, so much held by Protestant exegetes, that Peter's faith is the Rock on which the church is to be built 'is an ancient view attested in many Church Fathers (Origen, Eusebius, Ambrose, Theodore of Mopsuestia, Chrysostom, etc.)'.[18] Indeed, this view is totally correct. It *is* Peter's confession in Christ as the Son of God which is to be the foundation of the Church. 'For nobody can lay down any other foundation than the one which is there already, namely Jesus Christ.' (Cf. 1 Co 3:11)

However does this undoubted truth, that Christian faith in Jesus as the Son of God first professed in the Gospels by Peter, is the foundation of the Church, exhaust the meaning of the words of Christ to Peter, 'You are Peter, and on this Rock I will build my church'? Here the Catholic exegete would justifiably take issue. The texts in Matthew where Jesus explained Peter's role, in my opinion, makes it clear beyond any reasonable exegetical doubt that Jesus is giving Peter the leadership of his Church.

## 9.6 THE MESSIAH AND THE ROCK

*First, it seems clear that in calling Simon Peter 'the Rock', Jesus is giving Peter a title in response to his naming Jesus with his title 'you are the Christ, the Son of the living God'.*

As Lagrange says, '*petros* does not exist as a proper name either in Greek, or in Latin, and it cannot be derived from the Latin *Petronius.*'[19] Jesus is saying "Simon, you are the Rock" in response to Peter's "You are the Christ....". To say that Jesus was simply giving Simon a nickname would be to trivialize the response of Jesus. That 'Peter' is a title agrees with the parallelism in the Fourth Gospel account of the call of the disciples:

| Matthew 16:15-18 | John 1:41-42 |
| --- | --- |
| He said to them, 'But who do you say that I am?' Simon Peter replied, 'You are the Christ, the Son of the living God.' And Jesus answered him, 'Blessed are you, Simon Barjona! For flesh and blood has not revealed this to you, but my Father who is in heaven. And I tell you, you are Peter, and on this rock I will build my church, and the powers of death shall not prevail against it. | He first found his brother Simon, and said to him, 'We have found the Messiah' (which means Christ). He brought him to Jesus. Jesus looked at him, and said, 'So you are Simon the son of John? You shall be called Cephas' (which means Peter). |

For his Greek-speaking readers, John gives a translation from the Hebrew or Aramaic of the titles, *Christos* for Messiah and *Cephas* for Rock. After the resurrection of Jesus and Pentecost, in the early Christian community, Peter was called by the Aramaic form of Jesus' title for Peter, Cephas (Jn 1:42, Ga 1:18, 2:9, 1 Co 9:5). However we note that Jesus called Peter by his actual name Simon.

In Matthew, there is a distinction in the Greek which would not be possible when Jesus addressed Simon and called him Cephas in Aramaic. *So I now say to you: You are*

*Peter (petros) and on this rock (petra) I will build my church...*
As Lagrange says, 'But petros applies more to a man, and petra applies more to the founder of the church. In Aramaic, one cannot make this distinction'.[20] The historical Jesus would have said 'You are Cephas, and on this Cephas I will build my church.'

For PNT,[21] this play on words in the Greek Matthew is yet another demonstration that Matthew is dependant on an earlier Aramaic tradition of Jesus' words. Matthew, by the time of the writing of his Gospel towards the end of the first century, a generation and more after the time of the historical Jesus, is already assuming that *petros* is a common name, and wishes to use *petra*, meaning 'small stone', as a description of the role of one who is himself so small and insignificant yet is given the power by Jesus to become the 'rock' on which the church is to be built. Foundation stones are not necessarily large, but are the key for the building to become a solid structure.

## 9.7 THE CONFESSION OF THE HISTORICAL PETER

*We argue that the historical Peter professed his faith in Jesus as Messiah during the public ministry of Jesus, even though it was perhaps only after the resurrection that he understood Jesus to be the divine Son of God.*

Beare in his commentary on Matthew rejects completely the idea that the historical Jesus claimed to be the Messiah. Thus we would not be surprised also to read that he rejects equally that the historical Peter claimed that Jesus was the Messiah. However, we have on the contrary concluded with Bockmuehl and N. T. Wright, that Jesus did claim to be the Messiah.[22] If Jesus claimed in his early ministry that the kingdom of God was associated with his healing and preaching ministry, as historical Jesus scholars admitted, and even was accepted as authentic by the *Jesus Seminar* (Lk

11:19–20)[23] then what meaning could this have but as Bockmuel says 'Messianic connotations'?[24]

That the historical Peter claimed that Jesus was the Messiah at least fulfils one of the criteria of authenticity, namely that of multiple attestation,[25] being both in John and, as we have seen setting out the texts in parallel, in all the Synoptic accounts, "You are the Christ, the Son of the living God." (Mt 16:16), "You are the Christ" (Mk 8:29), and, "The Christ of God," he (Peter) said (Lk 9:20).

Bultmann is equally convinced as is Beare that Peter's confession of faith in Jesus is a 'legend of faith'.[26] However, Bultmann interprets Peter's confession not so much as Messiah rather as Peter understanding Jesus as the Hellenistic 'archetypal man'.[27] However is it not possible that during Jesus' public ministry on earth, Peter understood Jesus as very much a Jewish Messiah, as we have posited,[28] which makes the text in John closest to the pre-death and Resurrection historical reality where Peter says simply to Jesus 'you are the Messiah'? I would suggest that it is most feasible that during the life of the historical Jesus Peter professed Jesus as a Messiah in Jewish terms; but that as time went on, as Jesus was transfigured on the holy mountain, walked on the water, and fed the multitude, even while the earthly Jesus was alive Peter began to consider that Jesus was more than just the Messiah. After the Resurrection, Peter's faith in the divinity of Jesus became secure. This would easily explain the different terms in the Synoptic accounts, a terminology which reflects Peter's own developing Christology.

When Peter understood the divinity of Christ, most clearly after the Resurrection, he would have had in mind not at all the Hellenistic 'archetypal man', but rather the Christ who said very much in Jewish terms 'I and the Father are One', and 'Before Abraham was, I AM'[29]. This seems to be a most reasonable conclusion after consideration of the critical evidence.

## 9.8 SIMON 'THE ROCK'

*In Jesus calling Simon 'the Rock', and giving him the power of the keys, is he giving Peter juridical and legal authority? At first sight, at least, it seems that he is. 'Binding and loosing' appears to be a juridical authority; but is that authority given to Peter alone, or also to the other members of the Twelve?*

If then we accept the authenticity of Peter's naming Jesus as Messiah, we now consider the response of Jesus in Matthew 'So I now say to you: You are Peter and on this rock I will build my community. And the gates of the underworld can never overpower it. I will give you the keys of the kingdom of Heaven: whatever you bind on earth will be bound in heaven; whatever you loose on earth will be loosed in heaven.' (Mt 16:18–19). Was Jesus here making Peter the leader of the church on earth, or as Vatican I would put it, giving him the 'primacy'?

We must assert that, even if the historical Jesus did not pronounce the above words, as Beare contends, Matthew is reflecting a very early Aramaic tradition, well before the end of the first century. This means that a community within the early church of sufficient significance to influence the writing of Matthew's Gospel believed that Peter was made the Rock on which the church of Jesus was to be built, and that the keys of the kingdom of heaven were to be given to him.

That Jesus made Peter the leader of the Church in calling him 'the Rock' coheres with Peter's role in John's Gospel. Bultmann, perhaps surprisingly, insists that the Gospel of John also considered that Peter had been made the leader of the Church by Jesus, when Jesus commanded Peter three times to feed his sheep (Jn 21:15–17).[30] If Bultmann is correct, therefore, we have two strong strands of tradition in the early Christian community, the Johannine and the Matthean, both of which see Peter as appointed by Jesus as leader of the Christian community.

In this designation of Peter, there is presented in the Gospels no rivals to his leadership. Some have seen in the elevation of the 'beloved disciple' in John a rival to Peter in the Fourth Gospel, you might say a 'Petrine' and a 'Johannine' party. However after a long discussion, PNT concludes that 'To speak of rivalry is probably an exaggeration, if it implies polemic or animosity, since that would not be true to the Johannine portrait of Simon Peter. At most, we might say that this community has placed its apostolic figure (the Beloved Disciple) on a pedestal by showing him to be of competitive importance with Simon Peter, the most famous figure from the ministry of Jesus known to the church at large.'[31]

Nevertheless, the Beloved Disciple in the Fourth Gospel is never given authority over the Church by the risen Jesus as is Peter in John. Nor is anyone else of the Twelve. We thus may now turn to Matthew's account, and ask whether Matthew sees Peter as being made leader of his church when he names Peter the 'Rock' and promises him the keys of the kingdom of heaven.

Prescinding, again, from the question as to whether or not the historical Jesus gave to Peter the power of the keys and the authority to open and close, it seems to me as exegetically almost as certain as we can be that Matthew is presenting Jesus as giving a juridical and legal authority to Peter. PNT makes the point that, whereas the power of binding and loosing is given also to the other disciples ('In truth I tell you, whatever you bind on earth will be bound in heaven; whatever you loose on earth will be loosed in heaven' Mt 18:8), Jesus' promise to Peter 'I will give you the keys of the kingdom of heaven…' is made to Peter alone.[32] PNT therefore asks the question as to whether the two powers, that of the keys and that of binding and loosing, are the same. 'If the two powers are the same, then all the disciples received the power of the keys.'[33] If, however, the 'power of the keys' has a meaning in addition to the power of binding and loosing, then that provides demonstration of the uniqueness of Peter's role, *vis à vis* even the other disciples.

## 9.9 MATTHEW 16 AND ISAIAH 22

*It is clear from a comparison between Matthew 16:18–19 and Isaiah 22:19–23 that Jesus is giving Peter the authority of the leadership of the Church in his place.*

PNT correctly realizes that a possible clue to understanding the power of the keys is 'that the verse is evocative of Isaiah 22:15–25, where Shebna, prime minister of King Hezekiah of Judah, is deposed and replaced by Eliakim on whose shoulder God places "the *key* of David; he shall *open*...and he shall shut."'[34] I have never understood why this link with Isaiah 22:15–25 is seen only as a 'possible key to understanding the power of the keys'. It seems to me that, if we set out the verses in parallel, it is the only possible understanding of the power of the keys. The prophet thunders a proclamation that the corrupt official Shebna is to be replaced by Eliakim son of Hilkiah:

| Matthew 16:19 and 16:18 | Isaiah 22:19-23 |
| --- | --- |
| I will give you the keys of the kingdom of heaven, and whatever you bind on earth shall be bound in heaven, and whatever you loose on earth shall be loosed in heaven.' And I tell you, you are Peter, and on this rock I will build my church, and the powers of death shall not prevail against it. | I will thrust you from your office, and you will be cast down from your station. In that day I will call my servant Eliakim the son of Hilkiah, and I will clothe him with your robe, and will bind your girdle on him, and will commit your authority to his hand; and he shall be a father to the inhabitants of Jerusalem and to the house of Judah. And I will place on his shoulder the key of the house of David; he shall open, and none shall shut; and he shall shut, and none shall open. |

The relationship between Isaiah and Matthew becomes clear when we simply reverse verses 18 and 19 of Matthew's account. Like Eliakim, Peter represents his disgraced predecessor Shebnah, but in this case his Lord Jesus.

As Lagrange says,

> This passage is applied by the Apocalypse 3:7 to Jesus himself ("Write to the angel of the church in Philadelphia and say, 'Here is the message of the holy and true one who has the key of David, so that when he opens, no one will close, and when he closes, no one will open'"). Jesus is the foundation, and Peter is the foundation; Jesus has the key of David and Peter has the key of David; the authority of Peter is therefore that of Jesus. The measures that he adopts on earth as faithful major-domo (cf. Lk 12:42) are ratified in heaven, that is to say by God. The idea can be found in Makkot 23$^b$, where three decisions of the tribunal below are confirmed by the tribunal on high (Wünsche, p. 195).[35]

Lagrange goes on to uncover the various meanings of 'binding and loosing'. 'Binding' could have the legal meaning of 'preventing' or 'permitting', or even of putting one into prison or releasing him.[36] But for Lagrange, 'It seems, therefore, to take these two words in the widest sense which takes in all possible applications to the power of the major-domo. He renders speculative solutions, he declares innocent or culpable, he punishes or he exercises mercy; after the new spirit taught by Jesus, these speculative solutions are not restricted to textual commentary according to the tradition; nothing prevents the inclusion of a legislative power'. For Lagrange, this implies necessarily that Peter has the 'doctrinal and juridical authority'[37] of a major-domo.

PNT concludes regarding the relationship between Isaiah 22 and Matthew 16:

> But the Isaian scene is only one suggestion for a possible background of vs. 19, and the thesis that the

power of binding and loosing is a specification of the power of the keys is only one possible approach.[38]

However, PNT does not give us any alternatives to a Catholic interpretation of Matthew 16:19; and, it seems to me, it would be difficult to find one. As it stands, the text clearly states that Matthew is presenting Jesus as making Peter his successor with the powers of a major-domo. This is a power which other disciples apparently are not given. Only to Peter are the powers of binding and loosing related to his overall authority over the house of Jesus as having the power of the keys, that is a doctrinal and legislative power.

## 9.10 DID THE HISTORICAL JESUS GIVE PETER JURISDICTION OVER HIS CHURCH?

*The historical Jesus gave the historical Peter jurisdiction over his church in succession to him. Jesus did in fact found a Church during his lifetime, even if its fulfilment only occurred after his death and resurrection.*

We now consider the thorny question of whether the historical Jesus actually told Peter that on him as Rock he would build his Church, that the gates of hell would not prevail against it, and that what he bound on earth would be considered bound in heaven, and what he loosed on earth would be considered loosed in heaven.

As we shall now see, PNT discusses at some length Cullmann's view of this text, granted the importance of Cullmann as a Protestant exegete and theologian. But also, Cullmann does not contest the meaning of the text as presented by the Gospel of Matthew. His view is that the Matthean redactor has given Matthew 16:19 the juridical meaning which the First Vatican Council insists that Jesus gave to Peter. However this rather takes us into the complex and perhaps never-ending discussion as to whether the historical Jesus said to the historical Peter 'You are Peter, and on this rock I will build my church...'

Moreover, Cullmann draws attention to the relationship between the house of the church (whose building was just mentioned and of which Peter is to be the rock foundation) and the heavenly house of which Peter receives the keys. According to Cullmann, the original meaning was that after the death and resurrection of Jesus, Peter would open the door to the kingdom of heaven by his preaching mission, letting people into the kingdom. In this he would differ from the Pharisees whom Jesus condemned (Matt 23:13) because they closed the door to the kingdom of heaven. The power of binding and loosing, then, would not be so much a specification of a broader power of the keys, but a later pre-Matthean reinterpretation. (Cullmann does not think that 19a was originally joined to 19bc.) A similar thesis of historical reinterpretation would be that the power of the keys originally referred to the power of forgiving sins through baptism, and that this power was later reformulated in terms of the rabbinic pattern of binding and loosing.[39]

Cullmann therefore thinks that the change from Protestant to Catholic took place at the very earliest stage of the apostolic revelation, from an historical Jesus who commanded his disciples only to preach, to a Matthew who added a 'Catholic redaction', turning what was originally only an authority to preach the Word into a juridical authority, such as exists in the Catholic Church today. This is *Urkatholikismus* ('original, early Catholicism') with a vengeance! New Testament criticism has pushed back and back the Catholic tendency which Luther saw in the mediaeval church to claim juridical authority.

Protestant critics such as Ferdinand Christian Baur, as we have seen, regarded this *Urkatholikismus* as reflected in the later New Testament writings such as the Pastoral Epistles, and even in the Acts of the Apostles.[40] Cullmann takes such critique back as far as it can go; to a distinction between the historical Jesus' authentic words and the glosses of the Matthean redactor. This adaptation of the message must have taken place early in the history of the infant church, at least before AD 80 and perhaps much earlier.

John P. Meier equally recognizes that Matthew 16:17–19 must be interpreted as giving Peter juridical authority over the church by Jesus. He even considers seriously that this unique saying in Matthew's account should be accepted as authentically from the historical Jesus:

> The key-like authority of Peter was to be exercised especially in teaching the Israel of the end time the true will of God, i.e., what was permissible or impermissible to do according to God's Law. This power is summed up in allied metaphors of binding (declaring an action illicit or invalid) and loosing (declaring it licit or valid). Peter's authoritative teaching, addressed to us here on earth, would be ratified by God in heaven and so would be a sure defence against the hostile powers of sin and death seeking to destroy the eschatological assembly.

Thus, a plausible case can be made that Matt 16:17–19 is a charge that the historical Jesus gave to the leader of the Twelve during the public ministry. To be sure, Matt 16:17–19 lacks multiple attestation of sources, but critics sometimes accept other sayings of Jesus that lack multiple attestation when the sayings cohere perfectly with Jesus' core message and mission (for example the Lord's Prayer or Jesus' saying on 'the finger of God' in Lk 11:20 par.). In the opinion of various conservative exegetes, Matt 16:17–19 should be accepted on such grounds. At the very least, such arguments show that the passage cannot be simply dismissed with a wave of the hand.[41]

Yet Meier concludes that this text must be post-Easter. Firstly, Meier sees evidence of Matthean redaction in the text, '…which may include even the whole of v. 17'.[42] Secondly, he sees Matthew's use of the word *ekklésia*, 'church' or 'community', as only occurring in the Gospel of Matthew in two texts, otherwise 'the word never appears in the Gospels. It rather occurs throughout Acts, almost all of the Pauline epistles, Hebrews, James, 3 John and the book of Revelation'.[43] *Ekklésia*, Meier argues, is very much a post-Easter word.

Earlier, we considered at least plausible Lagrange's view that Jesus would have founded a Church in his own lifetime.[44] With a large following, perhaps thousands of followers, including 'publicans and sinners', Jesus as the kind of Chief Rabbi of his *qahal* would have exercised authority in that community, perhaps even having ad hoc courts to settle difficult disciplinary matters. Matthew 18:17, 'But if he refuses to listen to these, report it to the ekklésia, and if he refuses to listen to the ekklésia treat him like a gentile or a tax collector' could therefore refer to a primitive kind of court where the Rabbi could excommunicate one who did not follow the Torah and the instructions of his Way. We have been so conditioned to seeing Jesus as a 'marginal Jew', with small groups following him whereas all the evidence tells us that he was recognized as a Rabbi, and that during his public ministry he had a huge following.

If we accept that Jesus did form an *ekklésia* during his lifetime, then what Meier calls Matthew's 'heavy redaction'[45] in 16:17–19 is easily understood. After the Resurrection, as we have seen, Jesus was seen by Peter as not simply the 'Messiah' as in John's Gospel, but as Matthew says 'The Christ, the Son of the living God'. The *ekklésia*, which during Jesus' lifetime was provisional and run according to fairly primitive principles, became more structured, particularly after Paul's Gentile mission. This would easily explain the post-Easter usage and meaning of *ekklésia* in most of the 114 references to the word in the New Testament. Matthew is recalling an authentic saying of the historical Jesus: but his mind is filtering it through his post-Easter understanding of the 'primacy' given to Peter by the Christian Church at the end of the first century.

I repeat that in our *apologia* for the primacy of Peter given by the First Vatican Council, we have not provided an argument which will carry total certainty in the exegetical community. We have also argued that such absolute certainty is not absolutely necessary. If the argument is plausible, then the living and developing tradition of the Church becomes itself an exegesis of the text.

Many modern Catholic exegetes might say that we do not have to demonstrate that the historical Jesus gave the primacy to Peter during his lifetime. Rather, the understanding of the primitive church is adequate. Certainly, if Jesus gave the primacy to Peter after his Resurrection and before his Ascension, as we have found is a reasonable interpretation of John 21:15–17, and even the Petrine text in Matthew is a projection back from a Resurrection decree of Jesus to Peter to a period during his public ministry, then we could say that Jesus in fact gave the primacy to Peter.

I submit, however, that such retrojective interpretations of Matthew 16:17–19 are entirely unnecessary. That text clearly denotes the giving of the primacy of jurisdiction of the Church to Peter; and it is most plausible to ascribe it as authentically from the historical Jesus, during his public ministry, albeit with Matthew's post-Easter redactional interpretation.

## 9.11 DID PAUL ACCEPT THE PRIMACY OF PETER?

*We have no undisputed evidence that Paul accepted the primacy of Peter in the infant universal Church. But neither do we have any evidence that Paul rejected Peter's primacy, only that he criticized Peter in Galatians for going back on his word that Gentile converts to the new faith could eat with Jewish Christians.*

While most New Testament scholars would not call themselves Hegelian, as with the Quest of the Historical Jesus, many of Baur's early critical conclusions about the New Testament have influenced much modern scholarship.[46] We have seen already that there is continued debate concerning the authenticity of the later Pauline epistles. PNT notes much debate concerning the historicity of Acts, and in particular the account of the Council of Jerusalem in Acts 15 of the restrictions placed by that Council on Gentile converts:

> In Paul's own account of his Jerusalem encounters he never mentions any such restrictive regulations. From Galatians 2:9–10 one would get the impression that at the decisive second visit to Jerusalem the Pauline argument for freedom had triumphed completely, under the one condition that "they would have us remember the poor, the very thing I was eager to do".[47]

The PNT Lutheran-Catholic group of scholars concludes: 'Having to choose, then between the Pauline indications and the account of the four regulations in Acts, most scholars suspect the historicity of the Lucan picture.'[48] On the other hand the group admits that there are contrary views, for example. J. Hurd gives what to me is a credible explanation, that Paul 'tried to introduce the Jerusalem decrees, thus arousing the opposition to which he addressed himself in the Corinthian correspondence'.[49] Is there not also the possibility that Paul simply ignored those regulations from the beginning, on the grounds that he was in charge of the Gentile mission? Ignoring Canon Law has not been entirely unknown in the two thousand Christian years. Is this the first example in Christian history?

The other big problem presented by critical scholarship is Paul's opposition to Peter in the letter to the Galatians. Paul complains that at first the Galatian Jewish Christians were eating with the Gentile converts.

> However, when Cephas came to Antioch, then I did oppose him to his face since he was manifestly in the wrong. Before certain people from James came, he used to eat with gentiles; but as soon as these came, he backed out and kept apart from them, out of fear of the circumcised. And the rest of the Jews put on

> the same act as he did, so that even Barnabas was carried away by their insincerity. When I saw, though, that their behaviour was not true to the gospel, I said to Cephas in front of all of them, "Since you, though you are a Jew, live like the gentiles and not like the Jews, how can you compel the gentiles to live like the Jews?" (Ga 2:11–14)

All admit that the fact that Paul represents himself as having the courage, or even the audacity, to oppose Peter, means at least that Paul recognized Peter as an important person in the Jerusalem Church. The problem seems to have been one not of authority but of 'Cephas as acting without principle... Whoever failed to act according to that truth deserved to be reprimanded...'[50] This incident is at least possibly consistent with Peter accepting that circumcision was not necessary then going back on what the Church had decided by separating out Jewish from Gentile Christians at table. This would also be consistent with Paul even recognising the primacy of Peter, yet seeing the need to reprimand his fellow apostle for going back on his word.

## 9.12 THE ROLE OF JAMES

*We also have no evidence that James the 'brother of the Lord' was the superior of Peter, only that James had an important function in the Jerusalem Christian community as an elder, and role possibly as chairman at the Council of Jerusalem.*

The third important question is the role of James, who it seems, makes the final judgement at the Council of Jerusalem ('My verdict is, then...' Ac 15:19). It seems that James, the Lord's relative, had some position of authority in Jerusalem 'The next day Paul went with us to visit James, and all the elders were present' (Ac 21:18). Was James a local leader, the elder of the Church in Jerusalem? And is that why he is allowed to make the canonical judgement giving some restrictions regarding Gentile converts? In this case, even if we accept the primacy of Peter, as today with a General Council, decisions are made by the President of the Council who is not the Pope.

PNT presents more than one possibility regarding the position of James:

- Peter and the other members of the Twelve....were not really local church leaders, 'once Jerusalem became big enough to require such caretakers. James was the first leader of the local church at Jerusalem (or at least for the Hebrew Christians) and remained there after Peter and the other members of the Twelve left the scene...'[51]
- Peter was a local leader in Jerusalem....James took Peter's place as the local Jerusalem leader..... [52]
- Peter was a universal leader, operating from Jerusalem as the centre of Christianity, and was succeeded by James 'when Peter left Jerusalem or even earlier'.[53]

PNT concludes, 'Whichever option one selects as best meeting the evidence, one should remember that Peter still had a position that James did not have—Peter was one of and, indeed ranked first among the Twelve. But James had a position that Peter did not have—James was the "brother of the Lord"'.[54]

Paul, therefore, never says explicitly that he accepts the primacy of Peter, nor does he see James as at any time the superior of Peter; but he sees Peter as someone important, perhaps the most important of the Twelve, and there is no evidence that he actually denied Peter's primacy, only that he criticizes in his letter to the Galatians, Peter's vacillation.

# 9.13 PETER IN THE LATER NEW TESTAMENT LITERATURE

*Similarly, all the evidence points to Peter being the leader of the church at the close of the apostolic era, and no evidence is decisively against it.*

All the complex arguments in PNT do not clearly deny the primacy of Peter in the post-Resurrection Church prior to Peter and Paul going to Rome to martyrdom. However we would have to say that the primacy was 'low key', even more than it was in the first four Christian centuries up to the Council of Chalcedon in AD 451. Paul, after all, was himself an apostle, was a founder of churches, exercising his own authority as one to whom the Good News had been revealed. We cannot imagine him welcoming another apostle telling him his business! The church was in its infancy. Yet there are points which are indicators where the institution of the papacy was due to go in its own good time.

These pieces of evidence are only 'straws'; but Baur built much more on far less evidence! If we accept the tradition that Jesus made Peter primate of the whole Church, as we have argued above, then these 'straws' come together, all consistent with such a leadership role for Peter, which was to come to its fruition as it developed in the early Christian centuries. This we will investigate in the next Chapter.

## 9.14 CONCLUSION

*If we had no evidence in the Gospels that Jesus handed on the primacy of jurisdiction of his universal Church to Peter, then we could not argue from the rest of the New Testament alone, apart from the Gospels, that Peter was given the primacy by the historical Jesus. On the other hand, the difficulties enunciated, which we have discussed concerning the Petrine primacy, in the New Testament can be answered with relative ease, presuming the Petrine primacy in the primitive Church. There are other indications in the New Testament which would support such a handing over of the Church by Jesus to Peter as his successor. Granted, therefore, that we accept the testimony of the Gospels, and in particular as we have demonstrated in this chapter the authenticity of the Primacy Text Matthew 16: 18–19, then we may also accept that the New Testament manifests the beginnings of a development towards the papacy of later centuries, a development which is itself authentic.*

As a footnote to the chapter, we might conclude that the foremost Protestant theologian of the twentieth century, Karl Barth admits '... that it is impossible to establish *from the Gospel any radical* objection either to the concentration of the apostolic function in Peter or to the possibility of a primacy in the Church, which might even be that of Rome'. This from a theologian 'who has often and vigorously proclaimed his opposition to the Papacy...'[55]

## Notes

1. Tanner, II, 812 (Latin), *812 (English).
2. http://www.newadvent.org/cathen/07674d.htm Immaculate conception. [accessed 21.02.2013]
3. http://en.wikipedia.org/wiki/Assumption_of_Mary [accessed21.02.2013].
4. The Agreed Statement issued by the Anglican-Roman Catholic International Commission on *The Gift of Authority* 3rd September 1998: 'The reception of the primacy of the Bishop of Rome entails the recognition of this specific ministry of the universal primate. We believe that this is a gift to be received by all the churches.' Paragraph 47. http://www.ewtn.com/library/Theology/Arcicgf3.htm [accessed 21.02.2013]. However, ARCIC never concluded with any clarity regarding the *nature* of that primacy. The agreed statement as it stands could mean no more than that the Bishop of Rome has a primacy of honour among all the bishops, or that he acts as chairman of their plenary assemblies, as does the Archbishop of Canterbury at the Lambeth Conferences.
5. Pope Paul VI, Encyclical Letter *Humanae Vitae*.
6. For example, the Editor of *The Tablet*, (21 August 2010), p. 2, who commented in the leading article regarding Pope Benedict XVI's imminent visit to England in September 2110, even summoning Newman, to be beatified by the Pope during that visit, to her aid. If he insists that Newman's treatment of liberty of conscience does not permit dissent from the teaching of the Magisterium, he will be widely interpreted as demanding a clampdown against, for instance, Catholic homosexuals, couples who use contraception, or Catholics not persuaded by the Church's position on female ordination. Pope Benedict said somewhat ominously in his remarks to the bishops of England and Wales in February that 'it is important to recognise dissent for what it is, and not to mistake it for a mature contribution

to a balanced and wide-ranging debate'. It is also important to recognise that Newman would have been amazed by—and presumably delighted by—the Vatican II Declaration on Religious Liberty: 'This Vatican Council declares that the human person has a right to religious freedom ... no one is to be forced to act in a manner contrary to his own beliefs ...'

7   Pope Paul VI, Encyclical Letter *Humanae Vitae*, 3 footnote. See Mt 7: 21.
8   Pope Pius XII, Apostolic Constitution *Munificentissimus Deus*, 44–45: 'For which reason, after we have poured forth prayers of supplication again and again to God, and have invoked the light of the Spirit of Truth, for the glory of Almighty God who has lavished his special affection upon the Virgin Mary, for the honour of her Son, the immortal King of the Ages and the Victor over sin and death, for the increase of the glory of that same august Mother, and for the joy and exultation of the entire Church; by the authority of our Lord Jesus Christ, of the Blessed Apostles Peter and Paul, and by our own authority, we pronounce, declare, and define it to be a divinely revealed dogma: that the Immaculate Mother of God, the ever Virgin Mary, having completed the course of her earthly life, was assumed body and soul into heavenly glory. Hence if anyone, which God forbid, should dare wilfully to deny or to call into doubt that which we have defined, let him know that he has fallen away completely from the divine and Catholic Faith.'
9   *Lumen Gentium*, the Dogmatic Constitution of the Second Vatican Council on the Church, para 25. Tanner, II, p. *869.
10  PNT, Preface, p. v.
11  PNT, p. 5.
12  Ibid., pp. 8–9.
13  JVG, pp. 222–223.
14  DV 9.
15  PNT, p. 93.
16  Ibid., p. 89.
17  Beare, *Matthew*, p. 354.
18  PNT, p. 93, n. 216.
19  Lagrange, *Matthew*, pp. 323–324.
20  Ibid., p. 324.
21  PNT, pp. 90–91.
22  See section 6.2 above.
23  Cf. BMG, p. 31.
24  Bockmuehl, 1994, p. 164.
25  BMG, p. 115.
26  HST, pp. 257*–258*.
27  Ibid.
28  Cf. BMG, p. 57.

29. Cf. *Ibid.*, pp. 245–249, and regarding the authenticity of John 8:58 and 10:30, cf. BMG, 261–264.
30. R. Bultmann, *John*, p. 712. Contrary to for example Lindars, PNT, p. 142, n. 303, Bultmann insists that this story is not a threefold rehabilitation of Peter after his denial, but rather 'is a variant of Peter's commission to be the leader of the community, Matthew 16:17–19, cf. also Luke 22:32.' PNT also has to admit: 'The threefold command to feed the sheep also seems to imply an authority over the sheep; especially if we recall that in the Old Testament the king was described as a shepherd'. PNT, p. 142. PNT only questions what kind of authority. But it is here surely that we can harmonise Matthew with John, and see this authority as having legal and disciplinary connotations.
31. PNT, pp. 138–139.
32. *Ibid*, p. 96.
33. *Ibid.*
34. *Ibid.*, pp. 96–97.
35. Lagrange, *Matthew*, p. 328.
36. *Ibid.*, p. 329.
37. *Ibid.*
38. PNT, p. 97.
39. *Ibid.*, p. 98.
40. See section 3.2 above.
41. MJ3, pp. 230–231.
42. *Ibid.*, p. 231.
43. *Ibid.*
44. See section 6.5 above.
45. MJ3, p. 231.
46. See section 3.2 above.
47. PNT p. 51.
48. *Ibid.*
49. *Ibid.*, p. 51, n. 118.
50. *Ibid.*, p. 30.
51. *Ibid.*, p. 48.
52. *Ibid.*
53. *Ibid.*, p. 49.
54. *Ibid.*
55. Quoted in Constanzo, p. 150, from H. Küng, *The Council and Reunion*, 1961, p. 138, in *Church Dogmatics*, vol.1 (Edinburgh: 1936), pp. 106–115.

# 10

# THE PRIMACY OF PETER

## PART TWO: THE EARLY CENTURIES

### 10.1 ESSENTIAL BIBLIOGRAPHY

In this Chapter, I must acknowledge my indebtedness to M. Winter, *Saint Peter and the Popes*.[1] The early chapters on the New Testament evidence have been to some extent made redundant by more recent New Testament research, but the chapters on the post-apostolic developing evidence of the primacy are brilliantly assembled. Winter explains his purpose at the beginning of his book:

> It has therefore been my intention to present to the English reader a comprehensive account of all the important aspects of the early papacy, as revealed by modern scholarship, without attempting to exhaust any one of them, since this would be impossible in one volume. My objective has been to supply an answer to the question 'Is the papacy to be ascribed to Christ, or is it merely a human instrument of government invented by the church?... I shall be well contented if these pages may present a contribution to the eirenical study of the papacy, an attempt to show that our attitude to the Roman primacy is perhaps not as unreasonable as might have been imagined.[2]

Also essential to the writing of this Chapter have been:

- P. A. Hughes, *History of the Church Volume 1, The World in which the Church was Founded* (London: Sheed and Ward, revised edition 1948).
- W. H. C. Frend, *The Early Church: From the Beginnings to 461* (London: SCM Press, Second Edition, 1982).
- J. N. D. Kelly, *Oxford Dictionary of the Popes* (OUP 1986).[3]

Kelly is able to critique the documents available concerning the popes in the early centuries, coming to a judgement in each case which is in no way unfair to the papacy, but which sets out critically the development of the idea of the primacy which I find totally convincing. In the hundred and fifty years after Newman made his epoch-making studies, leading to his writing *The Development of Christian Doctrine* and becoming a Catholic (see Chapter 2), more documents are available, for example from the Vatican, to historians such as Kelly, to give a balanced view of the progress of the papacy. See Kelly, pp. x–xiii, where he lists his sources such as the *Liber Pontificalis,* which he judges to be often biased, yet nevertheless 'indispensable for the history of the papacy'.[4] For a complete history of the popes, Kelly has used and recommends F. X. Seppelt, *Geschichte der Päpste* (Munich, 1954–59).

## 10.2 STAGES OF THE DEVELOPMENT OF THE IDEA OF THE PRIMACY

*In the writings of the early Fathers, for example Irenaeus, the emphasis was upon Rome as the 'apostolic see', that is the city of the 'glorious apostles Peter and Paul'. The Bishops of Rome were seen as successors of both Peter and Paul, and thus the authority of Rome was unique in Christendom for that reason, and not explicitly for the primacy of Peter. The primacy of Peter alone became more and more important during the controversies of the post-Nicene church. First during the Arian controversy, and then most of all during the disputes concerning the Hypostatic Union and Monophysitism, the Bishop of Rome was seen as having the primacy given to him in Matthew 16:13–23 over the Churches of both East and West.*

Earlier on in this book, when we were discussing Modernism, we outlined the view of the Liberal Protestant Harnack, 3.2 who saw the evolution of the church as a movement towards 'primitive Catholicism', *(Urkatholikismus)* which movement however was from purity of motive in the earliest days to more and more organisation which stifled the natural brotherhood of the early days. The Reformers had identified such corrupt institutionalisation as revealed most of all during the Middle Ages; but Harnack saw this movement towards such fossilisation as taking place in the early years of Christianity:

> The first period which lasted until the middle of the second century was the period of pristine purity and brotherhood. This was succeeded by an era of organization which came to an end roughly at the close of the third century with the definitive establishment of Episcopal government. The third period which he described was that which opened with the Constantine toleration, and from then onwards the church tended to assimilate many of the institutions of the imperial government. This period was never supplanted in the East, but for the Western church Harnack postulated a fourth stage of progress which was the papal epoch, when the Bishop of Rome was able to increase his power owing to the collapse of the Empire in the West.[5]

For Harnack therefore, the papacy represented the final stage of institutionalisation, which he saw as having a political origin, the Papacy replacing the Roman Empire in the West. We would agree with Harnack that there was indeed development in the early Church, and we would have to agree again with him that the Papacy became politically powerful in the West, the Pope sometimes co-operating and sometimes clashing with the Holy Roman Emperor as one of the 'two swords' of the Christian Empire.

But we would read that development differently from Harnack. We would see the primacy of the Bishop of Rome as the development of the understanding of Matthew 16:17–19, with Jesus naming Peter as the Rock. The earliest church was not without organisation, as we have seen, but governed by Peter, Paul, and the Apostles. The Pope was truly the successor of Peter and Paul. What in fact developed was the working out of the implications of that primacy in the identification of the Pope's authority over all the other bishops of Christendom, particularly where the faith of the Church was concerned as expressed in the General Councils. Our line of development would be traced thus:

- **The apostolic age** We have argued to the authenticity of Matthew 16:13–20. Contrary to Beare, there is no evidence that Peter's primacy was ever questioned in the apostolic age, even though we cannot demonstrate that for example Paul explicitly acknowledged such authority. From the viewpoint of the historical Jesus, we have argued that, if Jesus was truly God become Man, he would most reasonably have been expected to provide an authority in place of his own after his death, Resurrection and Ascension.
- **The second century AD** During this early post-apostolic period, the Bishop of Rome was acknowledged as the successor of the 'glorious apostles Peter and Paul'. For this reason, Rome, in Irenaeus' terms, was seen as the See where the true faith was to be found.
- **The third century.** In this century, we see the beginning of the use of the primacy text in Matthew, to denote the authority of the Bishop of Rome, in particular Tertullian, (c. AD 160 to c. 220).

- **The fourth century.** In this century, we see the successive bishops of Rome alluding to the Petrine text when defending the orthodox faith against Novatianism, Pelagianism, and most of all Arianism. They begin to use their authority not only in the Western Church, but also over the Eastern bishops. It is remarkable how consistent the Bishops of Rome were time after time in supporting the orthodox faith.
- **The fifth century.** During this century, Pope Celestine concerning the Nestorian controversy (Ephesus 431), and Pope Leo the Great concerning the Monophysite controversy (449 the 'Latrocinium' and 451 Chalcedon), exercised their doctrinal and executive authority over the General Councils of the Church. The primacy text was used precisely as the First Vatican Council uses it.
- **Conclusion.** We argue that this use of the primacy text is precisely an example of genuine doctrinal development, where the meaning of a text of scripture is gradually revealed in the course of history. The primacy of the Bishop of Rome therefore is not an accident of history, still less to be explained as the growth of the power of Rome replacing the old Roman empire (although this was a factor in strengthening the influence of the Pope), but a genuine working out of the meaning of Matthew 16:13–20 in the life of the Church.

We will reach the same conclusions as J. H. Newman, when he wrote his life-changing work *The Development of Christian Doctrine*. The reader is referred again to **Chapter 2** of the present book. Newman saw the exercise of papal authority, particularly by Leo the Great, against the Monophysites, at the Council of Chalcedon 451 as an exercise of primacy over the whole body of bishops worldwide, which primacy was recognised by all those bishops. Because of the importance of this text in the life of Newman, we quote again, from that relevant paragraph in *The Development of Christian Doctrine*:

> ... but the historical account of the Council is this, that a formula which the Creed did not contain, which the Fathers did not unanimously witness, and which some eminent Saints had almost in set terms opposed, which the whole East refused as a symbol, not once, but twice, patriarch by patriarch, metropolitan by metropolitan, first by the mouth of above a hundred, then by the mouth of above six hundred of its Bishops, and refused upon the grounds of its being an addition to the Creed, was forced upon the Council, not indeed as being such an addition, yet, on the other hand, not for subscription merely, but for acceptance as a definition of faith under the sanction of an anathema, — forced on the Council by the resolution of the Pope of the day, acting through his Legates and supported by the civil power.[6]

In this chapter, we will revisit the evidence in the light of critical studies since Newman's conversion in 1846.

## 10.3 THE HISTORICAL JESUS AND THE APOSTOLIC AGE

*We have argued to the authenticity of Matthew 16:13-20. Contrary to Beare, there is no evidence that Peter's primacy was ever questioned in the apostolic age, even though we cannot demonstrate that for example Paul acknowledged such authority explicitly. From the viewpoint of the historical Jesus, we have argued that, if Jesus was truly God become Man, he would most reasonably have been expected to provide an authority to replace his own after his death, resurrection and ascension.*

The reader is referred back to **Chapters 8** and **9**, where we argue for the historical authenticity of Matthew 16:13-23, and for the primacy of Peter as at least present in its undeveloped form in the New Testament period. We briefly rehearse these arguments now.

We began our investigation by stating that we cannot exclude at least *a priori* the possibility that the conferring by the historical Jesus of the primacy upon the historical Peter is the actual meaning of Matthew 16:17-19. We first set out the text in Matthew 16:13-23, together with its parallels in Mark 8:27-33 and Luke 9:18-22. We accepted the critical conclusion that Matthew's Gospel cannot be dated later than the end of the first century.

Regarding Matthew's added response, 16:17-19, where Jesus makes Peter the rock on which he would build his church, we note the critical consensus that this added response is an Aramaic addition, which clearly pre-dates the written Gospel, and reflects at least one section of the early Palestinian Christian community which held that Peter had a special role in the Church given to him by the Lord Jesus. We noted that there is no other church leader who is given such a primacy by Jesus in the literature of the New Testament, whether or not the historical Jesus actually said 'You are Peter, and on this Rock I will build my church.' We noted also that according to scholars such as Bultmann, John 21:15-17, where the risen Jesus says to Peter 'Feed my sheep', this was a reflection of the faith of the Johannine community that Jesus had made Peter the leader of his church.

We then attempted to demonstrate that it is at the very least plausible that the historical Jesus gave Peter this authority while Jesus was still on earth. First, it seems clear that in calling Simon Peter 'the Rock', Jesus is giving Peter a title in response to Peter's naming Jesus with his title 'you are the Christ, the Son of the living God'. This giving of a title to Simon Peter by Jesus is multiply attested, in Matthew 16:15–18 and in John 1:41–42, and therefore fulfils one at least of the criteria of authenticity.

We argue that the historical Peter professed his faith in Jesus as Messiah during the public ministry of Jesus, even though it was perhaps only after the Resurrection that he understood Jesus to be the divine Son of God. With Bockmuehl, and against Beare, we claim that Jesus during his lifetime claimed to be the Messiah. Thus Peter's profession of the Messiahship of Jesus was not, *pace* Bultmann, confession of Jesus as the 'divine man', but very much a Jewish understanding of Messiahship, and therefore credible historically.

We accepted willingly the patristic interpretation of Matthew 16:15–18 which sees the promise of Jesus that on Peter he will build his church as a reference to the confession of Peter's faith that Jesus was Messiah. However, we argued strongly that, when Jesus called Simon 'the Rock', and gave him the power of the keys, the power of binding and loosing, he was giving Peter juridical and legal authority, not only together with the Twelve, but also over the other apostles. This seems to be demonstrable from a comparison between Matthew 16:18–19 and Isaiah 22:19–23, the replacement of a ruler of Israel by another who is then given the keys of the kingdom with the word of the prophet in the name of YHWH. Thus in Matthew, Jesus is giving Simon Peter similar juridical authority to succeed him after his death and resurrection.

The question now arises as to whether this text in Matthew giving Peter the keys of the kingdom is post-Easter in origin or from the historical Jesus during his lifetime. Meier, while admitting that Matthew 16:18–19 cannot be dismissed out of hand simply because it is only in Matthew's account, argues that its use of the word *ekklésia* makes it Matthew's redaction rather than from the teaching of the historical Jesus. We argued earlier with Lagrange, **6.5**, however, that Jesus did found a kind of church, and saw it as such, during his own lifetime; but that after the Resurrection and in the usage of the New Testament, the term *ekklésia* was much more explicit in meaning, in particular taking the membership of the Gentiles into its orbit. However again, if, as we have demonstrated in BMG, the historical Jesus was truly God become man, was cognizant of that fact, and was aware also of his own salvific plan for the world, then his intention to found a Church to be built up after his death, and his expression of that intention in Aramaic language, making Peter his successor in terms of his jurisdiction, is most credible.

The question remains as to how far the primitive church recognized Peter's primacy in the immediate post-Easter period. The majority of scholars recognize that Peter played a leading role in the Jerusalem church immediately after Pentecost, as is reflected in the Acts of the Apostles. Paul himself after his conversion recognized the doctrinal authority of the 'Twelve' and made sure that his own teaching squared with theirs. Even among the Twelve, Paul recognized Peter as having been entrusted with the Gospel to the Jews, as he had been entrusted with the Gospel to the Gentiles.

In the letter to the Galatians, Paul rebuked Peter for compromising with the Gospel by submitting to pressure for Jewish Christians not to eat with Gentile converts, and for advocating circumcision in some cases (although Paul himself had had Timothy circumcised!) But even granted the dispute among critical scholars, there is nothing to contradict explicitly Acts 15, where at the council in Jerusalem, the assembly followed Peter, who from his experience with the Gentile Cornelius, agreed with Paul in his teaching that Gentile converts did not have to be circumcised. There is no explicit evidence that Paul recognized the primacy of Peter, but again there is no text of Paul that denies that primacy. Some have argued that James, the 'brother of the Lord', did exercise primacy in Jerusalem in the early days of the church. Acts 15 sees James as a kind of president of the assembly, as a Jewish authority in the church solving the practical issues relating to Gentile observance of the Jewish law. But this does not necessarily mean that James had the primacy over the whole church at any stage, and there is no explicit New Testament evidence that he ever did.

At that early stage, each apostle, whether a member of the Twelve, or with a special church founding commission such as Paul (by divine revelation) or Barnabas (the Holy Spirit in the community), exercised his own authority in his own church community. The primacy of Peter would have existed as part of the tradition based upon the words of Jesus preserved in the Gospel of Matthew. That tradition could even possibly have been unknown in certain areas of the primitive church. But it was never contradicted according to all the evidence we have, and thus remained to emerge quite legitimately as the Church's understanding of the revelation of Jesus during his lifetime on earth.

## 10.4 THE SECOND CENTURY

*During this early post-apostolic period the Bishop of Rome was acknowledged as the successor of the 'glorious apostles Peter and Paul'. For this reason, Rome, in Irenaeus' terms, was seen as the apostolic see where the true faith would be found.*

Few scholars now doubt that Peter went to Rome, and was martyred there. Both Peter and Paul were martyred during the reign of the emperor Nero, according to the historian Eusebius, c.260 to c.340, 'probably in the persecution of 64'.[7] Regarding Peter in Rome, however, Kelly asserts:

> Nothing is known of the length of his residence: the story that it lasted twenty-five years is a 3rd-century legend. Ignatius assumed that Peter and Paul wielded special authority over the Roman church, while Irenaeus claimed that they jointly founded it and inaugurated its succession of bishops. Nothing, however, is known of their constitutional roles, least of all of Peter's as presumed leader of the community.[8]

According to the testimony of Irenaeus, attested by the historian Eusebius, Linus (c. AD 66 to 78) was the first Bishop of Rome, 'entrusted with his office by the Apostles Peter and Paul after they had established the Christian church in Rome'.[9] Kelly is skeptical as to what 'Linus's actual functions and responsibilities were ... for the monarchical, or one-man, episcopate had not yet emerged in Rome'.[10] Granted the evidence of Irenaeus, however, which is not disputed, it does seem reasonable to conclude that Linus was a successor of the apostles Peter and Paul and, parallel with Ignatius of Antioch, a single bishop with authority over the Church of Rome. We have earlier argued that the threefold ministry, and the monarchical episcopate, testified in Ignatius of Antioch at the close of the first century AD came into operation after the death of the respective apostle, and that this was the universal practice, even if that practice was not always explicit. This would be the most logical interpretation of the evidence, a role which in actual history Linus most probably assumed gradually as the Petrine and Pauline communities came more and more together to face the increasing persecution of the imperial authorities in Rome.

Presumably during the days when the apostles Peter and Paul still lived in Rome, they would have ruled their own communities as their apostolic leaders. Paul would temperamentally have ensured this! After the martyrdom of Peter and Paul, presumably the two communities, Pauline and Petrine, would have come together under a single ruler. As we have argued earlier with Hughes, and against Kelly, in **8.10**, we have no evidence for any other kind of rule in Rome, nor were the 'Pauline' and 'Petrine' communities in conflict with each other. It is testimony to the smooth transition to monarchical episcopacy in Rome that there was always considered in tradition one bishop of Rome. The writing of the later history of Rome might have idealized this process, but we have no reason to think that it was not the reality that one bishop succeeded in Rome from the apostles onwards.

For Irenaeus, this bishop of Rome derived his authority from being the successor of both 'glorious apostles' Peter and Paul. It will be useful to quote again from the statement of Irenaeus, to which we first drew attention above:[11]

> But since it would be too long to enumerate in such a volume as this the successions of all the churches, we shall confound all those who, in whatever manner, whether through self-satisfaction or vainglory, or through blindness and wicked opinion, assemble other than where it is proper, by pointing out here the successions of the bishops of the greatest and most ancient church known to all, founded and organized at Rome by the two most glorious apostles, Peter and Paul—that church which has the tradition and the faith with which comes down to us after having been announced to men by the apostles. For with this Church, because of its superior origin, all churches must agree, that is, all the faithful in the whole world. And it is in her that the faithful everywhere have maintained the apostolic tradition.[12]

Winter aptly comments:

> His account of the foundation of the Roman church, and the list of the bishops of Rome, mentions both Peter and Paul as the founders. Possibly this appears prejudicial to the position of St Peter, but since it was only the intention of Irenaeus to establish Apostolic connexion for his churches it would be outside his aim to differentiate between the Apostles.[13]

Irenaeus therefore is not affirming the primacy of Peter explicitly, but rather the primacy of Rome as the Apostolic See, because it transmits the authentic tradition from the 'glorious apostles Peter and Paul'. No other diocese in the world has such a powerful pedigree. That is why, says Irenaeus, if you wish to find out what the apostolic tradition is you do not need to search the world, but simply to ask the bishops of Rome, the successors of Peter and Paul. Thus the first references to Rome are to it as the prime Apostolic See. At this stage of the development of doctrine of the church, therefore, there was little reflection on the Petrine texts and discussion of the primacy of Peter. Each church that had an apostolic founder looked to that apostle for true doctrine and morality and presumably had a bishop who succeeded that apostle. As Hughes argued, we have no evidence that any other rule applied throughout the church.

## 10.5 THE THIRD CENTURY

*In this century, we see the beginning of the use of the primacy text in Matthew, to denote the authority of the Bishop of Rome, in particular Tertullian, (c. AD 160 to c. 220). However at this stage, the Pope did not exercise universal primacy based upon Matthew 16, nor was that universally accepted, even in the West.*

The third century was a period of spasmodic persecution in Rome, with a high proportion of the popes being martyred, ruling for only a short time, but of the consistent and relentless growth of the number of Christians throughout the known world and in the city.

However, Winter says, 'there is reason to believe that the Roman church applied the text of Matthew 16:16 to the primacy of St Peter as early as the beginning of the third century.'[14] Furthermore, in the century before the Arian crisis, according to Winter, 'The opinion of the anti-Arian fathers is therefore quite clear. Peter is regarded as the senior Apostle, and the foundation of the church. In their minds this honour is in no way incompatible with the position which Christ occupies, nor does the excellence of Peter's faith blind them to the fact that something more is indicated in the texts of Matthew and John'.[15]

The early third century Father of the Church, the North African theologian of great brilliance Tertullian sees the role of Peter as binding and loosing. 'Three distinct powers are alluded to, the roles of being the foundation, and the key bearer, together with the competence to bind and loose'.[16]

Kelly sees the short reign of Pope Stephen I (12 May 254 to August 257)[17] as significant in this respect. There was a fierce theological controversy[18] as to whether Christians who had apostatized under persecution had to be re-baptised. This view was vigorously promoted by the antipope the heretic Novatian (251 to 258)[19] who led a schismatic church in Rome itself, teaching that there was no forgiveness for serious sins after baptism. But Novatian was condemned by a Roman synod called by the orthodox Pope Cornelius.[20] Pope Stephen I then took an aggressive attitude promoting the Roman view that baptism could not be repeated if administered in the name of the Trinity. Those who had apostatized only required 'absolution by the laying on of hands'.[21]

Nevertheless, even in the West, not all bishops accepted the superiority of the Roman See over the bishops of the world.[22] Cyprian had a series of disagreements with Pope Stephen I, concerning the question of the validity of heretical baptisms. The pope made a 'definite declaration that if the rite be duly administered the person of the minister does not affect its validity',[23] '... but at the next meeting of the African bishops (1 September 256) a joint reply was sent to the pope. 'None of us', said St Cyprian in his opening speech and alluding to the pope, 'poses as bishop of bishops ... each bishop has the right to think for himself and as he is not accountable to any other, so is no bishop accountable to him'. The Council unanimously supported St Cyprian in 257.[24]

There was therefore a fierce argument between Pope Stephen I and Bishop Cyprian of Carthage on the rebaptism of heretics.[25] The Pope refused to see Cyprian's legates, and Stephen was blamed for splitting the Church. As Kelly notes, 'It is interesting that he was accused of "glorying in his standing as bishop and as claiming to hold the succession from Peter, on whom the foundations of the church were laid"'. He was in fact the first pope, as far as is known, to find a formal basis for the Roman primacy in the Lord's charge to the apostle Peter cited in Matthew 16:18.[26] Thus clearly, by the middle of the third century, the Pope was beginning to claim that the Petrine Primacy text applied to him as Bishop of Rome. But also clearly, not all held this interpretation, even in the West, Cyprian disagreed with it.

## 10.6 THE FIRST HALF OF THE FOURTH CENTURY

*In this period, we see the new Christian Emperor Constantine taking over the rule of the Church by summoning Councils, most notably the Council of Nicaea 325, where he supported the orthodoxy of Athanasius of Alexandria to define the full divinity of Christ. However, then the Emperor was influenced by the semi-Arianism of Eusebius of Nicomedia to attempt a compromise formula, discrediting Athanasius.*

The huge political and religious change which happened in the Roman Empire of the fourth century was the Edict of Milan (AD 313) by which the Emperor Constantine ended centuries of persecution of Christians, and made Christianity a legal religion. Almost as seismic a change in the Roman Empire was that Constantine in 325 moved his capital from Rome to Constantinople, and 'determined to make Constantinople the future capital of the empire, and with his usual energy he took every measure to enlarge, strengthen, and beautify it.'[27]

After the Edict the Emperor almost immediately took charge of the rule of the Church since presumably as Emperor he saw himself as its ruler. He called the Council of Arles in 314. The Pope was not its chairman, as the Emperor appointed Chrestus, Bishop of Syracuse to oversee its progress, and with the Bishop of Arles its president. The Council admitted the Pope as primate of the West.

Then, most significantly, the Emperor called the Council of Nicaea (325) to solve the problem raised by the heresy of the Alexandrian priest Arius, who denied the divinity of Christ. The Pope was invited as were the rest of the bishops; but he declined to attend, pleading old age, sending instead two priest representatives. However they affixed their signatures to the decrees above all those present except Ossius of Cordoba who was the presiding bishop of the Council, thus granting some primacy at least of honour to the Apostolic See.

The Creed of Nicaea was proposed authoritatively throughout the Empire as the Catholic faith:

> We believe in one only God, the Father, Almighty, maker of all things visible and invisible; and in one only Lord, Jesus Christ, the Son of God, the sole-begotten of the Father, that is to say of the Father's substance, God of God, Light of Light: true God of true God; begotten not made, consubstantial with the Father (*homoousion tou Patri*), by whom all things were made who for us men and for our salvation came down, became incarnate, became man, suffered, was raised again on the third day ascended back to heaven and will come again to judge the living and the dead; and in the Holy Spirit. As for those who say 'There was a time when He did not exist; before He was begotten. He did not exist; He was made from nothing or from another substance or essence; the Son of God is a created being, changeable, capable of alteration,' to such as these the Catholic Church says Anathema.[28]

As Kelly says, 'in the fifth and sixth centuries, the idea was to gain credence that Ossius had been commissioned by the pope, and even that the council had been summoned by the pope with the emperor in concert; but these are legends without historical foundation'.[29] By the fifth century, legends were developing about Pope Sylvester (314 to 331)[30] that he had converted Constantine, cured him of leprosy, and imposed on him the penance of setting Christians free and closing pagan temples. However we would have to admit that, in reality, the primacy text in Matthew was not seen by the newly converted Christian Emperor, or by the Eastern bishops, as making the Bishop of Rome the head of all the bishops and the ruler of the church. The fact that legends about the Pope developed by the fifth century was itself proof of the rapid growth of papal claims in the century following Nicaea.

In reality, the Emperor was less interested in orthodoxy, and much more interested in the unity of the Empire. Constantine was baptised by the semi-Arian Eusebius of Nicomedia. Eusebius was against the formula of *homóousios* as not in scripture, preferring to say that Christ was of 'like substance' (*homoiousios*) with the Father. Eusebius had a great deal of influence with the Emperor, and thus enabled the heresy to continue.[31] A Council in 331 deposed Eustathius Bishop of Antioch, on the grounds according to Eusebius of Nicomedia that he was a Sabellian, that is one who denied divine persons in the Trinity, while Eustathius actually supported Nicaea. The Emperor supported Eusebius and confirmed the deposition of Eustathius.[32] The Emperor went on to depose orthodox bishop after orthodox bishop and replace them with Eusebians.

Thus, for the first time, a heresy entered the Church and was able to survive for decades, through 'Caesaro-papism'. The dispute with Arianism raged from Nicaea onwards Frend contends, 'Against the devotion of Athanasius one must balance the statesmanship of successive Roman emperors, and the equally strongly held beliefs of the majority of bishops in the East. Constantius II (337 to 361) and Valens (364 to 378) believed that religious unity was essential to the survival of the Empire. Constantine sought to found that unity on broad agreement and to exclude troublemakers'.[33] The Eastern bishops 'dreaded Sabellianism (the modalist view of the Trinity) even more than Arianism.'[34] The Eusebians were able to accept the formula *homoiousios*, 'of like substance', whereas the Arians did not accept that the Son was of like substance with the Father, thus they were *anhomoiousios*.

Constantine accepted the decision of the Council of Nicaea as binding: 'The decision of three hundred bishops must be considered no other than the judgement of God'.[35] However in order to achieve unity in the Empire, the

Emperor was prepared to allow interpretations which contradicted the formulae of Athanasius agreed at Nicea. Regarding the Bishop of Rome, Frend claims 'Rome never quite deserted the Sabellianism of the third century popes.'[36] However, concerning the third century popes and Sabellianism, Kelly realises that the question is more complex concerning the debate about Modalism.[37] In fact, Popes supported Athanasius, not because they were Modalists, but because they were orthodox homóousians

However Frend is correct to note an important trend as the fourth century proceeded: 'Pilgrims went more and more to the tomb of Peter in Rome'. Instead of the Emperor, the Bishop of Rome was to be regarded as the court of appeal in ecclesiastical causes '[38]

The Emperor had challenged the orthodoxy of Athanasius. And so, in 339, Athanasius escaped to Rome, as again he had been expelled from his See by his enemies.[39] An alliance now built up between successive Popes and bishops defending orthodoxy to establish the doctrine and often the discipline of the Church, which in a short while would over-trump even the power of the Emperor. The primacy of Peter as stated in Matthew was to become the proof-text of this alliance.

Already Pope Saint Julius I (337–352) was an important defender of Nicaean orthodoxy, and of its champion Saint Athanasius. The followers of Eusebius of Nicomedia, who were of course Arianisers, had held a Council at Antioch in Syria in the summer of 341. They reaffirmed their condemnation of Athanasius, and devised a Creed which omitted the phrase regarding Christ, 'one in being with the Father' (*homóousios patri*).[40] But Pope Julius strongly resisted this Arian move, and defended Athanasius.

The question of the authority of Rome was quite naturally linked with the question of orthodoxy. After the death of Constantine the Great (337) the two new Emperors who replaced him, Constans and Constantius, convened a general council of East and West at Serdica (Sophia) in 342.

But when the Western delegation to that council insisted on Athanasius and a supporter of Athanasius, Marcellus taking part, the eastern delegation withdrew. The eastern delegation excommunicated leading Western bishops, including the pope. However the Western majority continued to meet as a council, and continued to vindicate the orthodox Athanasius and condemn the Eusebians. That same council gave a deposed bishop the right to appeal to the pope.[41] By now, there was a conflict between East and West, and the Pope was claiming more and more authority as orthodox doctrine was challenged.

The situation between East and West regarding ecclesiastical authority before the middle of the fourth century was by no means simple, as Winter explains. There was, he said, differentiation in terms of papal power in the three regions: Italy, the West, and the East.[42] 'Rome was the mother church of all Italy'.[43] Italy was almost certainly evangelised by Rome. 'It would appear that the Bishop of Rome was the only bishop in Italy until the middle of the second century'.[44]

As Winter remarks,

> Rome enjoyed a position of special respect in the West, because it was the only Apostolic church there, and moreover it was the centre from which the whole of the West was ultimately evangelised ... However, only in the time of Justinian (483–565) was the title of patriarch applied to Rome in view of its relationship to the West ... the Eastern zone presents the simplest explanation of all. No part of the East was evangelised from Rome, nor was there any lack of Apostolic Churches to give prestige to the Oriental empire. As a result, the Bishop of Rome intervened in the affairs of the Eastern Church only with his full papal authority. This accounts for the comparative scarcity of such interventions and, as will be seen later, the momentous character of those incidents.[45]

Differences between East and West were cultural, the former Hellenistic, the latter Latin. The power of the emperor was great in the East: 'Thus the East imitated completely the imperial pattern without pausing to consider whether it would be suitable for the church.'[46]

Winter concludes, 'As the fourth century drew to a close the authority of the Pope over the churches of the West was assured, and was maintained in a state of stability which would survive the collapse of the Roman political power.'[47] However, the second half of the fourth century saw the Bishop of Rome intervening more and more even in the East, continuing a process begun in the first half of that century, based upon the Matthean primacy text, most of all in order to ensure orthodoxy.

## 10.7 THE SECOND HALF OF THE FOURTH CENTURY

*In this period, we see the successive bishops of Rome alluding to the Petrine text when defending the orthodox faith against Novatianism, Pelagianism, and most of all Arianism. They begin to use their authority not only in the Western church, but also over the Eastern bishops. It is remarkable how consistent the Bishops of Rome were time after time in supporting the orthodox faith. It was this consistency, and not first and foremost the place of Rome as the old capital of the Empire, which led to the increase of the authority of the Bishop of Rome on the basis of the Matthean primacy text.*

The successor to Pope Julius as Bishop of Rome (337–352), who was a vigorous supporter of the Nicene Creed, was Liberius (352–366).[48] Now the sole Emperor Constantius II (337–61) attempted to bring the Western bishops into line with the Arianisation of the Empire. The Pope proved to be weak in the face of Arian pressure that was supported by the Emperor, and in order to return to Rome signed a compromise creedal formula in 358 which omitted the homóousios, and acquiesced in the excommunication of Athanasius. The Emperor wanted the Pope to go back to

Rome, but only on condition that he ruled jointly with Felix his archdeacon who had ruled in his absence. Liberius did not send delegates to the Synod of Rimini (359) at which 'the western bishops were eventually browbeaten into accepting an Arianising creed'.

Liberius had a great deal of trouble with Felix II, the anti-pope (355–365)[49] who was always in opposition to him. Felix was the archdeacon, and the favourite of the Emperor. He 'was consecrated by three Arianising prelates, not in a church but, according to Athanasius of Alexandria (d.373), in the imperial palace, presumably in Milan, and entered into communion with the Arianising party favoured by Constantius'.[50] However Constantius was convinced that it was necessary to restore Liberius, and attempted to maintain him with Felix as rulers of the Church of Rome. However the people threw out Felix, and proclaimed 'One God, one Christ, one bishop'.[51] Liberius remained as Pope in the Lateran palace from 358 and Felix was relegated to the suburbs. However, Felix, 'through being confused with Roman martyrs bearing the same name was eventually venerated as a martyr himself, with his feast on 29 July. As his legend developed, he was believed to have been a courageous defender of the Nicene faith and to have laid down his life for it, while Liberius was represented as a traitor to orthodoxy and a persecutor of the faithful'.[52]

All this emphasises the need for a critical reading of the sources.[53] There is no doubt that we can accept the word of Athanasius as to the Arianising nature of Felix, and the orthodoxy of Liberius, even if the latter was weak. In exile, and the prisoner of the Emperor, Liberius vacillated, and wrote letters 'which suggest that he was ready to pay almost any price to return home'.[54] However, with the death of Constantius (361), Liberius was free to resume his role as defender of orthodoxy, and 'Finally in 366, when eastern bishops were seeking western support, he granted them communion on the strict condition that they accepted the

Nicene creed'.⁵⁵ Thus Liberius, although weak, began a process of popes intervening in the East on doctrinal matters.

His successor, Pope Saint Damasus (366–384)⁵⁶ was the first Pope explicitly to base his claims to power on the Petrine text. He became pope after the killing of the followers of Ursinus, the deacon of Liberius, who also had been elected pope as a rival to Damasus.⁵⁷ He was described by Basil as 'impossibly arrogant'. Wealthy Roman lifestyle was popular among the Roman pagan upper class newly converted to Christianity. Damasus repressed heresies, including Arianism. 'Damasus was indefatigable in promoting the Roman primacy, frequently referring to Rome as the 'apostolic see' and ruling that the test of a creed's orthodoxy was its endorsement by the pope. For Damasus this primacy (of Peter) was not based upon decisions of synods, as were the claims of Constantinople, but exclusively on his being the direct successor of St Peter and so the rightful heir of the promises made to him by Christ (Mt 16:18)'.⁵⁸

As Winter says, at this time St Jerome (347–420) gives us 'the clearest and most carefully thought out theory of St Peter. In this matter he was helped by his thorough knowledge of the Biblical languages as well as a solicitude to establish the meaning of the text rather than any rhetorical or homiletic elaborations.' Jerome was not fazed by 1 Corinthians 10:4 which referred to Christ as a rock. Jerome interpreted 'the gates of hell' as the Church's security from heresy rather than a promised immortality.⁵⁹ Jerome's biblical learning was communicated to Rome, since he was commissioned by Pope Damasus himself to produce a translation of the Greek New Testament into official Latin,⁶⁰ and no doubt became part of the legacy of the Pope's own growing understanding of the meaning of the Petrine text.

This meaning was clearly not limited to the Pope's authority over the West, but also referred to his authority over the whole church. The African, Optatus of Milevis, who died in 370 or thereabouts '…. makes it quite clear that Peter has a special function as Teacher for preserving the unity of the church.'⁶¹ 'You cannot fail to be aware that in Rome the Episcopal Cathedra (chair) was conferred first on Peter, in which chair has presided Peter the head of all the apostles (whence he is called 'Cephas'), and in this chair unity is safeguarded for all'.⁶²

The Pope's exercise of doctrinal authority to defend orthodoxy was not limited to the condemnation of Arianism, but extended also to Apollinarianism. Apollinarius was Athanasius' auxiliary bishop, who adopted an extreme homóousian position, claiming that Christ was so much of one substance with the Father that his human soul was replaced by the Logos. 'One of the letters of Damasus which is difficult to date exactly, but which can be assigned to the period between 377 and 381, answers a request from a group of Easterns. It appears from the term of the reply of Damasus that it was a request, from the priests of the church of Berytus that their bishop, Timothy, would be deposed because of his Apollinarianism. In reply to this appeal Damasus asks them why they should keep asking about this matter, '… since he was deposed here, by a judgement of the Apostolic See, in the presence of Peter Bishop of Alexandria, at the same time as his master Apollinarius'.⁶³ As Winter comments, 'Since all this took place at the instigation of St Basil, it serves as an indication that he recognised some measure of superiority for the See of Rome.'⁶⁴

In the fifth century, Patriarch Cyril of Alexandria was orthodox as was Athanasius, but his successor Dioscoros of Alexandria was not. What was remarkable about Rome was how successive Popes, in spite of faults, weaknesses, and even pride and cruelty, maintained the orthodox faith against every type of heresy.

After a half century which began, in 353, that saw the Arian Emperor Constantius left 'sole master of the Roman world',⁶⁵ and Councils were called which deposed Athanasius. 'In 357, when even these had been deposed and Liberius, the Pope, was in exile, there was not one orthodox bishop left in any important see of the world. It appeared as if the Arian victory was complete.'⁶⁶ However by the end of that century, the Pope was habitually referring to the Petrine texts in order to establish doctrinal orthodoxy throughout the Empire.

For instance Pope Siricius (384–399) was according to Kelly, the first Pope to use imperial edicts as models for papal edicts. 'In fact he was an experienced, forceful pontiff who, though inevitably overshadowed by St Ambrose, Bishop of Milan (374–397) was as fully aware as Damasus I of Rome's primatial status and his own role as successor of St Peter.'⁶⁷

Some historians have claimed, with Harnack, that it was the model of the structures of imperial Rome which ensured the progress of the authority of the papacy at this time. We do not have to deny that popes, especially powerful aristocrats such as Damasus, used imperial language and symbolism to describe their own role, and provided a replacement for the declining power of Rome, which was tangible at this point. But the Pope could never have challenged the power of the New Rome Constantinople unless it had a source of its own authority to match the authority of the Emperor. This source of authority became more and more necessary, and the resources of the Emperor less and less adequate, as the Catholic Church attempted after the Arian crisis to establish worldwide unity on its own doctrinal terms and in uncompromising fashion. That the Pope did on the basis of the Petrine primacy; and its acceptance on the part of the East was a huge step forward for the papacy of the fifth century. That this authority was never seriously questioned by the Eastern patriarchs is at first sight surprising and significant.

## 10.8 THE FIFTH CENTURY

*During this century, Pope Celestine regarding the Nestorian controversy (Ephesus 431), and Pope Leo the Great concerning the Monophysite controversy (449 the 'Latrocinium' and 451 Chalcedon), exercised their doctrinal and executive authority over the General Councils of the Church, The Petrine text is used precisely as the First Vatican Council uses it, giving the Bishop of Rome that primacy which it claims Jesus gave to Peter during his lifetime.*

St Innocent I (401–417) set the tone of that whole century in promoting papal claims: 'At a time when the western empire was crumbling under barbarian invasions, he seized every opportunity of asserting the primacy of the Roman See, making more substantial claims for the papacy than his predecessors. As a result he not only proved one of the outstanding popes of the early centuries, but has sometimes been saluted as "the first pope"'. He wrote authoritative letters on the canon of scripture, the canon of the Mass, to the bishops of the west, insisting on Rome as the norm.[68] In the East, he supported John Chrysostom to continue as bishop when he was persecuted and deposed as Bishop of Constantinople. He rebuked John of Jerusalem for allowing atrocities in his diocese after the destruction of Jerome's monasteries by hooligans. He condemned the heretic Pelagius and his companion Caelestius, thanking his correspondents for referring to him for judgement, even though he had not been asked to do so! Thus the pope was able to advance the Holy See's doctrinal authority. 'No previous pope had previously enunciated the view that the apostolic see possessed supreme teaching authority'.[69] In this claim, of course, Innocent was only drawing out what was implicitly understood at least from Damasus onwards.

Pope Zosimus (417–418) continued to uphold papal claims, and to condemn Pelagianism, but according to Kelly his short reign 'was marred by blunders'.[70] His successor Saint Boniface (418–422)[71] was 'an unswerving supporter of orthodoxy' against Pelagius, and supported Augustine, who dedicated a treatise on Pelagianism to the grateful pontiff.[72] Boniface asserted 'It has never been lawful for what has once been decided by the apostolic see to be reconsidered'.[73] By this time, therefore, the Pope is acting with complete confidence in asserting the primacy of his See.

This primacy was first most obviously and unambiguously exercised by Pope St Celestine (422–432).[74] Both Cyril, on the side of the hypostatic union, and Nestorius on the side of denying Mary the title of *theotokos*, submitted their positions to him during the Nestorian controversy, and Pope Celestine treated both as appealing to him. He condemned Nestorius' views at a Roman synod, and instructed Cyril to carry out the sentence of excommunication if Nestorius did not recant. Celestine left Cyril to carry out this excommunication at Ephesus in 431, leaving the door open for John of Antioch to return to communion provided that he accepted the decree of Ephesus and disavowed Nestorius. 'In his correspondence and through his legates at the council Celestine repeatedly asserted, with an unprecedented insistence, the pope's claim, as successor and living representative of St Peter, to paternal oversight of the whole church, eastern no less than western'.[75]

It is the statement of the papal and Petrine claims made by the legate Philip at the council of Ephesus which is most obviously the use of the primacy text to impose the Pope's orthodoxy on all the bishops, a claim which, it is significant to note, was not challenged or questioned by anyone at that Council: 'There can be no doubt, indeed it has been known by all generations, that the holy and most blessed Peter, prince and head of the apostles, support of the faith, and foundation of the catholic church, received from our Lord Jesus Christ, the Saviour and Redeemer of the human race, the keys of the kingdom, and to him was also given the power of binding and loosing sins'. [76]

The death of Pope Celestine followed quickly upon the Council of Ephesus, Pope St Sixtus reigned from 432 to 440.[77] He notably achieved reconciliation in 433 between Cyril and John of Antioch. Cyril's anathemas issued against Nestorius contained some exaggerated language, which could and was interpreted later as implying a Monophysite position.[78] Avoiding mention of Cyril's anathemas, he (Sixtus) insisted that John of Antioch and others sharing his views only needed to accept the decisions of Ephesus and disavow Nestorius to be restored to communion. Sixtus attributed the success of the Symbol of Union to the Apostle Peter 'guarantor of true faith and present in himself'.[79]

We have already considered Pope Leo the Great and the Council of Chalcedon (451) which overtrumped the *Latrocinium*, the Robber Council of 449.[80] We saw how the legates of Pope Leo defended the orthodox doctrine of the two natures of Christ at the Council of Chalcedon, and how the Council Fathers declared 'Peter has spoken through Leo'. This clear and definitive exercise of the primacy was understood by Leo as his sermons manifest, so that in his pronouncements we attain the fulfilment of the doctrine of the primacy. Kelly sums up Leo with his usual perception:

> An energetic and purposeful pontiff, Leo infused all his policies and pronouncements, especially his anniversary sermons, with his conviction that supreme and universal authority in the church, bestowed originally by Christ on PETER, had been transmitted to each subsequent bishop of Rome as the Apostle's heir. As such, he assumed Peter's functions, full authority, and privileges; and just as the Lord bestowed more power on Peter than on the other apostles, so the pope was 'the primate of all the bishops', the Apostle's mystical embodiment.[81]

## 10.9 CONCLUSION

*We have here returned to Newman's position regarding the development of the papal primacy, which led him to visible union with the Catholic Church.*

> If such be the nature of the case, if we may so speak reverently, that an Infinite Wisdom, which sees the end from the beginning, in decreeing the rise of an universal Empire, should not have decreed the development of a sovereign ruler. Moreover, all this must be viewed in the light of the general probability, so much insisted on above, that doctrine cannot

> but develop as time proceeds and need arises, and that its developments are part of the Divine system, and that therefore it is lawful, or rather necessary, to interpret the words and deeds of the earlier Church by the determinate teaching of the later.[82]

We have now reached the formula of the First Vatican Council, which Leo and all successive popes explicitly claim:

> 1. We teach and declare that, according to the gospel evidence, a primacy of jurisdiction over the whole Church of God was immediately and directly promised to the apostle Peter and conferred on him by Christ the Lord.

Using Newman's biblical hermeneutic, therefore, it is quite legitimate to argue that the meaning of the Petrine text in Matthew was only understood over the course of four centuries, as the outbreak of heresy and of the attempt by the Emperor to compromise the doctrines of the Church caused Popes particularly from St Damasus onwards to insist upon the Petrine text as giving them universal primacy over both east and west. The meaning of this text also, as we have seen, became clear as the studies of scripture by Jerome explored the Semitic meaning of Matthew 16:17–19, making clear to him that the power of binding and loosing was a rabbinic term giving legal authority to Peter. We have also argued to the authenticity of what we have called the 'Matthean addition', that the historical Jesus most plausibly gave Peter the authority given to him in that text, even though we cannot necessarily argue to Matthew 16:17–19 being the *ipsissima verba Jesu*. The meaning and import of this text was part of the developing understanding of the whole Church guided by the Holy Spirit.

## Notes

1. M. Winter, *Peter and the Popes* (London: Darton, Longman and Todd, 1960).This book is not easily obtained, but gathers together in an accessible form the evidence from the first four centuries.
2. Winter, *Peter and the Popes*, pp. v–vi.
3. We depend quite heavily, and without apology, on Kelly's *Dictionary of the Popes*. Kelly himself represents the best of Oxford Anglo-Catholicism, totally loyal to the dogmatic Councils of the Church, and by no means hostile to the papacy. He accompanied the then Archbishop of Canterbury Michael Ramsey to meet the Pope as Ramsey's theological consultor.
4. ODP, p. xi.
5. Winter, p. 114.
6. DCD, p. 312, cf. 2.4 above.
7. ODP, p. 6.
8. *Ibid*.
9. *Ibid*., pp. 6–7.
10. *Ibid*., p. 7.
11. See section 7.1 above.
12. St Irenaeus, *Against Heresies* 3:3:2.
13. Winter, p. 40.
14. *Ibid*., p. 50.
15. *Ibid*., p. 58.
16. *Ibid*., p. 40.
17. ODP, p. 20.
18. P. Hughes, p. 116.
19. ODP, pp. 18–19.
20. *Ibid*., p. 19.
21. *Ibid*., p. 20.
22. P. Hughes, p. 112.
23. *Ibid*., p.115.
24. *Ibid*., p.116
25. ODP, p. 20.
26. *Ibid*., p. 21
27. http://www.newadvent.org/cathen/04295c.htm [accessed 31.03.2013].
28. P. Hughes, p. 192. (Cf. W. H. C. Frend, *The Early Church: From the Beginnings to 461* (London: SCM Press, Second Edition, 1982), p. 141, who gives a different translation. 'There was when he was not', and last sentence 'Catholic and Apostolic Church', p. 141). Tanner I, p. 5. "*tous de legontas én pote hote ouk én kai prin yennéthénai ouk én....Eos autem qui dicunt: erat quando non erat, et; priusquam nascerunt non erat*". Frend, *Early Church*, p. 137, quotes historian Socrates quoting in turn

Arius, *én hoti ouk én*.
29 ODP, p. 28.
30 *Ibid*.
31 P. Hughes, p. 192.
32 *Ibid.*, p. 194.
33 Frend, *The Early Church: From the Beginnings to 461*, p. 146.
34 *Ibid.*, p. 147.
35 *Ibid.*, p. 148.
36 *Ibid.*, p. 151.
37 'Callistus's reign (217–22) was marred by bickering with the aggressive antipope, who accused him of modalism and of laxity in discipline, but whom he seems never to have formally censured. The former charge can be dismissed, for he excommunicated Sabellius, the intellectual leader of modalism, who maintained that Father, Son, and Holy Spirit do not represent real distinctions in the Godhead but successive modes of its self-revelation. This did not satisfy Hippolytus, who jeered that he had only passed the sentence out of fear of himself and was still a modalist. In fact Callistus was trying to steer a middle course between modalism, which he rejected, and Hippolytus' teaching that the Word is a distinct hypostasis or person, which he viewed as ditheistic.' See ODP pp. 13–14. St Hippolytus Antipope, AD 217–235, Kelly, ODP, pp. 14–15. Hippolytus wrote in Greek, thus his writings are lost.
38 Frend, *The Early Church: From the Beginnings to 461*, pp. 151–153.
39 *Ibid*, p. 151.
40 ODP, pp. 29–30.
41 *Ibid.*, p. 30.
42 Winter, p. 133.
43 *Ibid.*, p. 134.
44 *Ibid.*, p. 134.
45 *Ibid.*, p. 135.
46 *Ibid.*, p. 138.
47 *Ibid.*, p. 169.
48 ODP, p. 30
49 *Ibid.*, pp. 31–32.
50 *Ibid.*, p. 32.
51 *Ibid*.
52 *Ibid*.
53 Kelly uses critically the *Liber Pontificalis* (ed. Paris: Duchesne, 1886–92), ODP, p. xi. 'A collection of papal biographies from St Peter to Pius II (d.1464), compiled in its first redaction in the middle of the sixth century and extended by later hands. While much of the material embodied, especially in the earlier section, is apocryphal,

54  ODP, p. 31.
55  Ibid., p. 32.
56  Ibid.
57  Kelly claims that Damasus consolidated his claims to the papacy 'by hiring a gang of thugs, storming the Julian basilica and carrying out a three-day massacre of Ursinians'. ODP, pp. 32–33.
58  Ibid., p. 33.
59  Winter, p. 62.
60  Redford, J. *Born of a Virgin: Proving the Miracle from the Gospels*, (London, St. Pauls, 2007), p. 47.
61  Ibid.
62  Winter, p. 67, n.1. Optatus of Milevis, *Adversus Parmen*, II, 2 in CSEL, Vol. 26, p. 36. He confused the Greek *Kephalé* (head) with *Cephas*, yet obviously was aware of the interpretation of Matthew 16 in terms of the primacy of Peter.
63  Winter, pp. 199–200.
64  Ibid., p. 200.
65  Ibid., p. 196.
66  Ibid., p. 196.
67  ODP, p. 35.
68  Ibid., p. 37
69  Ibid., p. 38.
70  Ibid.
71  Ibid., p. 39.
72  Ibid., pp. 40–41.
73  Ibid., p. 41
74  Ibid.
75  Ibid., p. 42.
76  Mansi, IV, col. 1295. Winter, p. 63.
77  ODP, p. 43.
78  The formula of Cyril was quoted 'One incarnate nature of God the Word'. Hughes states that Eutyches 'had taken this formula in its monophysite sense...', although Hughes insists that the monophysite interpretation of the term *physis* 'finds no warrant in St. Cyril', P. Hughes, p. 252.
79  ODP, p. 43.
80  See section 2.4 above.
81  ODP, p. 43.
82  DCD, p. 155.

[The opening fragment before note 54 reads: "the work is in the main based on valuable sources, and while it is often biased it is indispensable for the history of the papacy.'"]

# 11

# THE INFALLIBILITY OF THE CHURCH

## 11.1 VATICAN I AND VATICAN II ON INFALLIBILITY

*The Texts of Vatican I and Vatican II are set out.*

> **THE FIRST VATICAN COUNCIL**
> DOGMATIC CONSTITUTION ON THE CHURCH OF
> CHRIST *Pastor Aeternus*
> Session 4: 18 July 1870
> Chapter 4.
>
> On the infallible teaching authority of the Roman Pontiff
> 8. Therefore, faithfully adhering to the tradition received from the beginning of the Christian faith, to the glory of God our Saviour, for the exaltation of the Catholic religion and for the salvation of the Christian people, with the approval of the Sacred Council, we teach and define as a divinely revealed dogma that when the Roman Pontiff speaks EX CATHEDRA, that is, when, in the exercise of his office as shepherd and teacher of all Christians, in virtue of his supreme apostolic authority, he defines a doctrine concerning faith or morals to be held by the whole Church, he possesses, by the divine assistance promised to him in blessed Peter, that infallibility which the divine Redeemer willed his Church to enjoy in defining doctrine concerning faith or morals. Therefore, such definitions of the Roman Pontiff are of themselves, and not by the consent of the Church, irreformable.

> **THE SECOND VATICAN COUNCIL**
> *DOGMATIC CONSTITUTION ON THE CHURCH LUMEN GENTIUM*
> Session 5: 21 November 1964
>
> Para 25, continued:
> Although the individual bishops do not enjoy the prerogative of infallibility, they nevertheless proclaim Christ's doctrine infallibly whenever, even though dispersed through the world, but still maintaining the bond of communion among themselves and with the successor of Peter, and authentically teaching matters of faith and morals, they are in agreement on one position as definitively to be held. This is even more clearly verified when, gathered together in an ecumenical council, they are teachers and judges of faith and morals for the universal Church, whose definitions must be adhered to with the submission of faith ... The infallibility promised to the Church resides also in the body of bishops, when that body exercises the supreme Magisterium with the successor of Peter. To these definitions the assent of the Church can never be wanting, on account of the activity of that same Holy Spirit, by which the whole flock of Christ is preserved and progresses in unity of faith...'

## 11.2 ESSENTIAL READING

- B. C. Butler, *The Church and Infallibility: A Reply to the Abridged 'Salmon'* (Catholic Book Club Edition) [Butler]
- P. Chirico, *Infallibility: The Crossroads of Doctrine* (London: Sheed and Ward, 1977) [Chirico]
- H. Küng, *Infallible? An enquiry,* Translated from the German by Eric Mosbacher (London: Collins, 1971). [INF]
- J. F. Costanzo, *The Historical Credibility of Hans Küng* (North Quincy, Massachusetts: The Christopher Publishing House, 1979). [Costanzo]

## 11.3 INTRODUCTION

*Hans Küng argues that the doctrine of the infallibility of the Church was introduced later into the Church under the influence of the Isidore Decretals later proven spurious.*

It might be argued with at least some justification that the problem of infallibility has only seriously been discussed in the Church in the nineteenth and twentieth centuries. The two catalysts for such debate were first the definition of papal infallibility in 1870, and then the controversy over the issuing of the papal encyclical *Humanae Vitae* issued by Pope Paul VI in 1968 condemning contraceptive intercourse. This latter debate has also raised the question concerning the authority of what is sometimes called 'non-infallible teaching', together with the kind of assent required for that teaching which is less than the 'assent of faith' due from every Catholic in response to defined doctrine. We will be discussing such 'religious assent of the mind' (*religio animi obsequio*'[1]) later, when we consider the implications of the debate following the publication of *Humanae Vitae*.

At the beginning, we will discuss the question of the time the Church took to be explicitly aware of its infallibility in matters of doctrine, and the lateness of its expression of this doctrine first of all in 1870. For Hans Küng, it is clear that the affirmation of the doctrine of the infallibility of the Pope does not go back before the thirteenth century, and was influenced by the Forged Decretals. Küng avers:

> Congar relies on the work of J. Langren, who assembled facts and documents to show that the Pope was not regarded as infallible from the seventh century to the twelfth.'[2]

> But this all changed with the Gregorian Reform... It was on such and similar statements that Gregory VII relied in the second half of the eleventh century for his monarchical conception of the Church...[3]

For Küng, Thomas Aquinas was to blame for 'demonstrating' to the Greeks in *contra errors Graecorum* that 'the Pope decides what is part of faith'. These ideas were taken over into his *Summa Theologiae*:[4]

> There is no doubt that St Thomas Aquinas, basing himself in good faith on the forgeries, as we may assume, thus laid the foundations for the Vatican I doctrine of infallibility.[5] Vatican I certainly cannot be blamed for not quoting the Council of Chalcedon, with its famous Canon 28, which granted New Rome (Constantinople) the same prerogatives as Rome itself...[6]

Chirico claims that 'Brian Tierney has shown that this teaching (on infallibility) was first formulated by Pietro Olivi (c. 1248 to 1298) for what were basically political reasons. From this he concludes that the doctrine can be discarded for it is post-biblical.'[7] And Küng concludes that, for the reason that the doctrine of infallibility is so poorly attested in the history of theology, it can be replaced by the concept of 'indefectibility', which is the presence of the Spirit in the Church (that is in the whole church, not only in the Episcopal and Papal Magisterium) without guaranteeing the inerrancy of propositions.

We cannot deal with any justification of this doctrine without examining related issues, which in our formulation of the problem have already been noted, either in this Introduction or earlier in our work.

## 11.4 DEFINITION OF TERMS

*'Inerrancy', 'Infallibility', and 'Certainty':* **Inerrancy** *is the absence of any error in a text either of the present or of the past.* **Infallibility** *means that a given individual or community in certain circumstances will never possibly be in error not only in the present but in the future.* **Certainty** *means that a given person is convinced that a given proposition is without error, without implying either inerrancy or infallibility generally regarding that person.*

Abbott (later Bishop) B .C. Butler wrote a reply to a republished and abridged edition of the famous (or infamous) 'Salmon's Infallibility', which was a vitriolic attack on the Catholic concept of an infallible church published in Dublin first in 1889, after the definition of papal infallibility by the First Vatican Council. The abridged edition was published in the 1950s, when the then Archbishop of Canterbury Dr Fisher expressed his concern in his own time at the growth of (*sic*) 'Fundamentalism and Roman Catholicism'.

Butler, himself a convert from Anglicanism, produced what he himself considered to be a brief and limited reply in his book *The Church and Infallibility: A Reply to the Abridged 'Salmon'*, but it is perhaps still the best treatment of the subject after fifty and more years. Butler wrote before the Second Vatican Council, and so did not have the clear expression of the statement of the infallibility of General Councils which we have just quoted. In terms of the definition of doctrine, he was limited to the definitions of Vatican I, which stated only the infallibility of the Roman Pontiff when he speaks *ex cathedra*. The First Vatican Council broke up, the bishops fleeing from the forces attacking Rome, before they were able to work on the wider ecclesiological questions which were their original intention.

However Butler is in no way restricted in his treatment of infallibility to the infallibility of the Pope. On the contrary, he produces a credible apologetic for infallibility. Butler, in introducing the subject, presents infallibility as a vitally important doctrine of the Church:

> First, then, I would point out that if the Church is not infallible, then the Church cannot claim our allegiance. This is so because the Church insists, and has ever insisted, upon acceptance of her infallibility as *a sine qua non* of Christian allegiance.[8]

Butler means of course that the Church *implicitly* demands our assent to its infallibility, long before it was ever explicitly discussed from the eleventh century onwards:

> It may therefore be useful to point out that when the modern Church claims to be 'infallible' she is only making the claim which the Church has always made—that her teaching is true and that 'heretical' teaching is, as such, erroneous.'[9]

Butler quotes 1 Thessalonians 2:13 that the message of Christ was received by the Thessalonians not as a human word, but as the word of God. Butler claims, therefore, that right from the beginning, the Church demanded the allegiance of its members on pain of excommunication, because she was proclaiming God's teaching and not some human thinking. The General Councils made this explicit in the fourth and fifth centuries in deciding on questions of Christology, Trinity, and Incarnation. The Church is claiming allegiance from its members not only concerning what it *has* defined as matters of faith, but what it *will* define in the future. The Church is implicitly claiming that she cannot be wrong at any time when she does define such matters.

It is worth considering how we could ever make a statement of faith unless we believed that the Church could not be wrong in this matter. There must always be a lingering doubt as to whether a given doctrine is true if we were not convinced that the Church could not be wrong in this matter. Particularly regarding the doctrines of faith which are revealed, and beyond although not contrary to reason, the certainty of faith requires belief in the infallibility of the Church, that the Church could not be wrong in this matter.

Dr Salmon had argued that 'The craving for an infallible guide arises from men's consciousness of the weakness of their understanding...'[10] Butler on the contrary quotes from Origen in the third century:

> Whereas there are many who think that they have the mind of Christ, and some of them hold views diverse from those of former times, let the Church's teaching (*ecclesiastica praedicatio*) be maintained, which has been handed down in one succession

from the Apostles and abides till the present day in the Churches. That alone is to be believed truth which in no respect disagrees with the ecclesiastical and apostolic tradition.'[11]

Salmon had introduced the circular argument that, if I claim that the Church is infallible, then I am arrogantly claiming infallibility for myself. But Butler distinguishes between 'certainty' and 'infallibility'. He quotes Newman in the *Grammar of Assent* in stating: 'We may conclude, then, that it is quite logical to say "I myself am not infallible, but I am certain that the Church is"'.[12] We are 'certain' in making the act of faith in the Church's teaching, not because we are infallible, but because we affirm with confidence that the Church is.

We also must distinguish between 'inerrancy' and 'infallibility'. We will be examining later Küng's objection that the language of faith cannot be infallible. But Küng attacks equally the idea of an 'infallible church' and an 'infallible Bible', against Fundamentalist Protestantism:

> Just as it is wrong in the case of the Church to link the work of the Spirit of God (in the sense of an *assistentia*) with any particular definitions by a Pope or council, so is it wrong in the case of Scripture to restrict the working of the Spirit of God (in the sense of inspiration) to any particular statement by an apostle or biblical author.[13]

On the contrary, the Second Vatican Council asserts in the inerrancy of the sacred scriptures in the Dogmatic Constitution on Divine Revelation:

> Therefore, since everything asserted by the inspired authors or sacred writers must be held to be asserted by the Holy Spirit, it follows that the books of Scripture must be acknowledged as teaching solidly, faithfully and without error that truth which God wanted put into sacred writings for the sake of salvation. Therefore 'all Scripture is divinely inspired and has its use for teaching the truth and

> refuting error, for reformation of manners and discipline in right living, so that the man who belongs to God may be efficient and equipped for good work of every kind'. (2 Tim 3:16–17, Greek text)[14]

Thus the Church will not countenance that there is any error in the Scriptures, since God is their author; although of course, the truth is that which God wished to assert through the scriptures, which has to be judged according to its literary genre. Thus the distinction between the inerrancy of the scriptures and the infallibility of the church is as follows:

- The inerrancy of the scriptures is due to the fact that God is their author, whereas infallible definitions of the Church are authored by either a Pope or Pope and Bishops together, with divine assistance, but not with divine inspiration.
- The content of infallible definitions is limited to faith and morals as given in divine revelation, whereas the inerrant statements of the scriptures are not limited to matters of faith and morals, as Leo XIII said in his encyclical on biblical inspiration. Rather, the inerrancy of the scriptures is due to the fact that whatever they intend to say God himself through the Holy Spirit inerrantly wishes to say. The content need not be faith or morals, but could be for example historical fact (for example the Resurrection), if such is for our salvation.
- The Scriptures are already written, therefore there is no question of their being 'infallible', which refers to the inerrancy of divinely revealed statements on revelation not only now, but in any future contingency, forever. Thus more appropriately, we speak of the 'infallibility of the Church' but 'the inerrancy of the sacred scriptures.'

Thus, to summarise:

1. 'Infallibility' refers to that gift which God has given through his Holy Spirit to his Church to proclaim the truth of revelation through the Magisterium of bishops united with the Pope, that truth being declared at any time without error.
2. 'Inerrancy' refers to the inspiration of the biblical books which have God as their author, and therefore always state without error precisely what, and only what, God wishes to say through those sacred books.
3. 'Certainty' is the gift of the Holy Spirit by which each member of the Church may have confidence in the infallible teaching of the Church.

## 11.5 INFALLIBLE OR 'INDEFECTIBLE' STATEMENTS OF FAITH?

*Küng denies that propositions of faith can be infallible. He therefore wishes to replace 'infallible' with 'indefectible'. However the Church has always maintained that language about God can be true, although always needing further development. It is difficult to see what intelligibility can be given to the concept of 'indefectibility', which seems to come from a form of Hegelian relativism.*

Küng's problem is not so much in the infallibility of the Church, or even in the infallibility of the Bible, but rather in the philosophical impossibility of infallible propositions:

> Just as there is no inherently infallible teaching office, so is there no inherently infallible teaching book in Christendom. The Church as the community of the faithful cannot make infallible propositions, but possesses a fundamental indefectibility in the truth.[15]

Likewise he states: 'Even though there are no inherently inerrant propositions in the Bible, it nevertheless contains true propositions attesting the gospel'.[16]

Küng wishes to replace 'infallible' with 'indefectible' regarding the confidence with which the Church may have regarding its teaching. But Küng never tells us how we could have indefectible statements of faith which were true and yet at least possibly erroneous.

Again, the problem is not with the infallibility of the Pope. Equally problematic for Küng is the infallibility of General Councils, which is the Orthodox position and as we have seen earlier, is the position of the Anglicans of the Oxford Movement. Regarding Orthodoxy, Küng states:

> If the infallibility of the Church is thus to be identified with the infallibility of propositions—laid down, not by the Pope, but by ecumenical councils—Orthodoxy, for all its opposition to Rome, exposes itself to the same difficulties from which the Roman doctrine suffers, arising from the artificial restrictions of the apostolic succession to the bishops, the questionable legitimacy of deducing the infallibility of the ecumenical councils from the infallibility of the Church, and finally, the question as to whether it is possible to make infallible propositions at all... The argument for the infallibility of ecumenical councils seems, however to overshoot the mark, for if a hundred office-holders can represent the Church infallibly, why should a single one theoretically be unable to do so?'[17]

Küng therefore does not accept the infallibility of ecumenical councils, 'meaning by that their ability to formulate infallible propositions'.[18] His position here is quite logical. If the whole Church in General Council can make infallible propositions, then nothing prevents an individual making infallible propositions. However Küng does not think that this is really the Orthodox position. 'To the Orthodox the sole 'criterion of truth' is God himself....'[19] Küng only gives one or two modern Orthodox theologians as evidence of this more nuanced approach to General Councils. Certainly, the impression given by the Orthodox over the centuries is that the Ecumenical Councils of the first thousand years, which the separated Eastern Christians accept, were without error, and were produced by an infallible Church exercising its infallibility in the General Council. Küng can say that the Orthodox position is more akin to his own only because Orthodoxy has never defined the infallibility of General Councils; but Orthodoxy certainly acts as if those Councils were infallible.

Certainly, the Councils themselves which the Orthodox accept, as well as those later which they do not, act as if the words they use are themselves expressive of the infallible truth of Christian faith. There was a long and acrimonious debate throughout the fourth century on the meaning of the expression 'consubstantial with the Father', which Athanasius insisted upon, but which many of the Eastern bishops following Eusebius of Nicomedia rejected as unscriptural.[20] As we said earlier, Eustathius Bishop of Antioch was deposed for Sabellianism, although in reality it was only because he accepted the *homóousios* formula. How can Küng say that Councils do not claim infallibility for their words, when clearly they in fact do, excommunicating those who do not accept a particular formula?

Of course, the Church would always admit the inadequacy of any language about God. Each dogmatic statement is open to further development. As Butler says, only repeating the words of Newman, 'And if Christianity is a living thing it is only to be expected that it too will develop.'[21] Thus the words used must always be supplemented, sometimes by words which appear contradictory. Thus those followers of Athanasius such as Apollinarius who over-emphasised the doctrine that Jesus was 'of the same substance (*homóousios*) with the Father' drew the false conclusion that therefore the human soul of Jesus was replaced by the soul of the logos; and those who over-emphasised Cyril's doctrine that the Incarnate Word was 'one person' (*mia phusis*) led to the false doctrine that the Word becoming flesh in Jesus was of a single divine-human nature, Monophysitism, rather than the orthodox doctrine of Chalcedon that the Incarnate Word was equally two natures divine and human after the Incarnation as before it.

It is also difficult to see how Küng's view would work in practice in the Church. If no verbal formulae are sacrosanct, inerrant, and the Church does not have power to make infallible statements, how can it exercise its doctrinal authority? We have seen in recent years denominations such as the Church of England hopelessly divided over moral issues, and over the ordination of women. If no statement of faith or morals is free from error, then what value has any of them?

The Church claims that we can make true statements about God, even if inadequate, and always needing further development:

> In defending the ability of human reason to know God, the Church is expressing her confidence in the possibility of speaking about him to all men and with all men, and therefore of dialogue with other religions, with philosophy and science, as well as with unbelievers and atheists.[22]

Jesus said to his apostles just before his arrest and crucifixion, 'However, when the Spirit of truth comes he will lead you to the complete truth, since he will not be speaking of his own accord, but will say only what he has been told; and he will reveal to you the things to come.'(Jn 16:13). This means, in turn, that we are able to make true statements about God when divine revelation in scripture and in tradition communicates that true knowledge to us; and in words.

The problem is that Küng has a view of revelation which is defective, linked to the German philosopher Hegel. Küng says that with Hegel comes the realisation that 'the truth lies, not in the individual steps, propositions and elements, but in the whole'.[23] However Hegel proposed a philosophy which claimed that the Absolute Idea changed itself constantly in the process of development. We have already noted Strauss' view that we can only have a representation (*Vorstellung*) of the truth, and not a concept (*Begriff*) of it, cf. 3.3. In spite of the frailty of human language, the Creed is recited in millions of churches throughout the world, with the same meaning as understood by the Church. This is in itself an answer to the Hegelian view of the essential changeability of the meaning of words.

However, as we have already investigated earlier in this study, Küng's view of infallibility is by no means independent of his view of the Church as such, and particularly with his view of the visible Church. To that concept of the visible Church we now turn.

## 11.6 THE VISIBLE CHURCH

*On the contrary, with Butler, we maintain that from the beginning there was one visible Church, and that Church was headed by the apostles, against Küng, who denies to the apostles any authority not given to the whole community of Christians.*

Butler begins his reply to 'Salmon's Infallibility' with denying that the main question between Protestants and Catholics is infallibility:

> I wish now to add a word about the chapter's main contention, namely that the chief issue between Protestantism and the Church is the latter's claim to infallibility. I do not believe that this is an accurate statement. The real issue, it seems to me, is the Roman Catholic Communion's claim to be the Church founded by Christ, to which all men are called by God to belong as of duty. And behind this issue there lies the question of what idea is held of 'the Church' — what sort of a thing is meant by 'the Church militant'. The ancient and modern Catholic answer to this question is that the Church on earth is an association of baptised persons.[24]

Butler first claims that no-one before the Reformation thought of the Church as anything but a communion of baptised Christians. Was there ever considered an 'invisible church'?

> No-one before Luther had been able to emancipate himself in conscience from the visible Church.[25] Primitive Christianity recognized no invisible Church on earth as distinct from the visible society of the baptised; no self-governing body in the local congregation apart from the authority of the whole Body of Christ; no assured gifts of grace outside the Catholic communion.[26]

Critical scholars today would contend that the primitive church of the first century was 'pluralistic'. We have already seen discussions where scholars could only consider the Church as the expressed religions consciousness of its members, as Pope Pius X defined as the Modernist position, cf. 3.5. But there is lacking any evidence that the documents of the primitive church, namely the New Testament books, recognised that there was any more than one visible church of which all were members.

It is here that we see the importance of the apostolicity of the Church. We are not surprised to see that Küng repeats his argument which he has already made in his study of *The Church* in his later book *Infallibility? An Enquiry*. He now argues:

> Thus it is plain that only someone who, over and above human testimony, is instructed by God, by the Holy Spirit, can authoritatively transmit the message. But the New Testament testifies that that is every Christian. Every believer, having been taught by God, can and should teach others; as recipient of the word of God, he can and should also be its proclaimer in one way or another.[27]

Küng, as we have already seen denies that expressing our faith in the 'apostolic church' means that we give to the apostles and their successors a special magisterium.[28] On the contrary, we argued that Paul in Corinth exercised direct rule over the Church at Corinth, demanding that the Corinthians Christians excommunicate a man 'when you are assembled, and my spirit is present.' (1 Co 5:4ff.). The first Christians were in one visible church because they were ruled by the apostles whom Jesus himself appointed; and these apostles exercised that authority, This does not change but is only confirmed after the apostles are succeeded in AD 96 by for example Clement of Rome. See the quotation from Clement, where he tells the Corinthians to 'submit to the presbyters'.[29]

## 11.7 THE PRIMACY AND INFALLIBILITY

*Among the apostles, as we have demonstrated earlier, primacy was given by the historical Jesus to Peter, which primacy was handed on to his successors as Bishops of Rome.*

Küng is quite clear as to the inextricable link between papal infallibility and papal primacy, but which he says, is again historically untenable:

> The definition of papal infallibility presupposes the definition of papal primacy.[30] ... The whole of the Vatican I argument for the existence of a Petrine primacy of jurisdiction, and *a fortiori* a continuation of the Petrine primacy, and above all its continuation in the Bishop of Rome, runs into grave difficulties from the standpoint of contemporary exegesis and history (as it did to an extent in the exegesis and history of the time), and no Catholic theologian has yet been able to dispose of these difficulties. They make any attempt to demonstrate a historical succession of the Bishops of Rome in a Petrine primacy a highly questionable enterprise.[31]

Not necessarily contrary to 'a really living primacy of service that would be more than a mere primacy of honour or of jurisdiction—a pastoral primacy in the spirit of the gospel, in accordance with Matthew 16:18, Luke 22:32 and John 21:15–17, and following the pattern, not of Leo the Great, Innocent III, Pius IX or Pius XII, but of Gregory the Great and John XXIII.'[32]

Just as regarding the distinctive nature and authority of the Apostles and their successors we have referred you to Chapter 8, so now in considering the primacy of the Bishop of Rome and in consequence his infallibility we refer you to Chapter 9. We have argued above[33] that Matthew 16:13–23 in its exegesis strongly supports the primacy of Peter. Luke 22:32 supports also the leadership of Peter 'but I have prayed for you, Simon, that your faith may not fail, and once you have recovered, you in your turn must strengthen your brethren'. As does John 21:15–17, where Peter responds to the three times Jesus asks him *'Do you love me?'* with intense affirmation *'yes'*. Jesus' response 'Feed my sheep' is noted by Bultmann in his commentary as giving Peter 'the leadership of his community.'[34]

It is difficult to know what Küng means when he speaks of 'a pastoral primacy in the spirit of the gospel'. What we in fact see from the beginning of the exercise of the papacy is the exercise of the authority of the Bishop of Rome, which again we have traced in Chapter Nine. This authority developed, and as we saw reached its zenith in the fifth century, with the authoritative exercise of Pope St Leo the Great at the Council of Chalcedon n 451. This was inextricably linked with infallibility, since Leo acted as if he were infallible, having doctrinal authority over the bishops of the whole world. Admittedly, the Pope's primacy was denied after the schism with the Orthodox; but Butler argues that that was not any advance in terms of the claims of Rome. On the contrary, he claims, it was a stand based upon what the Council of Chalcedon, as an ecumenical council, had actually agreed in 451

Rome never withdrew from the position she had assumed for herself before the Council of Chalcedon, and which the letter of the Council recognized as hers by right. It was six hundred years later that there occurred, in the time of Michael Caerularius, Patriarch of Constantinople, the tragic breach between East and West which has yet to be healed. We may legitimately ask when, and by whom, during the period AD 451 to 860 the claims of Rome were contested, refuted or denied? Is it not true that what happened from time to time — sadly often, in fact — was that a virtual denial of these claims was involved in some heresy or compromise with heresy, which separated the East from the centre of unity and threw it into the arms of the Empire; and that a return to orthodoxy went always hand in hand with the acceptance of the Roman formula of faith and conditions of communion? Again the typical case is... When the Eastern bishops accepted the Emperor Zeno's Henotikon, a formula designed to reconcile those who had broken away from Catholic unity because they rejected the Leonine and Chalcedonian Christology — and to reconcile them by passing over Leo and Chalcedon in silence — Rome refused the Henotikon and excluded those who accepted it from Catholic communion; and when, after over thirty years, the schism was healed, it was by the Eastern bishops' signing the formula of Hormisdas, including the following:

> We cannot ignore the declaration of our Lord Jesus Christ when he said: 'Thou art Peter', etc. Moreover, the truth of his words is shown by actual fulfilment, since in the Apostolic See the Catholic religion has always been preserved without spot. So, as it is our aim to be parted in no way from that faith and hope, we anathematize all heresies ... Wherefore I hope that I may deserve to be with you in one communion, such as is defined by the Apostolic See, where the permanence of the Christian religion is intact and genuine, promising that in future those separated from the communion of the Catholic Church, that is not agreeing with the Apostolic See, are not to have their names recited in the sacred mysteries (i.e. the liturgy).[35]

How can a primacy over all the bishops of the world, as exercised by Pope Leo the Great at Chalcedon, and as claimed by successive Popes before him, and accepted by such as Patriarch Cyril of Alexandria at the time of the Nestorian heresy, imply anything less than infallibility, when its exercise is continuous throughout the centuries regarding matters of divine revelation?

## 11.8 THE FALSE DECRETALS

*The False Isidorian Decretals are not the source of the doctrine of the infallibility of the Pope. These Decretals only promoted the Pope's temporal power over the whole of Europe as against Caesaro-Papism. Regarding the doctrine of infallibility and primacy, the False Decretals say no more than was exercised in the fifth Century by Leo the Great.*

Some have argued that it was the False Decretals of Isidore which were the foundations of the modern papacy claiming primacy and infallibility. An example of one claiming such is Abbé Gette:

> Adrian sets before the Emperor the example of Charles, King of the Franks. 'Following our advice,' he says, 'and fulfilling our wishes, he has subjected all the barbarous nations of the West; he has given to the Roman Church in perpetuity provinces, cities, castles, and patrimonies which were withheld by the Lombards, and which by right belong to St Peter; he does not cease daily to offer gold and silver for this light and sustenance of the poor.'
>
> Here is language quite new on the part of Roman bishops, but henceforth destined to become habitual with them. It dates from 785; that is, from the same year when Adrian delivered to Ingelramn, Bishop of Metz, the collection of the False Decretals. There is something highly significant in this coincidence. Was it Adrian himself who authorized this work of forgery? We do not know; but it is an incontestable

> fact that it was in Rome itself under the pontificate of Adrian, and in the year in which he wrote so haughtily to the Emperor of the East, that this new code of the Papacy is first mentioned in history. Adrian is the true creator of the modern Papacy. Not finding in the traditions of the Church the documents necessary to support his ambitious views, he rested them upon apocryphal documents written to suit the occasion, and to legalize all future usurpations of the Roman see. Adrian knew that the Decretals contained in the code of Ingelramn were false. For he had already given, ten years before, to Charles, King of the Franks, a code of the ancient canons, identical with the generally received collection of Dionysius Exiguus. It was, therefore, between the years 775 and 785 that the False Decretals were composed.[36]

One fact is immediately to be noted. The intended effect of the False Decretals was to increase the *temporal power and wealth* of the papacy. Regarding the spiritual authority of the Pope, as Constanzo says: '... these forgeries do not excel in inventing new ideas; what they did was to give certain fundamental theses, already largely accepted, a historical twist and foundation.'[37]

Regarding the papal primacy, the Isidorian Decretals give the Pope no more power than Leo had already exercised at the Council of Chalcedon. What in fact the Decretals do is to counter Caesaro-Papism with an increase of the temporal power of the Pope. The third Canon of the Council of Constantinople had decreed that 'However, the bishop of Constantinople is to have honorary pre-eminence over the bishop of Rome, because Constantinople is the new Rome.'[38]

As Hughes says:

> The canon, though it tacitly admits the new unheard-of-principle that the honour should be according to the see-city, offers, it is true, no more than a title of honour. It does not make any exception for Constan-

tinople in the matter of jurisdiction as settled by the preceding canon. For all his new honour the Bishop of Constantinople remains, in jurisdiction, the simple suffragan of the Metropolitan of Heraclea, with no authority beyond the limits of his own see. The council had merely done for him what Nicaea had done fifty years earlier for Jerusalem.[39]

The *Isidorian Decretals* only continue the age-long struggle of the Pope in his temporal strife with the Emperors. The Catholic Encyclopaedia of the early twentieth century as usual gives us a judicious opinion concerning the effect of the Decretals, not over theology, but over the mediaeval view of the ancient church:

> In the domain of theology and canon law, Isidore's forgeries never had any serious consequences. Having said this, we are free to confess frankly that in lesser spheres than those of theology and law, the false decretals have not always exercised a fortunate influence. On history, for instance, their influence was baneful. No doubt they do not bear all the blame for the distorted and Legendary view the Middle Ages had of ecclesiastical antiquity. During the Middle Ages it was almost an impossibility to consult all the sources of information, and it was difficult to check and control those at hand. It was not easy to distinguish genuine documents from apocryphal ones. And this difficulty, which was the great stumbling-block of medieval culture, would have been always an obstacle to the progress of historical study. It must be admitted that Isidore's forgeries increased the difficulty till it became almost insurmountable. The forgeries blurred the whole historical perspective. Customs and methods proper to the ninth century stood out in relief side by side with the discipline of the first centuries of the Church. And, as a consequence, the Middle Ages knew very little concerning the historical growth of the rights of the papacy during those first centuries. Its view of antiquity was a very simple one, and

> perhaps it was just as well for the systematizing of theology. In the main, it was no easy matter to develop a historical sense during the Middle Ages. The absence of such a sense is all the more remarkable when we consider what civilization owes the Middle Ages in the realms of philosophy, theology, and architecture.[40]

In this work, we have been careful to base all our conclusions on the better sense of the ancient history of the Church which modern study has given us. For Küng, Aquinas was to blame for 'demonstrating' to the Greeks in *contra errors Graecorum* that 'the Pope decides what is part of faith'. These ideas, Küng asserts, were taken over into his *Summa Theologiae*.[41] 'There is no doubt that St Thomas Aquinas, basing himself in good faith on the forgeries, as we may assume, thus laid the foundations for the Vatican I doctrine of infallibility.'[42] On the contrary, Aquinas' logical mind must have fastened on to the fact that if the Pope can decide what is part of faith, which authority is based upon the Petrine texts again as used in the fifth century Council of Chalcedon, the Pope's infallibility is clearly implied. If the Isidorian Decretals had never appeared, no doubt his theological view would have been the same. This brings us on to a consideration of the First Vatican Council and its definition of the infallibility of the Pope.

## 11.9 THE FIRST VATICAN COUNCIL

*As Küng agrees, nearly all the bishops at the Council accepted the infallibility of the Church. Nor did they object to the doctrine of the infallibility of the Pope. The only debate was as to whether that definition would be 'inopportune'. From accepting the infallibility of the Church, and the full primacy of the Pope, it was but a short and logical step to defining his infallibility.*

We have already discussed Newman's view of the First Vatican Council, and the debate concerning the definition of papal infallibility, **2.8**. Newman, as we have shown, was an 'inopportunist'; that is to say, he believed that to define papal infallibility was inopportune, at a time when Europe would consider that such a definition would revive papal secular claims at a time when its temporal power was clearly on the wane. Newman also thought that Ultra-Montane extremists would use papal infallibility as an instrument of papal power beyond what the Church taught that the Pope could exercise his being the successor of St Peter.

Küng is obviously disgusted with the definition of papal infallibility at Vatican I. On the one hand, he admits that what came eventually to be accepted was a formula with clear distinctions.[43] Küng admits that the final definition of papal infallibility was not what the extreme Ultra-Montanes wanted. Later, when we discuss the encyclical *Humanae Vitae*, we will clearly see the conditions of an infallible definition of doctrine was not met in Pope Paul VI's encyclical, whereas, for instance, they were clearly met in Pope Pius XII's definition of the Assumption of the Virgin Mary. Küng admits that the definition of papal infallibility at Vatican I was carefully formulated, to prevent what some have called 'creeping infallibility'.

However Küng wanted a much more radical discussion of papal infallibility at Vatican I, and even more at Vatican II. 'The historical problem that is disclosed here is not concerned just with the 'opportuneness' of the definition of infallibility, as has often been stated in the past, depriving the question of sting; it is also concerned with its truth.'[44] For him, it was totally unacceptable that Vatican I in its definition of papal infallibility '... merely repeated the notorious phrase *non autem ex consensus Ecclesiae* without amending it. But did this solve all problems? Neither the pro-infallibility party nor the anti-infallibility Gallicans can have gone to the heart of the matter'.[45] This question, continues Küng, was not solved at Vatican II, which effected 'a lazy compromise with the Curial minority'.[46] The Pope can issue single-handed definitions which are infallible. For

Küng, it was no help at all that 'infallibility on the lines of Vatican I was now formally extended to the episcopate...'[47] Vatican II has not changed the fact that the Pope 'himself decides, with the means that seem appropriate to him, what the meaning of this revelation is and what the true beliefs of the Church are'.[48] That would also mean, as Vatican II added, that a General Council of the Church, united with the Pope, can similarly issue an infallible definition of a doctrine, as of course it has many times during the long history of the Church. After such definitions, which according to the First Vatican Council, 'are of themselves, and not by the consent of the Church, (*non autem ex consensus Ecclesiae*) irreformable', the whole Church is bound to accept them. No further discussion is possible.

However anyone who looks at the historical evidence can clearly see that that is precisely the way in which the Ecumenical Councils of the fourth and fifth century acted. After the definition that Jesus was 'of one substance with the Father', there was no further debate either expected or allowed. The 'consent of the Church' was not required, precisely because the Church had decided through its Magisterium the Ecumenical Council of Nicaea. Küng realises that this is the problem, not papal infallibility as such. It is precisely that the Church's Magisterium, either in the form of a General Council, or in the form of a pronouncement by the Pope, can make judgements deemed infallible, and the consent of the Church is not required, because the magisterial organ of infallibility itself represents the Church with its knowledge of divine revelation given by the Holy Spirit. The Church has already consented through the infallible declaration itself.

The bishops realised that once an infallible church was admitted, it was but a short road to the doctrine of the infallibility of the Pope. The authoritative intervention of Pope Leo the Great's legates at the Council of Chalcedon demonstrates historically the infallibility of the Pope himself over the Council, annulling the decisions of the previous 'Robber Council' in 449. It was this authoritative exercise of the Pope which led Newman ultimately to the Catholic Church, as we have seen, whose infallibility he had come to see as necessary in order for genuine doctrinal development to occur.[49] Newman already accepted implicitly papal infallibility when he became a Catholic twenty years before the First Vatican Council. That is why he only objected to the definition of 1870 as 'inopportune', but not as untrue.

Küng also admits that the nearly all the bishops at the First Vatican Council accepted that the Church was infallible. Butler adds that only a few bishops at that Council were of the view that subsequent consent was necessary:

> So, too, with the doctrine of the Pope's infallibility. By the middle years of the nineteenth century the effect of the great schisms in the medieval West was decaying, and practically the only point at issue between Catholic theologians was, not whether the Pope was the organ and spokesman of the Church's infallibility, but whether or not his determinations of theological controversies depended for their validity upon the subsequent consent of the Church. The uncertainty was almost at an end before the Vatican Council met, and Manning stated that perhaps not more than a dozen of the hundreds of bishops there assembled still held the Gallican view that this subsequent consent was necessary.[50]

Küng freely admits that the vote for papal infallibility at the First Vatican Council was free and was not forced. 'The decisive factor was that there was no need to bring pressure to bear on the majority, for the definition was in complete harmony with its ideas'.[51] Küng simply uses this freedom of the Episcopal vote at Vatican I as further proof of his thesis, that the Church is not infallible in its General Councils, since it was an error so to define it!

That the explicitation of the doctrine of the infallibility of the Pope, indeed of the infallibility of the Church which underpins it, was late in the Church's history need not at all be denied. Once more, it is in the development of doctrine that the Church's infallibility becomes manifest in history, as with every other doctrine so developed. It is clear as crystal that for two thousand years, the Church has always acted as if its doctrines are true, even if always in need for further development. It has never admitted that there is any falsehood or error in those doctrines. That is the reason why the doctrine of the infallibility of the Church and the infallibility of the Pope and of General Councils was eventually defined, because it always was implicitly part of the 'deposit of faith'. Indeed, the very fact that there is a 'deposit of faith' itself implies that the Church is infallible in teaching that deposit of faith. Just as Küng sees the proof of the errors of the Ecumenical Council in defining infallibility, so the Church sees the development of the doctrine of infallibility as truly an exercise of the infallible Magisterium.

## 11.10 INFALLIBLE FALLACIES?

*The Church has never gone back on a defined doctrine to deny it, or to reverse its conclusions. Objections put forward are always of teaching which has not been solemnly defined.*

Küng says:

> For a long time Catholic apologetics was able very successfully to ward off the calling into question of infallibility by resorting to the basically simple expedient of arguing either that no error had been committed or — if in the last resort it could not be denied, reinterpreted, rendered innocuous or belittled — that it was an issue in which infallibility had not been at stake.[52]

We would submit that Küng is completely right here!

Historical objections to the doctrine of infallibility, namely times when Popes or others have apparently been mistaken, are sometimes trawled out. We will set out one or two examples, and briefly answer those objections. For more detail, you can look at pamphlets which are specifically designed for this purpose:

1. As regards Galileo, the magisterium of the Church seems to have first condemned him for his scientific views, and later retracted. Church authorities did not behave very intelligently. But the condemnation of Galileo was never claimed to be an infallible statement.
2. Pope Honorius was condemned for Monothelitism that is that Jesus had two natures, divine and human, but only one will. But Pope Honorius only gave Monothelitism as a personal opinion, not as an infallible statement.[53]
3. The ninth century schism of Photius. However this schism was the result of the East rejecting that doctrine of infallibility which the Eastern bishops had accepted implicitly in the Ecumenical Councils of the fourth and fifth centuries.[54]
4. Cyprian of Carthage with the African Bishops disagreed with the Pope, as we freely admitted in our earlier chapter.[55] It is quite possible that Cyprian did not accept the primacy of the Pope, but only a primacy of honour. The primacy of the Pope had not at that stage been formally defined as a doctrine of the Church.

## 11.11 HUMANAE VITAE

*The controversial Encyclical of Pope Paul VI, Humanae Vitae was clearly not an example of the exercise of papal infallibility, as for instance was the definition of the Assumption of the Blessed Virgin Mary, 1950. Some theologians have seen the condemnation of contraceptive intercourse as an exercise of the infallible ordinary magisterium of the bishops united with the Pope. Others have seen that moral condemnation as an example of non-infallible teaching of the Pope, which the Second Vatican*

*Council maintains should be obeyed by all the faithful with obsequium not fides, 'faith'.*

In the summer of 1968, Pope Paul VI issued what for some became the notorious encyclical *Humanae Vitae* ('Of Human Life') at the conclusion of an investigation by a Papal Commission into the whole question of the use of artificial means to prevent conception. The Pope rejected the findings of the majority of the Commission, which stated that the recently researched and marketed anovulent pill was not contraceptive in the sense condemned by the Church, but an extended use of the 'safe period'.

In *Infallible: an Enquiry*, Küng asks what turned the Pope against a change in this matter? Clearly, he explains, emphasis on the magisterium and the teaching office of the Church.[56] 'The permissibility of birth control could have been granted only subject to a condition totally unacceptable to the Pope and Curia, namely the disavowal of the traditional teaching of the Church and of the last three popes in particular, the admission of an error in the teaching of the Church.'[57]

The majority group on the Commission gave two reasons for the possibility of change; a new historical situation, and that the teaching on contraception was not infallible. However for Küng, the conservatives 'have a convincing case. They point out that essentially the same arguments in favour of birth control were accepted by the Lambeth Conference of Anglican bishops in 1930, and that the encyclical *Casti Connubii* was written in reply to those arguments.'[58] Küng further points out:

> In short, if Paul sanctioned birth control, there would be no evolution, but simply contradiction between him and Pius XI, no continuity, but discontinuity...[59]

> Nor do the conservatives deny that Pius XI's was not inherently an infallible doctrinal statement. But they claim that the point is a diversion from the central issue, the immorality of contraception, as maintained and proclaimed—and this is the decisive

point—by the united stand of the teaching office, popes and bishops, at any rate in recent decades, up to the (so 'confused' from the Roman point of view) times of Vatican II.[60]

## 11.11.1 Infallibility of *Humanae Vitae*

Now what is clear from the outset, and what is agreed by all theologians for and against the encyclical, is that *Humanae Vitae* does not fulfil the conditions of an infallible statement of faith. In this, Küng is quite right. To demonstrate this point, we will set out what is such an infallible statement of faith, namely the declaration of the Assumption of the Blessed Virgin Mary by Pope Pius XII:

> **APOSTOLIC CONSTITUTION OF**
> **POPE PIUS XII**
> ***MUNIFICENTISSIMUS DEUS***
> **DEFINING THE DOGMA OF THE ASSUMPTION**
> *November 1, 1950*
>
> 44. For which reason, after we have poured forth prayers of supplication again and again to God, and have invoked the light of the Spirit of Truth, for the glory of Almighty God who has lavished his special affection upon the Virgin Mary, for the honour of her Son, the immortal King of the Ages and the Victor over sin and death, for the increase of the glory of that same august Mother, and for the joy and exultation of the entire Church; by the authority of our Lord Jesus Christ, of the Blessed Apostles Peter and Paul, and by our own authority, we pronounce, declare, and define it to be a divinely revealed dogma: that the Immaculate Mother of God, the ever Virgin Mary, having completed the course of her earthly life, was assumed body and soul into heavenly glory.
>
> 45. Hence if anyone, which God forbid, should dare willfully to deny or to call into doubt that which we have defined, let him know that he has fallen away completely from the divine and Catholic Faith.

Clearly, in comparison with the definition of the Assumption of the Blessed Virgin Mary, the Pope is not defining in *Humanae Vitae* that contraception is taught as wrong by his infallible definition:

1. That contraception is wrong is not, as with the doctrine of the Assumption, declared and defined to be 'a divinely revealed dogma' by the Pope. Rather, *Humanae Vitae* states: 'This kind of question requires from the teaching authority of the Church a new and deeper reflection on the principles of the moral teaching on marriage—a teaching which is based on the natural law as illuminated and enriched by divine Revelation'.[61]
2. Thus the teaching on the morality of conception is proposed by the Pope rather as 'constant teaching' rather than as 'divinely revealed dogma'. *Humanae Vitae* continues: '…The Church, nevertheless, in urging men to the observance of the precepts of the natural law, which it interprets by its constant doctrine, teaches that each and every marital act must of necessity retain its intrinsic relationship to the procreation of human life.'[62]
3. In concluding *Humanae Vitae*, Pope Paul VI once again clearly refers to the status of the teaching in that encyclical: 'Venerable brothers, beloved sons, all men of good will, great indeed is the work of education, of progress and of charity to which We now summon all of you. And this We do relying on the unshakable teaching of the Church, which teaching Peter's successor together with his brothers in the Catholic episcopate faithfully guards and interprets.'[63] The status of *Humanae Vitae* is therefore that the Pope refers to the unshakable teaching of the Church, which the Pope teaches together with the universal Catholic episcopate, but again not 'divinity revealed dogma'.

4. Finally, there is lacking in *Humanae Vitae* any anathema usually concluding a doctrine infallibly defined, as with the dogma of the Assumption: 'Hence if anyone, which God forbid, should dare willfully to deny or to call into doubt that which we have defined, let him know that he has fallen away completely from the divine and Catholic Faith.'[64]

## 11.11.2 An Exercise of the Infallible Ordinary Magisterium?

The question regarding the magisterial status of *Humanae Vitae*, however, is still a disputed point among moral theologians. As such, it is an interesting example of the exercise of Magisterium. The question is:

1. Was *Humanae Vitae* an exercise of the infallible ordinary Magisterium of the Church? If so, the obedience of faith is necessary as the only suitable response of every member of the Church. We have already quoted the text from LG 25 which asserts the infallibility of the ordinary Magisterium '...Although the individual bishops do not enjoy the prerogative of infallibility, they nevertheless proclaim Christ's doctrine infallibly whenever, even though dispersed through the world, but still maintaining the bond of communion among themselves and with the successor of Peter, and authentically teaching matters of faith and morals, they are in agreement on one position as definitively to be held.'
2. Or was *Humanae Vitae* not an exercise of the infallible Magisterium, but having the lesser status of common authoritative but non-infallible teaching? If so, the obedience of faith is not required, but rather what Vatican II calls 'the religious assent of mind and will' (*religiosum voluntatis et intellectus obsequium*)'. Also from LG 25: 'This religious submission of mind and will must be shown in a special way to the authentic magisterium of the Roman

Pontiff, even when he is not speaking *ex cathedra*; that is, it must be shown in such a way that his supreme magisterium is acknowledged with reverence, the judgments made by him are sincerely adhered to, according to his manifest mind and will. His mind and will in the matter may be known either from the character of the documents, from his frequent repetition of the same doctrine, or from his manner of speaking.'

## a. Those who consider it to be a declaration of the infallible ordinary Magisterium.

Küng, who of course is arguing against the infallibility of the Church, sees *Humanae Vitae* as such a declaration. He claims 'Nor do the conservatives deny that Pius XI's was not inherently an infallible doctrinal statement. But they claim that the point is a diversion from the central issue, the immorality of contraception, as maintained and proclaimed—and this is the decisive point—by the united stand of the teaching office, popes and bishops, at any rate in recent decades, up to the (so 'confused' from the Roman point of view) times of Vatican II.'[65] The conservative minority therefore appealed to the *magisterium ordinarium* for example the existence of God or the prohibition of killing the innocent.[66] The conservative case was that 'the moral impossibility of contraception had been taken for granted for centuries... From the point of view of the ordinary Magisterium of the Pope and the bishops, it was therefore *de facto* an infallible moral truth, even though it had not been defined as such.'[67] This position that *Humanae Vitae* was taught by the ordinary Magisterium with its gift of infallibility, was most notably advocated by the Catholic moral theologians Ford and Grisez.[68] This view seems to find support in the Vatican 1997 *Pontifical Council for the Family 'vademecum* for confessors concerning some aspects of the morality of conjugal life: "The Church has always taught the intrinsic evil of contraception, that is, of every marital act intentionally rendered unfruitful. This teaching is to be held as definitive and irreformable. Contraception is gravely opposed to marital chastity; it is contrary to the good of the transmission of life (the procreative aspect of matrimony), and to the reciprocal self-giving of the spouses (the unitive aspect of matrimony); it harms true love and denies the sovereign role of God in the transmission of human life.'" Proponents of this view find it difficult to see how a doctrine is presented by the Church 'to be held as definitive and irreformable' if it is not at the same time infallibly taught.

## b. Those who consider that *Humanae Vitae* is not infallibly taught, but is an example of the authentic teaching of the Pope.

This view is espoused by Fr George Woodall among many others. His position is that the doctrine on contraception is taught at least at the highest level of authoritative Magisterium, a position supported by the references to *obsequium* in *Humanae Vitae*, acknowledging that it may be taught infallibly on the basis of universal ordinary Magisterium, but that, without certainty as to the latter, no-one is obliged to hold to its being infallibly taught. They are obliged 'at least' to the highest degree of *obsequium* concerning contraception. Woodall's argument is that it is up to those who think that *Humanae Vitae* is a document published with the authority of the infallible ordinary Magisterium to prove that it is so. He does not think that the teaching that contraceptive intercourse is intrinsically evil is *certainly* from the infallible Magisterium.

The question is still an open one. *Humanae Vitae* at the very least, as an act of the Pope authentically teaching Catholic morals, requires our *obsequium*. Indeed, for many, the 1997 *Vademecum for Confessors* tips the balance towards that teaching being part of the infallible ordinary Magisterium. Although that document is from the Pontifical Council for the Family, not therefore at the doctrinal level of authority of the Pope and of the Congregation for the Doctrine of the Faith, yet it clearly states in its Presentation at the beginning that 'We are happy to put this document in the hands of priests, a document that has been prepared at the request of the Holy Father with the aid of the competent collaboration of professors of theology as well as some pastors. We thank all those who have offered their contribution to making this document possible. We are especially grateful to the Congregation for the Doctrine of the Faith and the Apostolic Penitentiary.'[69] This document says that the teaching that contraception is intrinsically evil is 'definitive and irreformable.' It is difficult to imagine a teaching closer to being part of the infallible ordinary Magisterium of the Church, since the Pope and the Bishops are 'in agreement with one position as definitively to be held', LG 25, this teaching being constant throughout the centuries. This view seems to be reinforced by an *allocutio* from Pope John Paul II on March 17, 1997, given to those participating in a course promoted by the Apostolic Penitentiary. The Pope refers to 'the immutable doctrine of the Church' regarding the teaching on the intrinsic evil of contraception in the objective moral order, which has been 'constantly taught' in particular now by the *Confessors' Vademecum*. This 1997 text, says the Pope, should be received *con fiducia ed interior disponibilità*, that is 'with fidelity and an interior openness'. If therefore the teaching of *Humanae Vitae* is not an example of the infallible ordinary Magisterium, then surely it is close to it! Paradoxically, it is the argument by Hans Küng which inclines me to the persuasion that the doctrine that a contraceptive act is intrinsically evil is infallible by an act of the ordinary Magisterium world wide.

## 11.12 CHIRICO AND INFALLIBILITY

*We discuss the detailed study of the philosophy of Infallibility by P. Chirico,* **Infallibility: The Crossroads of Doctrine** *(London: Sheed and Ward, 1977). We find much* *to commend in his work, but find his concept of 'universal meanings' difficult to understand as the philosophical basis of infallibility.*

Bishop Butler's fine little book limits itself to answering the objections of the revised edition of Salmon's diatribe against infallibility, as we have seen in this Chapter. Butler does not attempt to provide a complete theological treatment of the subject. Father Peter Chirico, SS, therefore is much to be commended in his attempt to outline what we might call a theology or a philosophy of infallibility. Chirico even received a positive review from a non-Catholic Professor of Religious Studies at Yale University, George Lindbeck, who concluded that 'the issues raised by this doctrine (of infallibility) are of great importance, not only to Roman Catholics, and not only to Christians, but to everyone who is concerned about the problems of transcultural communication and unity in a pluralistic world.'[70] We have moved, thankfully, a long way therefore from the polemicism of Salmon.

In writing *Infallibility: The Crossroads of Doctrine*, Chirico states 'I wholeheartedly accept the teaching of Vatican I on infallibility; however, I recognize in accord with the document Mysterium Ecclesiae issued by the Sacred Congregation for the Doctrine of the Faith with the approval of Pope Paul VI on June 24, 1973, that "it sometimes happens that some dogmatic truth is first expressed incompletely (but not falsely), and at a later date, when considered in a broader context of faith or human knowledge, it receives a fuller and more perfect expression."[71] I believe that Vatican I expressed incompletely, but not falsely, the doctrine of infallibility.'[72] It is strange, perhaps, that, publishing his book in 1976, Chirico does not include an explicit treatment, even exegesis, of Vatican II on Infallibility, para 25 of LG. In his book, he shows awareness of the teaching of Vatican II, however, and provides a very gentle and persuasive response to Küng, even an apologetic for infallibility.

## 11.13 AGREEMENTS WITH CHIRICO

*We agree with Chirico that the charism of infallibility of the Church is not in itself a supernatural revelation, but rather is at root a natural gift of the human mind, which develops as part of the Church's consciousness of her mission.*

Chirico declares that he is attempting to offer 'a unifying hypothesis...'[73] In studying the various aspects of infallibility, he avers 'Some of these universal aspects can be known simply through reflection on ordinary human experience; others can be known only in reliance upon the apostolic witness... it is the very nature of the reality expressed by dogma that permits infallibility...'[74] Chirico is attempting, if you like to 'de-mystify' infallibility. 'My basic point here is that there is a natural infallibility of the human mind which operates in certain limited cases of universal meanings.'[75]

We must immediately register agreement with Chirico that the gift of infallibility is not an extraordinary revelation given to either the Pope or the Pope and Bishops together. Whether we are dealing with definitions concerning revealed doctrine, as with the doctrine of the Assumption, or whether we are dealing with the truths not of apostolic revelation but of the 'natural law', assuming for the moment that Grisez and Ford are right in arguing that *Humanae Vitae* was such an exercise of the infallible ordinary Magisterium, the Church clearly teaches that there is no specific revelation given to those who have the charism of infallibility, only *assistance* from the Holy Spirit to ensure infallibility. Chirico is therefore quite right in locating the gift of infallibility as being what we might call the purification of a natural gift already in human nature rather than in a specific 'bolt from heaven'. It cannot be a divine revelation since, as DV 4 insists that 'no new public revelation is to be expected before the glorious manifestation of our Lord Jesus Christ (cf.1 Timothy 6:14, Titus 2:13.)'. Infallible statements can therefore only be, as the next paragraph DV 5 explains, '...a deeper understanding of revelation'.

I therefore also completely agree with Chirico when he defines that 'Infallibility refers to the generic process by which the Church comes to certitude about saving reality'[76] The Church's consciousness about a doctrine to be infallibly declared is correctly seen as a developmental process. Newman became a Catholic precisely because increasingly he saw the need for development beyond the language of the New Testament, since the New Testament cannot comprise 'a delineation of all possible forms which a divine message will assume when submitted to a multitude of minds.'[77] 3.3. Together with the concept of the development of doctrines, Newman saw the need for an authority with the power infallibly to decide upon those doctrines, 'thereby separating them from the mass of mere human speculation, extravagance, corruption, and error, in and out of which they grow. This is the doctrine of the infallibility of the Church; for by infallibility I suppose is meant the power of deciding whether this, that, and a third, and any number of theological or ethical statements are true'.[78]

Finally, we must assert with Chirico that the extent of infallibility regarding the doctrines of the Church is of course limited to doctrines which are salvific, concerning faith or morals. The Church does not claim infallibility regarding scientific hypotheses, weather charts, or any matters which do not relate to the message of salvation.

Chirico is surely also correct in seeing the developmental process as a dialogue taking place within the Christian community, both verbal and non-verbal. 'Dialogue is really the summary process by which the various elements we have so far mentioned are integrated, complemented, and corrected.'[79] In this, there is also the 'ontic-creativity phase' of dialogue. This is the reality of non-verbal communication. 'In the latter alternative, the interpreter so masters the actually expressed thought of the author that he is capable of detecting what the author thought but never expressed.'[80]

Chirico gives as an example of the gradual consciousness within the Church that slavery was immoral. 'However — and this is the point we have been making — such an effect does not take place unless the reader already possesses within himself an experiential continuum that is capable of being stimulated by the text'.[81] We have already seen how time was required to develop the Christological definitions of Chalcedon, and Newman describes how the doctrine of Purgatory developed from the need to purge the Christian from post-baptismal sin. 3.2. The Holy Spirit therefore works within the Christian community, which dialogues with itself and with the world, until the time is ripe for the definition of a doctrine.

## 11.13.1 BUT WHAT ARE 'UNIVERSAL MEANINGS'?

As I have already indicated, there is much in Chirico's treatment of infallibility which is to be highly commended. However, I find Chirico's concept of 'universal meanings' difficult to understand. He says 'Thus to ask if there are universal meanings is to ask if there are aspects of human development that are common to all men.'[82] But are there universal meanings, he asks? 'Only a final concrete reality that was absolutely unchangeable could be totally universally true.'[83] 'Basically, infallibility has to do with the mind's grasp with certitude of a universal meaning.'[84]

Chirico writes, 'Hence the man of Christian faith lives and acts and reflects in the recognition of all the universal meanings that pre-existed Christ. In addition, however, he recognizes in dependence on the apostolic witness that these meanings are now fulfilled in the Christ who touches them all.'[85] For example regarding the Assumption of Mary: 'Assumption refers to the completion of the whole person, indicated in a long-accepted psychology as body and soul.'[86] In this Chirico is attempting to explain how for him both those doctrines which are prior to Christ (for example the Church's certainty that we can come to know the existence of God, and the doctrines of the natural law) and those which come from the revelation of the Incarnation, death, and Resurrection of Christ itself, are rooted in 'universal meanings', that is to say fundamental concepts which presumably are in us as human beings.

It is here that I must register disagreement with Chirico, when he says: 'No persons persist over the life of the Church; no concrete operational structures have eternal validity; and despite what certain older apologists may have thought, no concrete organisational constitution has distinguished and will distinguish the universal Church of all the ages.'[87] 'Hence the Church of prior ages cannot be said to be identified with the Church of subsequent time by the possession of the same set of achieved universal meanings.'[88] 'It is this continuity of generating meaning which constitutes the enduring identity of the Church'[89] This 'set of meanings' 'is also what grounds the possibility of infallibility as I shall attempt to show in great detail'.[90] But is Chirico not contradicting himself here? Cannot the 'continuity of generating meaning' include the idea of developing 'concrete operational structures' such as the threefold ministry, and thus contribute thereby to the 'enduring identity of the Church'? We have hopefully demonstrated in great detail on the contrary in Chapters 7 to 9 that the threefold ministry and the primacy of Peter were of the essence of the Church and defined its nature. For that reason, the Church holds infallibly to such 'concrete operational structures'.

Chirico never in fact tells us what those 'universal meanings' are, still less does he give us examples of them. I feel that perhaps the fundamental problem with Chirico is that he wishes to find absolute statements infallibly known as logically necessary as the basis of the concept of infallibility. On the contrary, as is clear from what we have already discussed, the whole idea of revelation is contingent and non-necessary from the viewpoint of logic. The Church has always taught that, for instance, the Incarnation was not absolutely necessary for us to be saved (God could have saved us simply by answering a prayer); the virgin birth was not necessary in order for Jesus to become God and Man; it was not absolutely necessary for him to die in order for us to be saved. Truths of Revelation, as Aquinas states, are usually in the realm of the *necessity of convenience* rather than of absolute necessity. Thus, as Newman again leads us to consider, Antecedent Probability 'the most important principle of verification of questions related to human life', 3.4. In assessing an historical revelation, therefore, the use of hypothesis and verification of hypothesis is the most apt. The real problem of infallibility, therefore, is as to how the human mind can come to certainty regarding such contingent salvific events, and even more how the Church, and in particular its Magisterium, can be infallible in its judgements concerning such contingent salvific events. I do not see Chirico's concept of 'universal meanings' as too helpful in answering these fundamental questions.

For brevity's sake, I will therefore offer my own solution to this question, and leave the reader to find more enlightenment than I have been able to find in the second half of Chirico's treatment of infallibility.

## 11.14 A PHILOSOPHY AND A THEOLOGY OF INFALLIBILITY

*The gift of infallible judgement is only a purification of the Capacity of the Human Mind to Attain the Truth about God and human nature. The apostles were given a supernatural revelation, both by understanding the life, miracles, and teaching, and by the death and above all of the Resurrection of Jesus. But their successors needed no extra faculty beyond the acceptance of the truths of revelation in faith, only needing this gift purified and developed in order for it to become in certain circumstances infallible. This charism of infallibility is limited to the teaching office of the Bishop of Rome in union with the whole body of Catholic bishops as successors of the apostles in order to preserve the unity of the Church in the one faith.*

As we have said above, there is much in Chirico's work to commend, most of all in the stimulus which he gives to us to consider a philosophy and a theology of infallibility. The following I suggest as a synthesis of the rationale underlying the Church's teaching that it cannot err when defining doctrine.

The gift of infallible judgement is only a purification of the Capacity of the Human Mind to Attain the Truth about God and human nature.

Chirico is correct in attempting to 'de-mystify' infallibility. But I would suggest that 'universal meanings' are inadequate as a philosophy of infallibility. Rather, the possibility of infallible propositions is based upon the capacity of the human mind to attain the truth. Chirico correctly insists that we can know God. 'Man can, therefore, know God—not, it is true, as the direct object of experience, but rather as the Mysterious One ever presupposed as the ground and ultimate term of that experience.'[91] But this knowledge of God is, in the teaching of the Church, grounded on the fact that we can know reality, and are not limited in Kantian terms to the knowledge of phenomena, appearances.

Pope John Paul II, in *Fides et Ratio*, bemoans the fact that modern philosophy has abandoned the search for objective truth:

> Abandoning the investigation of being, modern philosophical research has concentrated instead upon human knowing. Rather than make use of the human capacity to know the truth, modern philosophy has preferred to accentuate the ways in which this capacity is limited and conditioned.
>
> In the wake of these cultural shifts, some philosophers have abandoned the search for truth in itself and made their sole aim the attainment of a subjective certainty or a pragmatic sense of utility. This in turn has obscured the true dignity of reason, which

is no longer equipped to know the truth and to seek the absolute.[92]

On the contrary, Vatican I insists on the fact that we can come to know the existence of God, and thus implicitly the natural law, by unaided reason. This it defines as a matter of faith.[93] This potentiality is in all of us as human beings. If we do not know this, this is not because our minds are not capable of it, but because of original sin or because of custom and environment. Thus the gift of infallibility is only a purification of a natural faculty of the human mind. What applies to the question of the existence of God applies also to the knowledge of the natural law. As Pope Paul VI states clearly in *Humanae Vitae*:

> No member of the faithful could possibly deny that the Church is competent in her magisterium to interpret the natural moral law. It is in fact indisputable, as Our predecessors have many times declared, that Jesus Christ, when He communicated His divine power to Peter and the other Apostles and sent them to teach all nations His commandments, constituted them as the authentic guardians and interpreters of the whole moral law, not only, that is, of the law of the Gospel but also of the natural law. For the natural law, too, declares the will of God, and its faithful observance is necessary for men's eternal salvation. [94]

That this knowledge is of the 'natural law' implies also that it is naturally known. If it is not known, it is not because the human mind is not itself capable of knowing the truth about God's commandments based in our nature. It is only because that mind is defective again through sin. Potentially, therefore, again the gift of infallibility is only a purification of a natural faculty. It is a charism, but a purification of a gift already potentially in human nature.

## 11.15 DEVELOPMENT AGAIN

*The apostles were given a supernatural revelation, both by understanding the life, miracles, and teaching, and by the death and above all of the Resurrection of Jesus. But their successors needed no extra faculty beyond the acceptance of the truths of revelation in faith, only needing this gift purified and developed in order for it to become in certain circumstances infallible.*

Again, therefore, regarding the truths of revelation infallibly known, I would conclude that for those given the charism of infallibility, no special gift apart from the purification of the natural faculty to know the truth is required.

Of vital importance regarding the gift of infallibility are historical judgements which, as we have seen above, are not necessarily logically necessary. They are contingent historical events.

We may take a particular example, that of the perpetual virginity of Mary. It is a dogma of faith that Mary did not have intercourse before, during, or after the birth of her Son Jesus Christ. But the New Testament evidence on its own is not finally persuasive.[95] The debate was early in the life of the Church. Helvidius in 382 first proposed that Mary gave birth to other children after Jesus, even though Helvidius accepted that Mary was a virgin when she first gave birth to Jesus. Epiphanius of Salamis, supported by the nineteenth-century Anglican scholar Bishop Lightfoot, on the other hand, held that Joseph had other children from a previous wife. Thus in this case, Jesus really did have 'brothers and sisters'.

The view of the Western Church, espoused by Saint Jerome, was that the 'brothers and sisters' of Jesus mentioned in the Gospels (Mk 6:3) were cousins or some less close relationship than children of the same natural father, Joseph.[96] This view was held by Protestant Christians such as Luther; but by now most Protestant scholars accept the Helvidian view in the light of critical studies.

The Magisterium of the Church does not insist on either the view of Epiphanius or of Jerome. It just insists upon the perpetual virginity of Mary:

> If anyone does not in accord with the Holy Fathers acknowledge the holy and ever virgin and immaculate Mary as really and truly the Mother of God, inasmuch as she, in the fullness of time, and without seed, conceived by the Holy Spirit, God the Word Himself, who before all time was born of God the Father, and without loss of integrity brought Him forth, and after His birth preserved her virginity inviolate, let him be condemned.[97]

The Lateran Council was not a fully ecumenical council, but was a council of the diocese of Rome. But clearly Pope Martin, who summoned and directed Lateran 649, considered that the definition of Mary as perpetual virgin was infallibly true, and this definition was confirmed by Pope Agatho addressing the Council of Constantinople III in 681, which Council of course did not contradict him. We may therefore consider that Popes Martin and Agatho in this case were acting as infallible from their Petrine Office. Such infallibility was not defined of course until many centuries later at Vatican I. From Constantinople III on, this doctrine of the perpetual virginity of Mary entered into the creeds of the Church, including that of Lateran IV 1215 and Lyons 1274. In 1555, Pope Paul IV reaffirmed this teaching against the heresy of Socinians,[98] early rationalists who denied the doctrine of the Trinity and the divinity of Christ on the basis that these doctrines were incompatible with reason, as was of course for them the virginity of Mary.[99] This doctrine was reaffirmed by Pope Paul VI as a matter of faith in his *Credo of the People of God*.[100]

The exegetical and historical evidence is not in itself totally persuasive. As I say in *Born of a Virgin*, 'The Perpetual Virginity of Mary is not contrary to Scripture, but cannot be demonstrated with certainty from Scripture.'[101] I then quote the Second Vatican Council on Revelation: 'Consequently it is not from Sacred Scripture alone that the Church draws her certainty about everything which has been revealed. Therefore both sacred tradition and Sacred Scripture are to be accepted and venerated with the same sense of loyalty and reverence.'[102]

There are complex and never-ending arguments for and against the possible meanings of, 'brothers and sisters' as 'cousins' or 'children by a former wife of Joseph'. The question for the Magisterium remains, however, as to how historical arguments which are not totally absolutely certain can be the basis of dogma.

We may first give the question of the primacy of Peter as another example. The complex discussion we have already had in Chapter 8 concerning whether the historical Jesus told the historical Peter that he was to have the keys of his Church is clearly disputed, as the ecumenical symposium *Peter in the New Testament* has underlined. We begin by asserting that we must hold at least to the *possibility* that the historical Jesus gave to the historical Peter the universal primacy.[103]

We admit that theoretically if historical arguments led to a given doctrine being incompatible with scripture, we could legitimately deny such a doctrine. We have argued that this is clearly not the case regarding the Petrine primacy. On the contrary, we have argued that the use of 'Messiah' in Matthew 16:15–18 and John 1:41–42 most likely means that Jesus is giving Peter (Cephas) a title in response to Peter's naming Jesus as 'the Son of the living God'.[104] We argue that the historical Peter confessed Jesus as Messiah, and that Jesus was giving him juridical authority.[105] We then argue that in comparison with Isaiah 22, it seems clear that Jesus in giving Peter the keys is handing over his own authority to Peter in his place.[106] We argue finally that it is most plausible that the historical Jesus founded a church during his lifetime and even more plausibly that he intended that Church to expand exponentially after his death and resurrection.[107]

On the other hand, I have made a significant disclaimer at the close of this argument for the historicity of the primacy given to Peter:

> I repeat that in our apologia for the primacy of Peter given by the First Vatican Council, we have not provided an argument which will carry total certainty in the exegetical community. We have also argued that such absolute certainty is not absolutely necessary. If the argument is plausible, then the living and developing tradition of the Church becomes itself an exegesis of the text.[108]

The charism of the Holy Spirit therefore acts simply to enable that ordinary processes of human reasoning are without error, including consideration of the contingent arguments of historical reasoning, which can never in themselves provide absolute certainty but can give us reasonable certainty.

In considering this process, we must also give sufficient scope for the possibility of oral tradition being handed on from Rome, the 'See of the glorious apostles Peter and Paul'. We see in the second century testimony of St Irenaeus:

> ...that Church which has the tradition and the faith with which comes down to us after having been announced to men by the apostles. For with this Church, because of its superior origin, all churches must agree, that is, all the faithful in the whole world. And it is in her that the faithful everywhere have maintained the apostolic tradition.[109]

Regarding the doctrine of the perpetual virginity of Mary, therefore, it is quite feasible that this doctrine was handed on in oral tradition from the Roman church. The vitriolic defence of this doctrine by Jerome against Helvidius could arise from the fact that Jerome spent time in Rome working on a new translation of the New Testament for the Pope.[110]

Again, this doctrine is not absolutely clear from the New Testament evidence, but it is at least a plausible interpretation of it. When Luke says that Mary 'gave birth to her first-born son' (Lk 2:7), this does not necessarily imply that children were born to Mary after Jesus, but simply that Jesus had the status of the first-born.

Regarding the Petrine primacy, we have seen that the text itself in Matthew 16 is quite open to the full Catholic doctrine of the primacy. That the popes took time to assert their primacy over the whole Church and manifest their infallibility when declaring matters of doctrine, as did Leo the Great in 452 at the Council of Chalcedon, is, as Newman argues, part of the logic of history. The popes needed no special revelation to understand their doctrinal authority, only the assistance of the Holy Spirit to lead them in time to the right interpretation of the text.

## 11.16 THE LIMITATION OF THIS CHARISM

*This charism of infallibility is limited to the teaching office of the Bishop of Rome in union with the whole body of Catholic bishops as successors of the apostles in order to preserve the unity of the Church in the one faith.*

Chirico would be fully in agreement with our interpretation of the doctrine of infallibility in not being a special supernatural revelation. He also realises the link that this doctrine has with the apostolic witnesses:

> ... just as the physical aspect of the act of laying down one's life (in Christian martyrdom) follows the natural physical laws of the universe, so too does the cognitive aspect of the act of infallible understanding follow the natural cognitive laws. What makes both acts supernatural is not that in some way the physical or cognitional laws of nature are superseded, nor that the actor has some implicit or explicit Christian intention in mind, but that both acts are performed in a mysterious union (explicitly recognized only in

dependence upon the apostolic witnesses) of faith with Jesus Christ risen from the dead.[111]

The key here is the link with the apostolic witnesses. The risen Christ gave his revelation to his chosen apostles, as we have argued previously throughout this book, in order to preserve unity in the truth. As the Second Vatican Council's Dogmatic Constitution on the Church states:

> This Sacred Council, following closely in the footsteps of the First Vatican Council, with that Council teaches and declares that Jesus Christ, the eternal Shepherd, established His holy Church, having sent forth the apostles as He Himself had been sent by the Father; and He willed that their successors, namely the bishops, should be shepherds in His Church even to the consummation of the world. And in order that the episcopate itself might be one and undivided, He placed Blessed Peter over the other apostles, and instituted in him a permanent and visible source and foundation of unity of faith and communion. And all this teaching about the institution, the perpetuity, the meaning and reason for the sacred primacy of the Roman Pontiff and of his infallible magisterium, this Sacred Council again proposes to be firmly believed by all the faithful. Continuing in that same undertaking, this Council is resolved to declare and proclaim before all men the doctrine concerning bishops, the successors of the apostles, who together with the successor of Peter, the Vicar of Christ, the visible Head of the whole Church, govern the house of the living God.[112]

Bishops, therefore, with their helpers, the priests and deacons, have taken up the service of the community, presiding in place of God over the flock, whose shepherds they are, as teachers for doctrine, priests for sacred worship, and ministers for governing. And just as the office granted individually to Peter, the first among the apostles, is permanent and is to be transmitted to his successors, so also the apostles' office of nurturing the Church is permanent, and is to be exercised without interruption by the sacred order of bishops. Therefore, the Sacred Council teaches that bishops by divine institution have succeeded to the place of the apostles, as shepherds of the Church, and he who hears them, hears Christ, and he who rejects them, rejects Christ and Him who sent Christ.[113]

Therefore, as we have consistently seen, the gift of infallibility is indissolubly linked with that of episcopal authority. Indeed, the role of the Bishop of Rome as the successor of Peter, and as having the primacy of jurisdiction over the whole worldwide body of bishops, is to unify the whole Church with all the successors of the apostles. Infallibility is thus a charism to serve the unity of the Church. All of us in our way represent Christ to the world; but the body of bishops, united with the Bishop of Rome as successor of Peter, are Christ to us in particular when they proclaim infallibly the truth of the revelation once given by Christ while on earth, and now continued in its saving mission. They speak with the full authority of Christ. That is the whole purpose of the charism of infallibility, for us to be certain as members of the Church in matters of faith and morals as to what the saving truth of Christ is. As we have seen above, this charism of magisterial infallibility is not a special revelation. It is rather the purification of a natural gift which we all have to know the revelation of Christ which was historically given. This charism of infallibility is given to the whole body of bishops in union with the Pope in protecting them from error when they become Christ to us in his teaching should it be necessary for the whole Church in the development of doctrine that infallible judgement be given.

## Notes

[1] LG 25, Tanner II, p. 869.
[2] INF, p. 94
[3] *Ibid.*, p. 95.
[4] *Ibid.*, p. 96.

5   *Ibid.*, p. 97.
6   *Ibid.*, p. 98.
7   Chirico, p. 226.
8   Butler, p. 4.
9   Butler, p. 44. See also INF, p. 216, note 36: 'For the earlier Catholic-Anglican dialogue, B. C. Butler, *The Church and Infallibility*, 1954, new edition, London, 1969, is important'. While seeming to quote Butler in his favour, Küng also seems completely unaware that Butler is in every way contrary to his own position since Butler accepts and promotes infallibility rather than just indefectibility! The new edition, 1969, does not at all alter substantially this position.
10  Butler, p. 42.
11  *Ibid.*, p. 43, from Origen third century.
12  *Ibid.*, p. 49.
13  INF, p. 177
14  DV, 11b.
15  INF, p. 180.
16  *Ibid.*, p. 181.
17  *Ibid.*, p. 166.
18  *Ibid.*, p. 169
19  *Ibid.*, p. 171.
20  See section 10.6 above.
21  Butler, p. 5.
22  CCC 39.
23  INF, p. 137.
24  Butler, p. 35.
25  *Ibid.*, p. 36, quotation from Canon A. J. Mason's article in H. B. Swete, ed., *Essays on the Early History of the Church and the Ministry*, 1921, pp. 9 ff.
26  *Ibid.*, p. 38 quoting Swete, *Essays on the Early History of the Church and the Ministry*, pp. xii f.
27  INF, p. 185
28  See sections 8.2. and 8.3 above.
29  See section 8.4. above.
30  INF, p. 77.
31  *Ibid.*, p. 79.
32  *Ibid.*, p. 79.
33  See section 8.4–10. above.
34  R. Bultmann, *The Gospel of John: A Commentary*. Transl. G. R. Beasley-Murray, [Oxford, Basil Blackwell, 1971], p. 712.
35  Butler, pp. 179–180
36  http://orthodoxinfo.com/inquirers/decretals.aspx [accessed 22.02.2013].
37  Constanzo, p. 162.

38 E. C. Frend, p. 209.
39 Hughes, pp. 229–30.
40 Abbé Guettée, *The Papacy: Its Historic Origin and Primitive Relations with the Eastern Churches* (New York : Carleton, 1866).
41 INF, p. 96.
42 *Ibid.*, p. 97.
43 *Ibid.*, p. 82.
44 *Ibid.*, p. 77.
45 *Ibid.*, p. 84. Cf. Section 3.8 above.
46 *Ibid.*, p. 85.
47 *Ibid.*
48 *Ibid.*, p. 86,
49 See section 2.5. above.
50 Butler, pp. 68–69.
51 INF, p. 107.
52 *Ibid.*, p. 28.
53 Cf. Butler, p. 199.
54 *Ibid.*, p. 208ff.
55 See section 10.5. above.
56 INF, p. 41.
57 *Ibid.*, pp. 42–43.
58 *Ibid.*, p. 44.
59 *Ibid.*, pp. 45–6.
60 *Ibid.*, pp. 46–47
61 Pope Paul VI, *Humanae Vitae*, 4.
62 *Ibid.*, 11.
63 *Ibid.*, 31.
64 Pope Pius XII, *Munificentissimus Deus*, 45.
65 INF, pp. 46–47.
66 *Ibid.*, p. 47.
67 *Ibid.*, pp. 48–49.
68 Cf. G. Woodall, *Humanae Vitae Forty Years On. A Commentary*. [Oxford: Family Publications, 2008]. p. 184. Quoting J. C. Ford, and G. Grisez, 'Contraception and the Infallibility of the Ordinary Magisterium'. Theological Studies, 39 (1978), pp. 258–312.
69 Pontifical Council for the Family, *Vademecum for Confessors* (1997).
70 Chirico, *Infallibility*, back cover.
71 A. A. S., 65 (1973) pp. 402–3.
72 Chirico, p. xix.
73 *Ibid.*, p. xii.
74 *Ibid.*, p. xiii.
75 *Ibid.*, p. xv.

76. *Ibid.*, p. xvi.
77. DCD, pp. 56–7.
78. *Ibid.*, pp. 78–9. See section 3.4. above.
79. Chirico, p. 21.
80. *Ibid*, p. 26.
81. *Ibid.*, p. 28.
82. *Ibid.*, p. 54.
83. *Ibid.*, pp. 56–7.
84. *Ibid.*, p. 63,
85. *Ibid.*, p. 87.
86. *Ibid.*, p. 88.
87. *Ibid.*, p. 108.
88. *Ibid.*, p. 109.
89. *Ibid*.
90. *Ibid.*, p. 110.
91. *Ibid.*, p. 69.
92. Pope John Paul II, *Fides et Ratio*, 5, 47.
93. Vatican I, Dogmatic Constitution on the Catholic Faith, Chapter 2 *On Revelation*. Tanner, II, p. 806.
94. Pope Paul VI, *Humanae Vitae*, 4.
95. There is an excellent discussion of all three views outlined in J. McHugh, *The Mother of Jesus in the New Testament* (London, Darton, Longman and Todd, 1975), pp. 200–254. McHugh's solution is that the word 'brothers' does not mean 'cousins' but 'blood-brothers', 'the first cousins of Jesus on his father's side', p. 200. McHugh therefore retains the dogma of the perpetual virginity, while giving at least a plausible if not a totally convincing explanation of *adelphoi*.
96. This is the view espoused by CCC 500.
97. Lateran Council of AD 649 as found in DS 503.
98. http://www.newadvent.org/cathen/14113a.htm (accessed 23.02.2013).
99. *Ibid*.
100. Pope Paul VI, *Credo of the People of God* (1968).
101. J. Redford, *Born of a Virgin* (London, St Pauls, 2007), p. 21.
102. DV 9.
103. See section 8.3. above.
104. See section 8.6. above.
105. See section 8.7.–8. above.
106. See section 8.9. above.
107. See section 8.10. above.
108. *Ibid*.
109. St Irenaeus, *Adversus Haereses*, 6.1.
110. The fact that Jerome defended so stoutly the perpetual virginity of Mary, and that this belief was part of the oral tradition of the Church

of Rome, does not imply that we must accept his particular interpretation of 'brothers' as first cousins of Jesus, cf. McHugh, *Mother of Jesus in the NT*, p. 227.

[111] Chirico, p. 165.
[112] LG 18.
[113] LG 20.

# EPILOGUE

Dear Reader,
You have ploughed through this book, for which patient endeavour I thank you. You have read the arguments for the truth we as Catholics believe revealed by God, that the historical Jesus came to earth to found the Church led by Peter and his successors the Bishops of Rome, and Paul the Apostle of the Gentiles. To Peter the historical Jesus gave his primacy, which included the gift of infallibility to the whole body of Catholic bishops united with him.

The purpose of founding this church was your salvation, and the salvation of the whole human race. This salvation is mediated through baptism into the Church, and the sacraments, most of all the Holy Eucharist, which we call the Mass. This saves us from the sin of the first parents of the human race, which scripture name as Adam and Eve. To save us, Jesus has left us the sacrament of his own body and blood, which above all makes us sharers in his divine nature, a superb gift of Christ.

If you are not already a Catholic, and would like to become a full member of the Church, if you are not baptised, then you will wish to follow a course of instruction called the Rite of the Christian Initiation of Adults, which takes place in your local parish. You will follow this course, and, if you wish to become a full member of the Church, you will be baptised and given the sacrament of Confirmation, followed by your first Holy Communion.

If you are already a baptised Christian of another Christian denomination, however, you will still follow a course of instruction, but there will be a simpler act of reconciliation into full communion with the Catholic Church recognising your baptism together with the conferring of the sacraments of Confirmation and the Eucharist. If you are a member of one of the separated Eastern Christian Churches, such as the Greek Orthodox Church or the Russian Orthodox Church, you will not need to receive any of the sacraments, since we recognise their validity. You will only need to profess your faith in the Catholic Church, and then continue to receive the Eucharist in full communion with the Catholic Church.

Life in the Church involves fidelity to the Law of Christ as expounded in the scriptures and in the Catholic Church, in daily preparation for heaven, most of all the law of love, which led Jesus himself to die for us. We are all sinners needing divine grace. Catholics commit sins even after baptism and being received into full communion with the Church. If those sins are serious, then Catholics are obliged to go to seek reconciliation with God and the Church through a priest in the Sacrament of Penance. We believe as Catholics that regular attendance at the Sacrament of Penance or Reconciliation is a great means of spiritual strength, even if sins are not serious but daily "venial" or less serious sins such as losing our patience.

Perhaps the most difficult area of life in the Catholic Church today is in the area of sexual temptation. All down the centuries, Catholics have needed to confess these sins. This is nothing new. The difference today is that society, and particularly British and European society, does not recognise as sin what the Church from its beginning, and from its roots in Judaism and the Old Testament, recognises as such.

We have already in this book discussed from an intellectual point of view the Encyclical *Humanae Vitae* of Pope Paul VI, issued in 1968. What the Pope himself foresaw, but which few saw at the time, even Catholics, was a profound change in the whole thinking of society about sex and the married relationship. This was due to the separation between the sexual act and its consequence in procreation. I quote here from the Encyclical:

> 8. Marriage, then, is far from being the effect of chance or the result of the blind evolution of natural forces. It is in reality the wise and provident institu-

tion of God the Creator, whose purpose was to effect in man His loving design. As a consequence, husband and wife, through that mutual gift of themselves, which is specific and exclusive to them alone, develop that union of two persons in which they perfect one another, cooperating with God in the generation and rearing of new lives.

11. God has wisely ordered laws of nature and the incidence of fertility in such a way that successive births are already naturally spaced through the inherent operation of these laws. The Church, nevertheless, in urging men to the observance of the precepts of the natural law, which it interprets by its constant doctrine, teaches that each and every marital act must of necessity retain its intrinsic relationship to the procreation of human life.

12. This particular doctrine, often expounded by the magisterium of the Church, is based on the inseparable connection, established by God, which man on his own initiative may not break, between the unitive significance and the procreative significance which are both inherent to the marriage act. The reason is that the fundamental nature of the marriage act, while uniting husband and wife in the closest intimacy, also renders them capable of generating new life—and this as a result of laws written into the actual nature of man and of woman.

Since 1968, there has been a sexual revolution which stems from society rejecting the above link between the unitive and the procreative dimension of the sexual act between man and woman. Condoms have been used more and more not only within married life, but as simply as a way of having sex without children. Thus more and more men and women do not marry, but live together for a time, and then decide to have children at some stage, or otherwise change their partner. Homosexual acts are no longer considered immoral, since having removed the procreative dimension of the sexual act, there is no reason in people's minds for a man not to have sex with a man and a woman not to have sex with a woman. Because contraception by means of condoms or an anovulent pill do not always work, in fact in human circumstances often do not work, abortion has become a means of contraception, the numbers of aborted babies, the destruction of life in the womb, in Britain running into millions over the past thirty years. This is at a time when natural methods of controlling fertility have become very effective and very sophisticated.

With this development, militant advocates of homosexual practice are pressing the government to make sexual acts between heterosexual couples and homosexual couples equal in law, and at the time of the publication of this book the government is preparing legislation to make homosexual marriage equal with heterosexual marriage. Those who oppose this proposed legislation are called 'bigots', and the threat hangs over those who oppose this legislation to be eventually arrested as criminals under human rights laws.

This takes place in a much deeper process of secularization in society, which profoundly affects morality. The lobby for assisted suicide finds its moral basis in a combination of Darwinian natural selection without any hope of a future life after death, and a consumerist feeling that I should be able to take my own life when I wish to. No person thinking in this way would say 'Thou shalt not kill' in this context. Therefore the Church is obliged to be 'counter-cultural'.

This situation has crept up on us unawares, as we begin the Year of Evangelisation. But one becoming a Catholic cannot afford to be unaware of the profundity of the change in our society in this new millennium. Every adult member of the Church needs to know Catholic teaching on this matter, which will not change essentially, even though some Catholics might think it will. The Church has faced opposition in the past two thousand years many times and in varying degrees of intensity. The Church's effective response has always been for each Catholic to know the teaching and the reasons for that teaching, and to follow that teaching to the very best of one's ability. When problems arise, again the approach is effective in the long tradition of the Church; the Sacrament of Penance or Reconciliation, and help from professional counsellors within the Church.

According to Paul's Second Letter to Timothy, Christians in those days did not always have matters easy. Timothy is exhorted:

> You then, my son, be strong in the grace that is in Christ Jesus, and what you have heard from me before many witnesses entrust to faithful men who will be able to teach others also. Share in suffering as a good soldier of Christ Jesus (2 Tm 2:1).

In this way, the Church got through the first two centuries despite her faithful being thrown to the lions in the Roman arena. We too can suffer just a little in the new millennium, and come through it equally effectively. The small amount of suffering you will have to go through will not seriously diminish your joy in having sought the Truth, in Jesus himself, and having found it (Mt 7:7).

# BIBLIOGRAPHY

*New Jerusalem Bible: Standard Edition* (London: Darton, Longman and Todd, 1974).

## Church Documents

*Decrees of the Ecumenical Councils.* II Vols. Tanner, N. P. (ed.) (London: Sheed & Ward & Washington: DC, Georgetown University Press, 1990).

*Catechism of the Catholic Church* (London: Geoffrey Chapman, 1994).

Pope Benedict XVI, *Jesus of Nazareth, Volume 1, From the Baptism in the Jordan to the Transfiguration* (London: Bloomsbury, 2007).

Congregation for the Doctrine of the Faith, *Dominus Iesus, Declaration on the Unicity and Salvific Universality of Jesus Christ and the Church* (London: Catholic Truth Society, 2003).

## Dictionaries

Cross, F. L. & Livingstone, E. A., (eds.), *The Oxford Dictionary of the Christian Church* (Oxford University Press, 1974).

Kelly, J. N. D. (ed.), *The Oxford Dictionary of Popes* (Oxford University Press, 1986).

## Books

Ball, D. M., *'I am' in John's Gospel: Literary Function, Background and Theological Implications.* JSNTS, (Sheffield Academic Press, 1996).

Barrett, C. K., *The Gospel According to John: An Introduction with Commentary and Notes on the Greek Text*, Second Edition (London: SPCK, 1978).

Bauckham, R., *Jesus and the Eyewitnesses: The Gospels as Eyewitness Testimony* (Cambridge: Eerdmans, 2006).

Beare, F. W., *The Gospel According to Matthew* (Oxford: Basil Blackwell, 1981).

Benoit, P., *Exégèse et Théologie*. Les Éditions du Cerf, (Paris: 1961).

Black, M., and Rowley, H. H., *Peake's Commentary on the Bible*, Revised Edition (London: Nelson, 1962).

Bockmuehl, M., *This Jesus: Martyr, Lord, Messiah* (Edinburgh: T and T Clark, 1994).

Brown, R. E., *The Gospel According to John XII–XXI A New Introduction, Translation and Notes* (London: Chapman, 1971).

Brown, R. E., *An Introduction to the New Testament* (London: Doubleday, 1997).

Brown, R. E., Donfried, K. P., and Reumann J., (eds.), *Peter in the New Testament: A Collaborative Assessment by Protestant and Roman Catholic Scholars* (Minneapolis: Augsburg Publishing House, 1973 and London: Geoffrey Chapman, 1974).

Brown, E., Fitzmyer, J. A., Murphy, R. E., (eds.), *New Jerome Biblical Commentary* (London: Geoffrey Chapman, 1989)

Bultmann, R., *Existence and Faith. Shorter Writings of Rudolf Bultmann*. (ed.) and Int. S. Ogden (London: Collins, 1961).

Bultmann, R., *Faith and Understanding*. Robert Funk (ed.), and translated by L. Pettibone Smith, (New York: Harper and Row, 1969).

Bultmann, R., *The History of the Synoptic Tradition*. Translated John Marsh. Revised Edition 1968.

Bultmann, R., *Jesus and the Word*. Transl. Louise Smith and Erminie Lantero. (London: Collins, Fontana Books, 1958).

Bultmann, R., *The Gospel of John: A Commentary*. Transl. G. R. Beasley-Murray (Oxford: Basil Blackwell, 1971).

Butler, B. C., *The Church and Infallibility: A Reply to the Abridged 'Salmon'* (Catholic Book Club Edition)

Butler, B. C., *The Church and Infallibility*. 1954, new edition, (London: 1969)

Chirico, P., *Infallibility: The Crossroads of Doctrine* (London: Sheed and Ward, 1977).

Clark, F., *Godfaring On Reason, Faith, and Sacred Being* (Washington, D.C.: Catholic University of America Press, 2000).

Costanzo, J. F., *The Historical Credibility of Hans Küng* (North Quincy, Massachusetts: The Christopher Publishing House, 1979).

Davis, S. T., *Disputed issues: contending for Christian faith in today's academic setting* (Texas: Baylor University Press, Waco, 2009).

Davis, S. T. et al, editors, *The Incarnation. An Interdisciplinary Symposium on the Incarnation of the Son of God* (Oxford University Press, 2002).

Dodd, C. H., *The Interpretation of the Fourth Gospel*. (Cambridge University Press, 1953).

Dunn, J. D. G,. *Jesus Remembered*, Volume 1, *Christianity in the Making* (Grand Rapids: Eerdmans, 2003).

Fitzmyer, J. A., *Essays on the Semitic Background of the New Testament* (London: Chapman, 1971).

Frend, W. H. C. *The Early Church: From the Beginnings to 461* (London: SCM Press, Second Edition, 1982).

Funk, R., Hoover, R. W., and the 'Jesus Seminar', *The Five Gospels The Search for the Authentic Words of Jesus* (New York: Scribner, 1993).

Goudge, H. L. *The First Epistle to the Corinthians*. Westminster Commentaries. Revised Edition, (London: Methuen, 1926).

Green, M. (ed.), *The Truth of God Incarnate* (London: Hodder and Stoughton, 1977).

Haffner, P., *Mystery of the Church* (Gracewing: Leominster, 2007)

Hahn, F., *The Titles of Jesus in Christology Their History in Early Christianity* (London: Lutterworth Press, 1969).

Hick, J., *The Myth of God Incarnate* (London: SCM, 1977).

Hodgson, P. C., (ed.), Strauss D.F., *The Life of Jesus Critically Examined* (London: SCM, 1973).

Hughes, P. A., *History of the Church Volume 1, The World in which the Church was Founded* (London: Sheed and Ward, revised edition 1948).

Johnson, T. L., *The Real Jesus: The Misguided Quest for the Historical Jesus and the Truth of the Traditional Gospel* (San Francisco: Harper Collins, 1997).

Kelly, J. N. D., *Early Christian Doctrines* (London: Adam and Charles Black, 1968).

Klijn, A. F. J., *An Introduction to the New Testament*. Transl. M. van der Vathorst-Smit. (Leiden: Brill, 1967).

Kümmel, W. G., *The New Testament: The History of the Investigation of its Problems*. Transl. McLean Gilmour S., Kee H. C. (London: SCM, 1973).

Küng, H., *Infallible? An enquiry*. Translated from the German by E. Mosbacher (London: Collins, 1971).

Lagrange, M.-J., *Évangile Selon Saint Matthieu* (Paris: Gabalda et Fils, Fourth Edition, 1927)

Latourelle, R. (ed.), *Vatican II Assessment and Perspectives, Twenty-Five Years After (1962–1987)*. Volume One, (New York: Paulist Press, Mahwah, 1988).

Lightfoot, J. B., *Saint Paul's Epistle to the Galatians: A Revised Text with Introduction, Notes and Dissertations*. Ninth Edition (London: MacMillan, 1887).

Marshall, I. H., *The Gospel of Luke: A Commentary on the Greek Text* (Exeter: Paternoster Press, 1978).

Meier, J. P., *Rethinking the Historical Jesus. Volume One: The Roots of the Problem and the Person* (New York: Doubleday, 1991).

Meier, J. P., *Rethinking the Historical Jesus, Volume Two: Mentor, Message, and Miracles* (New York: Doubleday, 1994).

Meier, J. P., *Rethinking the Historical Jesus, Volume Three, Companions and Competitors* (New York: Doubleday, 2001).

Moule, C. F. D., *The Origins of Christology* (Cambridge University Press: 1977).

Moulton, J. H., and Milligan G., *The Vocabulary of the Greek Testament. Illustrated from the Papyri and Other Non-Literary Sources* (Michigan: Eerdmans, 1930).

Neuner, J., and Dupuis, J., *The Christian Faith in the Doctrinal Documents of the Catholic Church* (London: Collins, 1983).

Newman, J. H., *An Essay on the Development of Christian Doctrine* (Notre Dame Series in the Great Books). Foreword by I. Ker.

Newman, J. H., *An Essay in Aid of a Grammar of Assent*. New Edition, edited and introduced by C. F. Harold (New York: Longmans, Green and Company, 1947).

Redford, J., *Bad, Mad or God? Proving the Divinity of Christ from St. John's Gospel* (London: Saint Pauls, 2004).

Redford, J., *Who Was John? The Fourth Gospel Debate After Pope Benedict XVI's Jesus of Nazareth* (London: Saint Paul's, 2008).

Redford, J., *What is Catholicism? Hard Questions, Straight Answers* (Huntingdon, Indiana: Our Sunday Visitor Publishing Division, 1997).

Redford, J., *Born of a Virgin: Proving the Miracle from the Gospels* (London: St. Pauls, 2007),

Robert, A. and Feuillet, A., *Interpreting the Scriptures* (New York: Desclée, 1969), French original, *Introduction à la Bible*, Volume 1 (Paris: Tournai, Desclée, 1959).

Robinson, J. A. T., *The Priority of John* (London: SCM, 1985).

Schaff, P. (ed.), *A Religious Encyclopaedia or Dictionary of Biblical, Historical, Doctrinal, and Practical Theology*, 3rd Edition, Vol. 1. (Toronto, New York & London: Funk & Wagnalls Company, 1894).

Schmithals, W., *The Office of Apostle in the Early Church* Transl. J. E. Steely (London: SPCK, 1971).

Schweitzer, A., *The Quest of the Historical Jesus. A Critical Study of its Progress from Reimarus to Wrede*. Transl. W. Montgomery (London: A. and C. Black, 3rd Edition, 1954).

Taylor, V., *The Gospel According to Mark*. Second Edition (London: MacMillan St Martin's Press, 1966).

Theissen, G., and Merz, A., *The Historical Jesus: A Comprehensive Guide* (London: SCM, 1998).

Wickenhauser, A., *New Testament Introduction* (New York: Herder and Herder, 1958).

Winter, M., *Peter and the Popes* (London: Darton, Longman and Todd, 1960).

Woodall, G., *Humanae Vitae Forty Years On, A Commentary* (Oxford: Family Publications, 2008).

Wright, N. T., *Jesus and the Victory of God Volume 2 of Christian Origins and the Question of God* (London: SPCK, 1996).

# SCRIPTURAL INDEX

## OLD TESTAMENT

**Genesis**
13:8        p. 173
14:6        p. 173
29:15       p. 173

**Exodus**
3           p. 106
3:14-15     p. 101
24:9        p. 184

**Leviticus**
1:13        pp. 177, 203
16:8        p. 166

**Joshua**
7:16        p. 116
13:1-21:5   p. 167
21:1ff      p. 167
24          p. 116

**2 Kings**
4:42-44     p. 62

**2 Chronicles**
8:14        p. 203
8:5         p. 177
24:11       p. 203

**Psalm**
110:1       p. 103

**2 Maccabees**
12:40-45    p. 39

**Isaiah**
14:12-15    p. 103
22          p. 314
22:15-25    p. 224
22:19-23    pp. 224, 246
40:3        p. 99
40-55       p. 99
43:16       p. 101

# NEW TESTAMENT

**Matthew**
| | |
|---|---|
| 3:13 | p. 52 |
| 7:7 | pp. 22, 327 |
| 7:21 | p. 236 |
| 8:20 | p. 139 |
| 9:2-3 | p. 103 |
| 10:2-4 | p. 142 |
| 10:2 | p. 152 |
| 10:3 | p. 168 |
| 10:5ff | p. 132 |
| 12:28 | p. 92 |
| 13:41 | p. 118 |
| 14:15-21 | p. 101 |
| 15:24 | p. 132 |
| 15:31 | p. 92 |
| 16 | pp. 7, 224-225, 251, 316 |
| 16:12-20 | pp. 215-216, 241, 243, 244 |
| 16:13-23 | pp. 245, 286 |
| 16:14 | 116 |
| 16:15-18 | pp. 245, 246, 314 |
| 16:16 | pp. 114, 221, 251 |
| 16:16-19 | p. 8 |
| 16:17 | p. 217 |
| 16:17-19 | pp. 117, 210, 217, 218, 228, 229, 230, 237, 242, 245, 266 |
| 16:18 | pp. 252, 260, 286 |
| 16:18-19 | pp. 222, 224, 234, 246 |
| 16:19 | pp. 137, 226 |
| 16:21 | p. 102 |
| 16:23 | p. 217 |
| 17:1 | p. 168 |
| 17:5 | p. 101 |
| 18:8 | p. 223 |
| 18:15-18 | p. 116 |
| 18:17 | p. 229 |
| 19:6 | p. 80 |
| 27:24 | p. 94 |
| 28:16-20 | pp. 130, 132 |
| 28:16 | p. 134 |
| 28:17 | p. 105 |
| 28:18ff | pp. 19, 150 |
| 28:18-20 | p. 150 |

**Mark**
| | |
|---|---|
| 2:5-7 | p. 103 |
| 2:14 | p. 168 |
| 2:25-28 | p. 93 |
| 3:14 | p. 152 |
| 3:16-19 | p. 142 |
| 3:18 | p. 168 |
| 6:3 | p. 12 |
| 6:7 | pp. 142, 144 |
| 8:27-33 | pp. 215, 245 |
| 8:29 | p. 221 |
| 8:33 | p. 217 |
| 9:2 | p. 168 |
| 9:33 | p. 217 |
| 9:35 | p. 205 |
| 14:60-64 | p. 105 |
| 14:64 | p. 102 |
| 16:8 | p. 132 |
| 16:9-20 | p. 132 |
| 16:14-16 | p. 131 |

## Scriptural Index

| | | | |
|---|---|---|---|
| 16:14 | p. 105 | 4:43b | p. 30 |
| | | 6:20 | p. 101 |
| **Luke** | | 6:67 | p. 142 |
| 2:7 | p. 31 | 8:58 | pp. 16, 17, 237 |
| 3:52 | p. 67 | 10:30 | pp. 17, 99, 237 |
| 5:20-21 | p. 103 | 10:31 | p. 100 |
| 6:13 | p. 134 | 10:33,36 | p. 103 |
| 6:14-16 | p. 142 | 12:20-24 | p. 133 |
| 6:15 | p. 168 | 13:16 | p. 132 |
| 7:37 | p. 93 | 13:39 | p. 139 |
| 9:1 | p. 144 | 14:9 | p. 17 |
| 9:18-22 | p. 45 | 16:13 | pp. 8, 282 |
| 9:18-23 | pp. 215, 216 | 19:26 | p. 171 |
| 9:20 | p. 221 | 19:38 | p. 133 |
| 11:19-20 | pp. 220-221 | 20:19-22 | p. 131 |
| 11:20 | pp. 92, 228 | 20:21 | p. 163 |
| 12:42 | p. 225 | 20:21-23 | p. 132 |
| 22:8 | p. 167 | 20:22-23 | p. 136 |
| 22:31-33 | p. 104 | 20:23 | p. 137 |
| 22:32 | pp. 29, 237, 286 | 20:24-27 | p. 105 |
| 23:2 | p. 94 | 20:31 | p. 13 |
| 24 | p. 131 | 21:15-17 | pp. 222, 230, 245, 286, 314, |
| 24:11 | p. 105 | | |
| 24:13 | p. 134 | 21:17 | pp. 19, 65 |
| 24:17 | p. 105 | | |
| 24:33 | p. 134 | **Acts** | |
| 24:36 | p. 134 | 1:2 | pp. 134-135 |
| 24:38-41 | p. 105 | 1:1-8 | p. 132 |
| 24:46-53 | p. 131 | 1:13 | pp. 142, 169 |
| 24:48 | p. 134 | 1:15-26 | p. 140 |
| 24:49 | p. 163 | 1:21-22 | p. 165 |
| | | 1:26 | pp. 135, 138, 155 |
| **John** | | 2:14 | p. 140 |
| 1:14 | p. 13 | 2:22 | p. 97 |
| 1:41-42 | pp. 219, 245 | 2:23 | p. 136 |
| 1:42 | p. 219 | 2:38 | p. 170 |
| 1:46 | p. 1 | 2:40 47 | p. 138 |

| | | | |
|---|---|---|---|
| 2:46 | p. 121 | 13:1 | p. 78 |
| 4:5 | p. 175 | **1 Corinthians** | |
| 4:23 | p. 195 | 1:1 | p. 165 |
| 4:12 | p. 7 | 3:11 | p. 218 |
| 5:34 | p. 145 | 5:1-5 | p. 171 |
| 6:2 | pp. 140, 143 | 5:14ff | p. 285 |
| 6:7 | p. 185 | 7:12 | p. 80 |
| 8:16 | p. 170 | 7:12-15 | p. 80 |
| 9:5 | p. 107 | 9:2ff | p. 164 |
| 9:10-15 | p. 146 | 9:5 | p. 219 |
| 9:11 | pp. 106, 145 | 11:3 | p. 3 |
| 9:15 | p. 129 | 12:3 | p. 20 |
| 10:13 | p. 140 | 15:5 | p. 140 |
| 12:2 | p. 167 | 15:7 | p. 169 |
| 12:17 | p. 169 | | |
| 13:1-4 | p. 164 | **2 Corinthians** | |
| 13:3 | p. 164 | 1:1 | p. 165 |
| 13:4 | p. 164 | 1:20 | p. 18 |
| 13:9 | p. 147 | 2:5-11 | p. 151 |
| 13:13 | p. 168 | 3:13 | p. 18 |
| 13:45 | p. 91 | 4:6 | p. 18 |
| 14:23 | pp. 175, 184 | 12:12 | pp. 156, 164 |
| 15 | pp. 58, 139, 140, 231, 247 | **Galatians** | |
| 15:13 | p. 169 | 1:1 | p. 165 |
| 15:19 | p. 232 | 1:8 | p. 146 |
| 15:22, 23 | p. 150 | 1:9 | p. 146 |
| 15:28-29 | p. 58 | 1:11-12 | p. 146 |
| 20:28 | p. 183 | 1:15-17 | p. 146 |
| 21:18 | p. 232 | 1:18 | pp. 146, 219 |
| 22:3 | p. 145 | 2:4 | p. 58 |
| 22:25 | p. 145 | 2:7 | p. 170 |
| | | 2:9 | pp. 167, 169, 219 |
| **Romans** | | 2:11-14 | p. 232 |
| 1:1 | p. 165 | | |
| 5:1 | p. 55 | **Ephesians** | |
| 11:1 | p. 145 | 1:1 | p. 165 |

*Scriptural Index*

| | | | |
|---|---|---|---|
| 1:22-23 | p. 117 | 5:1-2 | p. 196 |
| 4:5 | p. 3 | 5:12 | p. 196 |
| 4:4-6 | p. 25 | | |
| 5:23ff | p. 118 | | |
| 5:25-27 | p. 22 | | |
| 5:29, 32 | p. 118 | | |

**1 & 2 Peter Chapter 8**

**Philippians**
2: 9-11    p. 106
3:5    p. 145

**2 John**
1:7    p. 161

**Colossians**
1:1    p. 165
1:18, 24    p. 118

**Revelation**
1:1-3    p. 207

**1 Timothy**
1:1    p. 165
3:1    p. 192
3:15    p. 19
5:19-20    p. 192
6:14    pp. 31, 305

**2 Timothy**
2:1    p. 327
3:16-17    p. 278

**Hebrews**
11:1    p. 20

**Titus**
1:1    p. 165
2:13    p. 302

**1 Peter**
3:14b-15    p. xi
4:10-11    p. 196

# Index of Names

## A
Adrian, Pope 288–289
Agatho, Pope 313
Ambrose, St 218, 262
Apollinarius, 4 261, 282
Aquinas, St Thomas 68, 274, 291, 309
Arius, 4, 66, 178, 253
Athanasius, 45–47, 253, 255–259, 261, 281–282
Augustine, St 263

## B
Ball, D. M. 99, 109
Barnabas, St 129
Barrett, C. K. 135, 137, 170–171
Barth, K. 26, 124, 235
Basil, St 260–261
Bauckham, R. 110, 142, `68, 171, 173
Baur, C. 57–58, 199, 227, 230, 234
Beare, F. W. 114, 116, 117, 119, 123–24, 170, 218, 220, –222, 236, 242, 244, 246
Benedict XVI, Pope 108, 110, 156, 235
Benoit, P. 122–124
Black, M. 110
Bockmuehl, M. 114–115, 123, 220, 236, 246
Boniface VIII, Pope 2–3
Boniface, St 263

Boslooper, D. T. 110
Bousset, 97, 106
Brown, R. E. 110, 124, 13, 170–172, 176, 190–193, 195–196, 205–207, 213, 236
Bultmann, R. 105, 122, 140, 156, 172, 221–222, 236–237, 245–246, 286, 319
Butler, B. C. 272, 275–277, 281, 283–284, 286, 294, 304, 319–320

## C
Celestine, Pope 243, 262, 264
Chirico, P. 272, 274, 303–313, 316, 319–20, 321, 322
Clark, F. 30
Clement of Alexandria, 38
Clement, Pope 202, 207
Constantine, Emperor 241, 253–257
Constantius II, Emperor 255–256, 258–259, 261
Constanzo, J. F. 272
Cornelius, Pope 252
Cross, F. L. 70
Cullmann, O. 213, 226–227
Cyprian, St 38, 252–253, 296
Cyril of Alexandria, 44

## D
Damasus, St, Pope 260
Davis, S. T. 102, 109, 110

Dioscorus, 43–44, 46, 54
Dodd, C. H. 99, 109
Döllinger, Dr 49, 83
Donfried, K. P. 213, 236
Dunn, J. D. G. 112, 123
Dupuis, J. 30, 70

**E**

Eichhorn, 56
Eusebius, (historian), 154, 168, 195, 198–199, 205, 207, 218, 248
Eusebius of Nicodemia, 253, 255–256, 281
Eutyches, 44–46, 269
Eustathius of Berytus, 44, 255, 281

**F**

Feuillet, A. 123
Fitzmyer, J. A. 110, 124, 189
Flavian, 44, 197
Frend, W. H. C. 240, 255–256, 267–268, 320
Funk, R. 30

**G**

Gette, Abbé 288
Goudge, H. L. 150, 171
Green, M. 30
Gregory the Great, Pope 286

**H**

Hahn, F. 110
Harnack, A. 63–65, 95, 154, 198–199, 241–242, 262

Hegel, G. W. F. 62–63, 69, 282
Hick, J. 15, 30
Hodgson, P. C. 69
Holtzmann, H. J. 59, 64, 67, 70, 95,
Honorius, Pope 296
Hoover, R. W. 30
Hughes, J. H. 109
Hughes, P. A. 201–202, 208, 240, 249, 251, 267–269, 289, 320

**I**

Ignatius of Antioch, St 36, 106, 161, 165, 176–177, 184, 196–202, 204–205, 206, 208, 248–249
Innocent I, Pope 263
Innocent III, Pope 286
Irenaeus, St 125

**J**

James, Apostle 101, 141, 166, 167–168, 173
James, brother of the Lord 141, 166, 168–169, 173, 231–233, 247
James, Son of Alphaeus 168–169
James, writer of Epistle 188, 207
Jerome, St 168, 207, 260, 263, 266, 312–313, 315, 321
Jesus, 4, 7–22, 26–27, 30, 31, 42, 53, 56, 67, 69, 70, 71, 74, 79–81, 85–87, 89–108, 109, 110, 111–123, 124, 129–136,

*Index of Names* 343

138–144, 146, 150, 152, 154–163, 165, 168–169, 170, 173, 186, 189–200, 204, 207, 209–210, 213–230, 234, 236, 242, 244– 246, 248, 254, 263, 266, 281–282, 285–287, 293, 296, 298, 305, 309, 311–312, 314, 316–317, 321, 322, 323–324, 327
John of Antioch, 264
John, St Apostle 101, 166–169, 173, 188, 197, 205, 207, 223
John the Baptist, 92, 98, 109, 165, 216
John of the Cross 25
John Chrysostom, St 205, 218, 263
John, Evangelist 16–18, 30, 65, 89, 97, 99, 101, 124, 132, 133, 135, 137, 142, 152, 160, 166, 170, 219, 221–223, 237, 245, 251
John Mark, 129
John XXIII, Pope 83, 286
John Paul II, Pope 5, 9, 68, 70, 303, 310, 321
Johnson, T. L. 20
Josephus, 90, 100
Julius I, Pope 256

## K

Kant, I. 68, 73–74, 310
Kelly, J. N. D. 202, 208, 240, 248–249, 251–252, 254, 256, 362–263, 265, 267–269
Kümmel, W. G. 69

Küng, H. 87, 177–186, 204, 206, 237, 272–274, 277, 279–286, 291–295, 297–298, 301, 303–304, 319

## L

Lagrange, M.-J. 117–119, 124, 219–220, 225, 236, 237, 246
Leo the Great, Pope 43–47, 82, 243, 262, 265, 286, 288
Leo XIII, Pope 66, 68
Lewis, C. S.17, 23, 26
Liberius, Pope 258–259, 261
Lightfoot, J. B. 153–156, 165–166, 168, 171, 172, 173, 198, 312
Livingstone, E. 70
Loisy, A. 63–65
Luther, M. 33, 38–40, 55, 64, 72–3, 178, 227, 284, 313,

## M

Manning, Cardinal 51, 294
Marshall, I. H. 132–133, 170
Martin, Pope 313
Meier, J. P. 100, 109, 141–144, 159–161, 171, 228–229, 246
Merz, A. 1, 109
Moule, C. F. D. 105, 110
Moulton, J. H.

## N

Nestorius, 264–265
Neuner, J. 70
Newman, J. H. 35–39, 41–52, 77, 86–87, 108, 110, 111–

113, 119–120, 122, 198, 235, 236, 240, 243–244, 277, 21, 291–292, 294, 306–307, 309, 316

## P

Papias, 196
Paul, St, Apostle 20, 23, 58, 80, 106–107, 115, 124, 126, 128–130, 133, 140, 145–153, 158, 161–169, 170, 172, 173, 175–176, 182–188, 190–194, 199, 201, 203, 206, 230–234, 235, 236, 240, 242, 244, 247–250, 285, 295, 315, 323
Paul IV, Pope 313
Paul VI, Pope 87, 211–212, 235–236, 273, 292–293, 296–297, 299, 304, 311, 320–321, 324
Peter, St, Apostle 7–8, 10–11, 19, 26, 42, 46, 48, 56–58, 68, 74, 80–82, 84–85, 67, 97, 101–102, 106, 114, 116, 125–126, 128–120, 137–140, 146, 160, 163, 166–169, 170, 173, 177, 179, 182, 188–189, 191–192, 194–195, 197, 199, 201–205, 209–210, 212–235, 236, 237, 239–240, 242, 244–252, 256, 260–266, 267, 268, 269, 271–272, 285–288, 292, 298, 300, 308, 311, 314–315, 317–318, 323
Philips, J. B. 23
Pius IX, Pope 49, 286

Pius X, Pope 61, 65–68, 70, 117, 284
Pius XII, Pope 83, 190, 207, 236, 286, 292, 298, 320
Polycarp, St 126–8, 196, 198, 205

## R

Reimarus, H. S. 56, 62, 69, 96, 98, 107, 114
Redford, J. 23–27, 30–31, 56, 89, 99, 110, 206, 208, 269, 321
Reumann, J. 213, 36
Robert, A. 123
Robinson, J. A. T. 110

## S

Salmon, Dr 272, 275–277, 283, 308
Sanders, E. P. 93, 98, 109
Schaff, P. 208
Schleiermacher, F. 57
Schmithals, W. 140–141, 147, 154–161, 171–173
Schweitzer, A. 56–57, 59–60, 64–65, 69, 95, 96, 109
Siricius, Pope 262
Sixtus St, Pope 264
Stephen I, Pope 251–252
Strauss, D. 42, 56–57, 6–63, 66–67, 69, 70
Sylvester, Pope 254

## T

Tacitus, 90–91, 94

Tanner, N. P. 30, 53, 206, 235, 236, 267, 318, 321
Taylor, V. 132, 170
Theissen, G. 91, 109
Theodoret, 46, 54, 205

## W
Ward, W. 51
Wellhausen, J. 58, 69
Wickenhauser, A. 189–190, 207
Winter, M. 239, 250–251, 257–258, 260–261, 267, 268, 269
Woodall, G. 302, 320
Wrede, W. 60, 69, 96
Wright, N. T. 99, 102, 104, 109, 114–117, 214, 220

## Z
Zosimus, Pope 263

www.ingramcontent.com/pod-product-compliance
Lightning Source LLC
Chambersburg PA
CBHW032016230426
43671CB00005B/101